ALSO BY DAVID HAJDU

Lush Life: A Biography of Billy Strayhorn

Positively 4th Street: The Lives and Times of Joan Baez, Bob Dylan,
Mimi Baez Fariña, and Richard Fariña

The Ten-Cent Plague: The Great Comic-Book Scare
and How It Changed America

Heroes and Villains: Essays on Movies, Music, Comics, and Culture

LOVE FOR SALE

FARRAR, STRAUS AND GIROUX   NEW YORK

LOVE
FOR
SALE

POP MUSIC IN AMERICA

DAVID HAJDU

Farrar, Straus and Giroux
18 West 18th Street, New York 10011

Library of Congress Cataloging-in-Publication Data
Names: Hajdu, David.
Title: Love for sale : pop music in America / David Hajdu.
Description: First edition. | New York : Farrar, Straus and Giroux, 2016. |
    Includes bibliographical references and index.
Identifiers: LCCN 2016017769 | ISBN 9780374170530 (cloth) |
    ISBN 9780374710507 (ebook)
Subjects: LCSH: Popular music—United States—History and criticism
Classification: LCC ML3477 .H3 2016 | DDC 781.640973—dc23
LC record available at https://lccn.loc.gov/2016017769

Designed by Abby Kagan

Our books may be purchased in bulk for promotional, educational, or business use.
Please contact your local bookseller or the Macmillan Corporate and
Premium Sales Department at 1-800-221-7945, extension 5442, or by e-mail
at MacmillanSpecialMarkets@macmillan.com.

www.fsgbooks.com
www.twitter.com/fsgbooks • www.facebook.com/fsgbooks

1   3   5   7   9   10   8   6   4   2

In memory of my sister, Barbara Ann,
and for my sister in spirit, Alisa Solomon

CONTENTS

LOVE FOR SALE

INTRODUCTION

Of the countless terms for categories of music, from "classical" and "blues" to the secret-password language of micro-genres like "doomcore" and "neurofunk," the least useful phrase I know is "popular music." It provides no information about the music itself: no suggestion of how it sounds or what sort of mood it might conjure, no indication of the traditions it grows from or defies, and no hint of whether it could be good for dancing, for solitary listening, or for anything else. All the term tells you about the music is the fact, or the assertion, that it's popular—that a lot of people seem to like it for some reason. The words "popular music" are like sociological taxonomy, a way of defining a body of creative work as a measure of the group of people to whom it appeals. What good is that, if you're not a sociologist?

I have always found the very notion of the "popular" off-putting, in part because I have never fully outgrown my early conception of popularity as something restricted to the girls I was afraid to talk to in the sixth grade. I can't help but think of anyone or anything popular as part of a world I don't belong in. This line of thinking is rooted, I admit, in a vain feeling of exceptionalism—*They all think they know what's cool, but I know better, and that makes me even cooler*—which, I suspect, is anything but an exceptional way to feel. It seems likely to me that a great many people—particularly Americans, being citizens of a society in which rugged individuals and rebels and outlaws and misfits have always been glorified—think of themselves as outliers or exceptions in one way or another. Nobody wants to feel like everybody—or just anybody—and because we know we are defined in others' eyes by our preferences in music, movies, TV shows, and other cultural products, most of us tend not to talk about popular music as our favorite music, no matter how deeply it has run through our lives.

I like to think of myself as a jazz fan who grew up on rock and roll. But the truth is not so simple. The jazz repertoire was built largely (though not solely) through the adaptation of popular standards—songs originally created by tunesmiths such as George Gershwin and Irving Berlin for the musical theater with the explicit goal of making hits. Gershwin's "I Got Rhythm," written with the lyricist Ira Gershwin in 1930 for the musical *Girl Crazy*, is the source material for more than a dozen other tunes in and out of jazz: Duke Ellington's "Cotton Tail," Charlie Parker and Dizzy Gillespie's "Anthropology," Thelonious Monk's "Rhythm-a-Ning," Sonny Rollins's "Oleo," among others, not to mention the *Flintstones* theme song. Pop always fed jazz and continues to do so today, with venturesome jazz artists such as Brad Mehldau, Bill Frisell, and the Bad Plus playing repertoires that mingle original works, compositions from the jazz canon, and rock tunes by the likes of Oasis, Soundgarden, Black Sabbath, Nirvana, and Rush. For a period around the middle of the twentieth century, when big-band swing was a musical craze, jazz and popular music were essentially the same thing.

Popular music—or "pop," in the term's most popular form, although the two expressions are not always perfectly interchangeable—has run very deeply in my life, as it has run through the lives of innumerable Americans over the course of more than a hundred years, since the mass audience for American popular culture first took form in the late nineteenth century. This book is an effort to come to terms with that history and its meaning. What are we talking about when we talk about pop, and what bearing has the music had on American life? Does popular music matter, really? And why is it so relentlessly romantic and sunny? Or am I wrong to think of pop that way?

Among the ironies of popular music is that it is a phenomenon of vast scale and intimate effect, a product of mass culture that reaches millions of people (or more) at one time and works for each person in a personal way. We could look, as an example, at the tune that qualifies by some measures as the most successful popular song of all time: "Yesterday." Composed by Paul McCartney and first released on a Beatles single in 1965, it would be broadcast in its many renditions more than seven million times before the end of the twentieth century. (The other side of the original release was "Act Naturally," a country-pop novelty that had been a hit for the Nashville star Buck Owens, warbled on the Beatles' record by Ringo Starr. In at least one early advertisement for the record, "Act Naturally" was promoted as the A side.) "Yesterday" made *The Guinness Book of World Records* as the most-recorded song in history, with more than three thousand versions on record. I can't think of a tune that more people of varied ages are more likely to know, aside from "Happy Birthday." Yet "Yesterday" carries grossly different meanings, including some personal meanings, for many people.

For McCartney himself, "Yesterday" stands as proof of his independent ability as a songwriter—evidence in refutation of the widespread view that he was at his best with the help of John Lennon. At various times, McCartney has attempted to have the songwriting credits to "Yesterday" reversed, to "McCartney and Lennon" instead of "Lennon and McCartney," the standard language for all the compositions John Lennon and Paul McCartney wrote during the time of their partnership, regardless of the weight of the contribution by either person.

For Lennon, after the breakup of the Beatles, the song was a gnawing, inescapable reminder of a past he was trying to leave behind to establish a new identity with Yoko Ono. "I go to restaurants," Lennon grumbled to *Playboy* in 1980, "and the groups always play 'Yesterday.'"

To Bob Dylan, the tune was a symbol of the pandering sentimentalism in music made in Tin Pan Alley before the revolution in songwriting philosophy that Dylan's work incited. When his first biographer, Robert Shelton, brought up that he had heard that Joan Baez was planning to record Beatles material, Dylan launched into a lecture about "Yesterday" and songs in its vein. "It's the thing to do, to tell all the teenyboppers 'I dig the Beatles,' and you sing a song like 'Yesterday,'" Dylan told Shelton. "God knows, it's such a cop-out, man. If you go into the Library of Congress, you can find—there are millions of songs like that written in Tin Pan Alley."

A quick search online brings up an account of Laura Binetti and Steven Blessing, a couple from Fort Myers, Florida, having chosen "Yesterday" for the father-daughter dance at their wedding. To me, considering this from the outside, the song seems an odd choice for the occasion, because it is about troubles being here to stay. Yet such is the ability of any tune to take on idiosyncratic meaning for any listener. My own parents' favorite song was "For the Good Times," Kris Kristofferson's bittersweet plea to share one last moment together, "now that it's over."

Searching online for another minute shows that the family of Meredith Ewart, who died in the World Trade Center on September 11, 2001, played "Yesterday" at her funeral.

On the evening before the attacks, September 10, my wife, Karen, and I were at an event Paul McCartney attended, and he and his girlfriend at the time, Heather Mills, talked with Karen and me for a while. When they walked away, Karen said to me, "I can't believe we were just hanging out with the man who wrote 'Yesterday.'" Karen, who is a jazz singer, loves the song, with reason—as Lennon once said, "That was a good one"—but I am sick and tired of it. I feel as though I must have heard all three thousand of those recordings that got "Yesterday" into *Guinness*. Like Karen, I admire it, and at the same time I resent it for its oppressive presence in my life. Its popular success has spoiled it for me. I can barely still hear qualities I heard in the song at various times in the past: the statement of generational pride in a rock-era composer's ability to write well in a style favored by his parents and grandparents, and the strangeness in the fact that a song so self-pitying could be a big hit.

I would much prefer to hear "Tell Me What You See," a minor Beatles song by Lennon and McCartney from the same period as "Yesterday," because it conjures one of my most precious memories. It was the song that happened to be playing on the tape deck in my car the first time I made out with Mary Jane Pence in high school.

Pop, the form with the largest of all music audiences, is a social art that works with every member of its enormous following in small, unique ways, and my conception of music as a writer is inextricable from my experience of music as a person. As the critic Alfred Kazin once noted, "If the critic cannot reveal to others the power of art in his own life, he cannot say anything useful or even human in its interest. He will scrawl, however learnedly, arbitrary comments on the text." I don't mean to gussy up the point by name-checking Kazin, but I simply cannot separate my individual experience with music from the music itself. When I hear "Tell Me What You See," I am equipped as a critic to tell you what I hear: an infectious folk-pop trifle indebted to the mid-1960s American sound of the Byrds. But to tell you what I feel, I need not only John Lennon and Paul McCartney but also Mary Jane Pence.

I'm from New Jersey. My mother was a waitress at a chrome-clad diner on Route 22, the old state highway that ran east to west across northern Jersey and was the main link between New York and Pennsylvania before the interstate was constructed. During my childhood, Route 22 stopped in the east at the Holland Tunnel and in the west at the bridge across the Delaware River, where drivers handed dimes to my father, who was a toll collector. The diner where my mother worked was located on the edge of our town, Phillipsburg, about five miles east of the bridge, and was called the Gateway, a word that suggests the way a lot of people tend to think of New Jersey. The state has always been widely perceived less as a place of its own than as a conduit for getting to a place interesting enough to be worth a trip through Jersey: from the East Coast, the gateway to the whole of America; from the west, the gateway to New York City and the urban Northeast.

The Gateway had a jukebox, hooked up to table stations with menus of song titles on those fun-to-swing metal-frame pages, right there in every booth, and my mom persuaded the amusement company rep to give her the worn-out records so she could bring them home to me. Through this arrangement, I built a superb collection of nearly unplayable copies of mid-1960s pop hits. I had "Hanky Panky" by Tommy James and the Shondells, which I treasured as the filthiest thing I had ever encountered; "Cool Jerk" by the Capitols, which I fantasized as being all about me; "I'm Your Puppet" by James and Bobby Purify, whose lyrics I pictured literally and found disturbing; and dozens of others among the most popular or most shoddily manufactured singles of the era. Nearly all the records I was given skipped from having nicks or scratches or were so battered from being overplayed with the steel-tipped needle in the jukebox that the music sounded like the dim radio broadcasts from West Virginia that my father tried to tune in on his plug-in radio at the kitchen table late at night so he could hear country music.

The flaws in the records never bothered me much, because we had no record player in our house during these years. (Later, I got a portable from Sears as my eighth-grade graduation present.) To play the

45s my mother brought home for me, I would have to walk across the alley and down a few houses to my cousin Dick's house and ask if I could use his record player. Deterred by boyhood lethargy, I generally stayed alone at home and sat on the floor of the basement with my piles of records, and I studied them. I examined and compared the labels; I learned the names of the songwriters and cross-checked the production credits. In the absence of the ability to listen to the music, I drew upon my memory of the work from hearing it on the radio and pored over the cryptic evidence of the particulars of its making. I began to learn to theorize.

As an adult writer, in the 1990s, I interviewed the Italian jazz pianist Romano Mussolini, and he recalled warmly how his father, the Fascist dictator, had nurtured his young child's interest in music, particularly American swing. According to his son, Benito Mussolini had a standing order for Blackshirt troops to confiscate any 78 rpm records that they found in enemy encampments. "He was very tough. He didn't care for the music. He brought me records because he knew they would give me happiness," Romano Mussolini said, and I told him my mother did the same thing for me.

A great many important artists and other notable figures came through the Gateway, according to my mom. Leonard Bernstein had the pudding and, by her account, adored it. "Leonard Bernstein loves pudding," my mother would always say. The Beatles once took one of the booths on the left of the entrance, she said—or maybe that was another one of those bands from England. She couldn't be sure. (There is a long-standing rumor that the Rolling Stones once ate at the Gateway, and chatter about that endures online.) The one almost notable musician in her regular clientele was a fellow Italian American from my hometown known as Red Mascara—an oddly transgressive-sounding pseudonym for a chemical-plant worker named Joseph Mascari. He had written an awful song called "I'm from New Jersey."

My mother's rank and skill earned her the dinner shift, from 3:00 to 11:00 p.m. Accordingly, I saw her only occasionally as a child. The walk from our house to the Gateway was more than two miles each way, and I made the trip alone by foot after school just a few times a year, including once in the spring of 1967 when I was twelve and my mother arranged for me to meet Mascara, the only composer she knew, Leonard Bernstein notwithstanding. I can date the occasion fairly accurately by the songs I remember playing on the jukebox while I waited in a booth for Mascara's arrival: "Epistle to Dippy" by Donovan, a spacey jumble of pseudo-poetic images—stuff about looking through crystal spectacles and riding the elevator in the brain hotel—which I studied in hopes of learning what it was like to take those drugs we were being warned against in health class; "Ruby Tuesday" by the Rolling Stones, a twee, un-Stonesish ballad about a mystery woman who disappears before her lover even learns her name; and, most memorably, its flip side, "Let's Spend the Night Together," a blunt entreaty for sex that I could hear only on the jukebox, because most AM radio stations refused to play it. I got three tunes for the quarter my mother gave me, which I think I realized even then was probably the sum of her tips from one or two customers.

Mascara sat down next to me in the booth, instead of across from me, and after saying a few words I don't remember now and likely didn't absorb then, in my panic from such unexpectedly close contact with a grown stranger and one involved in music, at that, he laid a copy of the song sheet for "I'm from New Jersey" in front of us on the Formica tabletop. One of us opened the sheet music, and I pretended to study it. Mascara, helpfully, proceeded to sing the tune for me. I learned much later that he would croon it to virtually anyone with little excuse; Mascara labored for decades, vainly, to have it adopted as the official state song, singing it to legislators and their staffs in the chambers of the Trenton statehouse.

Having just listened to "Let's Spend the Night Together" on the jukebox, I recognized "I'm from New Jersey" as anachronistically corny and dumb, a bouncy flag-waver of the sort that George M. Cohan had made a cliché more than half a century earlier. The melody is as easy to

sing and as strident as the tune of "You're a Grand Old Flag." The lyrics
are discernible to a child as childish, and yet they have one odd, original element: Mascara devised the song to be customized for any municipality, as long as the name of that municipality could be sung with
no more than three notes. The sheet music reads,

I'm from New Jersey and I'm proud about it
[blank] is my home
I'm from New Jersey and I want to shout it
No matter where I roam.

In the second line of the stanza, the blank is intended to be filled
in with the name of the singer's hometown, and the presence of that
blank is a minor wonder. With the expedient cogency of an insur-
ance form, one phrase in the song sheet for "I'm from New Jersey"
gives expression to the elusiveness and contingency of identity, the
blankness in one's sense of belonging that is certainly part of what it
means to be from New Jersey but is hardly exclusive to any single
place. I wondered, as I was growing up, where do I belong? What
[blank] is my home?

Looking back, I see that it was not my town that filled the blank
for me, but the imagined landscape of pop music. That's where I lived
in my heart and mind and where, in a contradiction of propositions I
could not see at the time, commercial products that were popular
among millions of other young people fed my adolescent feelings of
alienation and exceptionalism. From the songs on both sides of those
piles of records in the basement, from the tunes I later listened to
alone in bed with the transistor radio my big brother handed down
to me, from the numbers I would fumble through on guitar in
after-school bands, and, later, in the songs I played in my car, I heard
about things I wasn't hearing about anywhere else. I learned how a
jerk could, by virtue of his coolness, be the heaviest cat there ever
could be. I learned how much fun it was to do the hanky-panky,

maybe even overnight together, even if the girl disappears in the morning without saying her name. I rode the elevator in the brain hotel.

As commercial products, pop songs are in the business of selling fantasies of love, sex, taboo kicks, and other titillations as a means of moving units. My older brother Chuck fancied himself a folk music purist and arbiter of authenticity and virtue in all things and, perhaps properly in his role as an older brother, teased me mercilessly about my musical tastes when I was a kid. One afternoon, he came after me with his transistor radio, which was playing a Peter, Paul, and Mary record called "I Dig Rock and Roll Music." It was intended as a parody but so persuasively emulated the bounciness of lite rock that it became a Top 10 hit in the autumn of 1967, a few months after my meeting with Red Mascara at the Gateway. The lyrics mock Donovan for being "tripped out" and scold the Beatles because "they have the word 'love' to sell you."

My brother latched on the latter point and told me, *Don't you realize they're only trying to sell you something?*

As a defense, I asked what harm there was in what they were selling, which was only love. I said, *What's wrong with that?*

Chuck, who had already graduated from high school when I was still twelve, thought about that for what seemed like minutes but was probably only a few seconds and grinned a grin I recognized. He was doing the hanky-panky in his mind.

Let's just drop the whole subject. You'll grow out of it, he said, and I naively feared that he might be right.

THE SHEET MUSIC ERA

THE ZENITH OF THE POPULAR MUSIC CRAZE

When I thought of pop songs as a young music fan—before digitization, downloading, and streaming—I thought of records. The music seemed inextricable from and in some ways even subordinate to the thing that contained it. A song I didn't know of as a record—a chant from the kids on the playground, a tune my mother hummed while she cut pie pieces—seemed as if it were not really a *real* song. It wasn't touchable, holdable—possessable. Nor did it seem legitimate in ways fundamental to the commercial society I lived in: it wasn't sellable, buyable—consumable.

In the period of my childhood and adolescence in the second decade of the rock era, the 45 rpm vinyl single served as the primary mechanism of distribution for pop songs to their principal audience of kids and young adults like me, and it was a good object. The 45 was cheap and easy to manufacture and to use: practical as a forum for relatively low-risk experimentation by new artists and independent labels; affordable for purchase on the budgets of income from babysitting and lawn mowing; transportable to parties in containers no bigger than lunch boxes; storable in cubbies within the limited confines of bedrooms shared with one or more brothers or sisters; collectible; tradable; and vulnerable to damage or wear to an extent that made a physical imperative of a pop song's essential temporariness. After all, popular music has always come and gone like fashion. A pop song might have the capacity to endure for years, and plenty have lasted for decades and longer. Yet if a song has this capacity, it's a secondary attribute, impressive but unessential.

The Beatles, I learned, had the same conception of songs as records that many children of the vinyl era have no doubt shared. "The boys got their musical education through the records they listened to in Liverpool," their producer George Martin said in an interview I did with him in the early 1980s. "They were always thinking in terms of records. Would the song fit on a single? Would it sound good on a 45 rpm record?" When Martin was supervising the production of "Paperback Writer," the Beatles single from the summer of 1966, he and the engineer Geoff Emerick mastered the record specifically so it would play as loud as a 45 rpm single could play without making the turntable needle fly off the grooves.

"Their publisher, bless him, had the Beatles songs transcribed for publication—I was distantly involved in that, although I wasn't paid for the work—and I think Paul and John found the published music terribly amusing," Martin said. "They absolutely never thought about musical notation. They thought it wonderfully strange to see their songs in notes on paper, as if they had been translated into an ancient language."

For me at the age of twelve, the sheet music to "I'm from New Jersey," being sheet music, struck me as a curiosity unconnected to popular songs as I knew them. Like the booster-club words and the bouncing-ball tune of the song, the material format of the song— printed notation—suggested a distant age in musical history. The days of sheet music were a time before hits, before multimillion sellers, before popular music became the common currency of young life—or so I thought when I was twelve.

In truth, as I learned in time, it was publication on song sheets that first brought mass popularity to American songs. There were monster hits on sheet music years before there were records.

By 1920, newspapers were already reporting that the "day of great hits" had passed. The "zenith of the popular music craze," when sales of hit tunes were estimated to have averaged one million copies per week, was understood to have occurred in the first decade and a half of the twentieth century. The transactional form of those song sales was not a recording in any format of sound storage but commercially published sheet music. The words and music of popular songs were presented in the same format as classical compositions, in formal notation: a treble staff for the melody line; the lyrics underneath it, with each syl-la-ble separated to match the notes of the tune; and below the words another pair of staves for piano accompaniment. The music would be printed on a large sheet of heavy cotton-fiber stock, folded in half like a greeting card and intended to serve much the same function as one, to provide mass-produced sentiments for use in the name of individual expression.

When commercial song sheets first came into widespread use, during the second half of the nineteenth century, the cover graphics were typically illustrative in a literal manner, depicting the lyrical content of the song: a pair of dancing polar bears for "Polar Bear Polka"; a young woman receiving a carrier dove for "The Carrier Dove." Then, in 1892, a portentously wily songwriter in Wisconsin, Charles K. Harris—soon to be famous as the father of the tearjerker but also historic as a great innovator of cross-merchandising and payola—wrote a mopey story-song, a paean to self-pity called "After the Ball."

Harris set up his own publishing operation to maximize the profits that were unapologetically the sole stimulus to his creative work. According to Harris, an established publisher had offered him ten thousand dollars for the right to print up "After the Ball," but he refused in order to control sales of the music himself. When a music hall star of the day named J. Aldrich Libbey came through Milwaukee, Harris offered to pay him five hundred dollars—enough for Libbey to have bought, say, a parlor grand piano—plus a cut of the royalties of the sheet music sales, if Libbey agreed to interpolate "After the Ball" into his touring show, *A Trip to Chinatown*, a successful musical comedy that had little to do with Chinatown. In exchange, Harris put a portrait of Libbey on the cover of the sheet music to the tune, and the enduring model for entertainment marketing as image brokering and favor trading was set.

Written in waltz time to an instantly learnable singsong melody in the mode of an Irish folk tune, "After the Ball" tells the tale of a lonely old man who explains to his young niece why he never married. He had once been in love, he tells the girl, but had his heart broken one night when, after the ball, he saw his beloved kissing another man. Many years later in the song, after the woman he had loved has died, the old uncle receives a letter from the other man, and it turns out that he was just her brother. The song is a cheap little cut-glass gem of Victoriana. It has melodrama, a twist ending, a contorted hint of the incestuous (as the uncle describes watching the brother and sister: "When I returned, there stood a man / kissing my sweetheart as lovers can"), and, at the heart of the overt tragedy in the story, a less-than-covert case for the Victorian ethos of blissful domestication. (To be unmarried is a kind of death only in a world where marriage is the most important thing in life.)

"After the Ball" had another dimension. In one of the last stanzas, the old uncle mentions, in contradiction to the rest of the song, that by abandoning his girl, he "broke her heart." Suddenly the man is not a lonesome victim but a heartbreaker, an agent of misbegotten punishment, and the story has become a lament of Victorian guilt and suffering.

During the first decade of its release, the sheet music to "After the Ball" was reported to have sold five million copies at thirty to forty cents per copy, or about eight to ten dollars a sheet in early twenty-first-century money. (Retail prices were left to the store owners to set and were not printed on the music at the time.) With the population of the United States at around seventy-six million in 1900, that is proportionally the equivalent of a song being owned (in any format) by more than eighteen million Americans a hundred years later. (The biggest hit of the year 2000, Santana's "Maria Maria," sold 1.3 million copies as a CD single.) During the first decade of the twentieth century, about a hundred songs were said to have sold more than a million copies apiece in sheet music, and the U.S. population was around ninety million. The country was smaller, and the hits were bigger.

Popular music had existed long before the success of a song could be quantified by sales statistics, of course. The songs embraced at any time by a significant share of the populace—the folk songs, the songs of social dance, holiday songs, wedding songs, the songs hummed by all people cutting pieces of pie—are songs widely used and well liked, music that is popular: popular music. A practical distinction can be made between such music and the music associated with formal or official institutions: religious music, patriotic music, and the music presented in opera houses and symphony halls. Yet that distinction has always been a matter of practicality. A great deal of religious music is used widely, often every week in worship services, and treasured by huge portions of the population. "Amazing Grace" has long been beloved among the populace and much sung; it is a very popular song. So is "Silent Night." So, for that matter, is "The Star-Spangled Banner," by virtue of the obvious if begrudging satisfaction that millions of people have taken in belting it out at ballparks. The operas of Rossini and Puccini have always attracted sizable audiences. By the self-evident fact of its popularity, all this is popular music.

The transformative phenomenon of the sheet music era was not popularization—songs of many kinds were already popular—it was industrialization, accelerated through mechanization on the production side and a vast expansion of the marketplace on the consumption end. Where popular music had existed, the popular music industry was born.

In the final decades of the nineteenth century and the first two decades of the twentieth, an unassociated group of music publishers coalesced and flourished in New York, at first on Union Square, by the vaudeville theaters, and then on a stretch of West Twenty-eighth Street between Sixth and Seventh Avenues derisively nicknamed Tin Pan Alley, for the noise made by all the singing and piano playing in the buildings. Some twenty publishing businesses were set up in rooms in a row of narrow brownstones overpacked with workers making music on the industrial model. Specialists handled each of the tasks involved, one and then another, from the lyricist to the composer to the music transcriber to the publisher to the song plugger, the last of whom peddled the sheet music to professional musicians to perform (for the promotional value in performances by stars of the day, such as J. Aldrich Libbey) and to store owners to sell to amateurs who provided entertainment for one another in their parlors. Tin Pan Alley was a mill district where music was produced by a means my aunts and uncles working in the piecework sweatshops of New Jersey would have understood.

"Nowadays, the consumption of songs by the masses in America is as constant as their consumption of shoes, and the demand is similarly met by factory output," reported *The New York Times* in 1910. "Songs may be properly classed with the staples, and are manufactured, advertised, and distributed in much the same manner as ordinary commodities."

Unlike the songs to come in another era of popular music, the age of recordings, the tunes of the sheet music age were created mainly for performance by the general public at home rather than for professional performance. With the rise of the middle class and the five-day workweek in America came an urge among the growing membership of that class to demonstrate their excellence by spending their newly discretionary money and time on luxuries such as fancy objects and the arts. They bought houses—rococo temples of domestic splendor that earned their later classification as Victorians—and acquitted them with carved-oak furnishings, lacy window dressings, and pianos that served as magnificent display racks for song sheets published with beautiful covers. Between 1890 and 1904, yearly piano sales in the United States grew from 32,000 to 374,000. In 1910, nearly three hundred American piano makers employed some twenty-five thousand people and sold about 375,000 instruments in one year's time. Women (and some men) and children (especially girls) in respectable families (or families aspiring to respectability) took music lessons, and most of the songs they sang and played at the piano were produced for them on Tin Pan Alley. A symbol of domestic refinement performed by girls or their mothers or aunts at the piano, generally speaking, popular music took on associations with femininity that it would carry forever. Indeed, the very notion of having a musical sensibility would be taken to suggest the presence of a feminine quality—in either women or men.

Just as the 45s I collected were not really the music but a handy system for delivery of it, sheet music was not the work itself; it merely contained a representation of the music in the coding of notation and words set by Linotype. This is obvious. Largely lost to us today, though, is the way the music of the song sheets came together in performance to make a complicated, elementally imperfect, partly commercial, partly homemade form of popular art. Without performance, there is no music, just the idea of music. (That the idea of music on its own can be a work of art is another matter and one that John Cage would lead the music audience to confront several decades after the Tin Pan

Alley era.) The fact that amateurs gave life to the songs of the sheet music age was fundamental to the work. The music was inseparable from the irregular character and the limits of everyday voices and rudimentary musicianship. Imperfect intonation, ragged (even ugly) tones, shaky accompaniment, multiple voices out of unison or in harmony that was imprecise or out of sync—imprecision, unprofessionalism, volatility, surprise: all these things were parts of the work as important as the words and music. On paper, Tin Pan Alley songs such as "In a Hammock Built for Two" and "When the Morning Glories Twine Around the Door" (both by the composer Harry Von Tilzer and the lyricist Andrew Sterling) were insufferably trite and formulaic. But no hits existed only on paper, and the uncertainty and messiness of home performances improved the music by complicating it.

Charles Ives, growing up in the song sheet era, found musical inspiration in the ardent faultiness and accidental atonality of amateur playing and singing. As the Ives biographer Jan Swafford described Ives's thinking, "He could not separate the music on the page from the way people sang or played it. Even the coarseness of amateur performance seemed to Ives a sign of authenticity. The mistakes were part of the music; sometimes the mistakes were the music of the ages."

The songs of the sheet music age were, by necessity, fairly easy to perform, and that fact allowed critics of the tunes to mistake them for being unnecessarily easy to write. As a reporter for the *Times* wrote, "The composition of popular songs, whether it be the words or the music, seems to be largely a matter of knack"—not inspiration nor expertise acquired through experience, formal learning or informal training on the job, or an understanding of the milieu, but "knack," something piddling and involuntary, a happy fluke. "The greatest hits do not display any considerable degree of literary or musical ability," the writer continued. "The words are generally inane and the construction not infrequently ungrammatical. The music is often such a simple tune as a child might conceive.

"The minstrels and ballad writers of old probably brought more talent to bear upon their work and took greater pains with it than do their latter-day successors. The former followed their vocation for the love of the thing, and looked for no greater compensation than the means of keeping body and soul together."

The Tin Pan Alley tunesmiths made up the first class of professional songwriters in American history. As good professionals, they catered to their market—often expertly, even artfully, however cynically—and were taken to task by the press of their day for pandering to the tastes of the public and for perverting those tastes with their scary urban ideas. The provenance of the Tin Pan Alley songs in New York City, at a time of bubbling fear of the effects of urbanism on America, figured significantly in the early criticism of popular music.

"Song writers, publishers and play producers recognize the fact that their public wants this music," reported the *New-York Tribune* in 1915. "And untrained 'composers' at once turn out thousands of the kind of song that at once debase all who sing and hear." The *Tribune* piece, like many others at the time, portrayed popular music as a crude, citified threat to the genteel values supposedly exemplified by traditional formal music, and it set up as an exemplar of those values one Olive Fremstad, a Swedish American opera star.

"American popular music is but another evidence of the frantic and insensate hunt for pleasure that motivates city life," Fremstad said, as the *Tribune* quoted her. "It is one of the many expressions of a devastating unthinkingness on the part of intelligent people. And pandering to this is a leering commercialism. [Popular songs] exude the vice in which and for which they were conceived. The popular music that is blandly introduced into drawing rooms, that is so guilelessly sung by our daughters, is vicious." Neither Fremstad nor the uncredited author of the article offered any titles as evidence.

Sweepingly, they asserted that commercial popular music, by nature of its commercialism, had to be corrupt and that the music, by nature of its popularity, could be broadly corruptive. Of course, the operas that Fremstad sang were also commercial works; the Metropolitan Opera, where she played the title role in the premiere of Richard Strauss's *Salome*, charged up to ten dollars for tickets. She and other critics of popular music (then and later) obviously had objections unrelated to commerce. There were clearly strains of both class bias and ethnic phobia in the feeling that the music of the Tin Pan Alley songwriters, those untrained (uneducated, unrefined—in a sense *unclean*) moneygrubbing city-dwelling tradesmen, should not be coming into our homes and touching the hearts and minds (*touching* in deep ways) of our young women. Irving Berlin: Wasn't he a *Jew*? Eubie Blake and Noble Sissle: Weren't they *Negroes*?

Looking at the song sheets for tunes that were popular over the course of the year before that *Tribune* article, I can picture someone like Olive Fremstad squirming in her corset. Sharing music in the parlor was still thought of as one of the most acceptable ways for proper young men and women to socialize, although rigidities of that sort were already fading, echoes of the Austen age carried out in ritual as symbols of Old World propriety still lingering in the middle-class American imagination. Many of the popular ballads published as late as 1914 and 1915 were sweetly romantic but laced with a strain of eros that was daring, if not radical, for its time. A pair of major hits of the day—"I Was a Good Little Girl till I Met You" (by the composer James W. Tate and the lyricist Clifford Harris) and "I'll Make a Man of You" (by the composer Herman Finck and the lyricist Arthur Wimperis)—were sly, titillating celebrations of sexual awakening that helped stir the larger awakening of post-Victorian society. For thirty to forty cents apiece, song sheets sold both love and sex to buyers for whom the latter was thought of as a new product. Even a few of the jokey novelty songs of the time, such as "Who Paid the Rent for Mrs. Rip Van Winkle" (by the composer Fred Fischer and the lyricist Alfred Bryan), had a slyly radical sauciness that their humor leavened.

When early critics of Tin Pan Alley saw devilry in "city life," they were not associating urbanism with blackness. That would come later, after the Great Migration of the period roughly between 1910 and 1930 brought nearly two million African Americans out of the post-Reconstruction South and into northern cities for industrial work, including labor in the music industry. Black identity, in the public consciousness informed in part by popular music, was still connected to the South and distorted by the minstrelsy prominent in popular entertainment since the songs of Stephen Foster in the mid-nineteenth century.

By 1915, minstrel songs were fading in popularity but still in circulation, with Irving Berlin having recently composed "The Minstrel Parade" and the mixed-race team of Bert Williams (the renowned African American minstrel star), Will Vodery (the African American composer and conductor later associated with *Show Boat*), and Jean Havez (a white gagman for stage productions and silent comedies) having just published "The Darktown Poker Club." Minstrelsy, duly infamous today for having propagated insidious stereotypes, was exempted from high-minded criticism in its time, because it was taken to be no threat to the public good—that is, to the welfare of the white people.

Minstrelsy took a variety of forms, and few races or ethnicities other than WASPs were spared its cruelties. The dime music halls of the Bowery, the center of American popular entertainment in its gestational years in the late nineteenth century, were founded on the principles of racial and ethnic parody and self-parody, through which the teeming population of working-class immigrants acted out, ridiculed, and popularized the stereotypes that codified their status as outsiders while sending up the standards of white "normalcy" that defined them as outliers. In addition to blackface minstrels, or "darkie" or "coon" acts, common in the early period of the turn of the century, there were "Hebe" acts, "Dutch" acts (mocking German immigrants), "Dago" acts, "Mick" acts, and "Chink" or "Chinee" acts, with the actors generally aligned to ethnicities by their performance skill rather than their genetic endowment. Joe Weber and Lew Fields, both Jews, did a Dutch act in the Bowery era; the DeVere Brothers, a white American team, did a Chink act; Tom Brown, the African American star of the minstrel show *A Trip to Coontown*, also did a Mick act, as well as a Dago act. The catalogs of sheet music publishers overflowed with songs of minstrelsy of multiple kinds, from the more than three hundred "Chinee" songs, most of which had to do with prostitution and/or the use of opium, to the more than six hundred "coon" songs, including "All Coons Look Alike to Me," by the African American minstrel performer Ernest Hogan, a song from 1896 that sold more than a million copies of sheet music, and Fred Fischer's "If the Man in the Moon Were a Coon," from 1905, which sold more than three million song sheets. (Hogan said before his death in 1909 that he had come to regret having written "All Coons Look Alike to Me," and he is more fittingly remembered as one of the creators of ragtime.) In their boiling-over outlandishness and ignorance, the ethnic songs of the sheet music era gave form to America's fascination with and terror of its own multiethnic identity. The songs are a lurid grotesquerie of cultural panic.

Along with titillating love songs and minstrel tunes, one of the most popular categories in early sheet music was the romantic travel song, which pretended to capture the spirit of foreign places and people in exoticizing platitudes. In 1914, again, Tin Pan Alley publishers produced "On the Shores of Italy," with music by Jack Glogau and lyrics by Al Piantadosi, "I'm on My Way to Mandalay," with music by Fischer and lyrics by Bryan, and "In Siam," by Manuel Klein, among others about many places. Through both the twisted flattery of minstrelsy and the demeaning romanticizing of the travel song, American popular music asserted its Americanism.

Olive Fremstad might have been onto something when she railed about the great threat of early twentieth-century songs being that they were "introduced into drawing rooms," violating the sacred space of the late-Victorian home. Because the tunes were being sung and played by their audience, they entered a space much deeper than the parlor—an internal space where music, in the act of being performed, works on the performer in psychophysiological ways. After all, the audience for sheet music was not really an audience; it was a vast body of performers, and words and music have an effect on us when they are internalized and sung, processed through the same part of the brain that generates speech (called Broca's area), and given form by the same throat and the same mouth that produce our own words. It is one thing to listen to a performance of "I Was a Good Little Girl till I Met You" or "I'll Make a Man of You"—or, dear God, "All Coons Look Alike to Me"—and another thing to have the words come off your tongue.

Today, the music of the Tin Pan Alley era is commonly mistaken to have traded mainly in universal sentiments. As commercial music intended not only for consumption but for performance by the public, the songs needed to appeal to as broad a swath of the public as possible. Yet universals and cultural vogues are different things, and popular music is nothing if not voguish. Tin Pan Alley songs reflected their market-oriented creators' conception of the public's tastes at the moment while contributing mightily to the making of those tastes. Pop songs, as cultural products, have always been part of the production of the culture.

When I was a kid in the 1960s, the essential simplicity of rock and roll, combined with the obvious social benefits of playing in a band— the girls liked the boys with guitars—led to a resurgence in amateur musicianship among young people. The home performance paradigm of the sheet music era returned, in a new way for new reasons.

The ability to read music was no longer an imperative for participation in musical culture, as it had been for people of my grandparents' time. To the contrary, the fact that rock and roll seemed to require no training to play, nor even much talent, was a source of its power as an emblem of raw purity and authenticity—values that flew against the complexity and the sophistication of the jazz-based music of my parents' era. Still, when my mother bought me my first guitar, a brown-sunburst plywood Silvertone acoustic from Sears, for twenty-eight dollars, she arranged for me to have lessons in music from one of her customers at the diner, a youngish, raffish man named Ray who was the leader of a local wedding orchestra. He came to our house for forty-five minutes once a week, and I remember suspecting then that my mother had a special arrangement with him to pay for my sessions. I took to music theory, unexpectedly, and quickly grew comfortable with the notation that I had thought of as outdated before I understood it.

One summer, four of my buddies and I put together a band and called it the Ryders. The bassist, Ernie Fazekas, owned no bass and played the low strings on a six-string electric guitar. Our inspiration was a Monkees cover band in town, and our repertoire consisted almost exclusively of tunes we picked out of a copy of the Monkees songbook that my teacher Ray bought for me. We were a copy of a copy of a copy of the Beatles. We practiced in the living room of our drummer's house, and we had to play with towels on the drums so as not to distress the patrons in the bar next door. After a few weeks of rigorous flailing, we got a booking as the entertainment at a birthday party for one of our coveted female classmates, Colleen Trembler, held at the town youth center. I set up my retractable chrome music stand and played the music as it was notated. At some point early in the show, the lead singer, Tootie Ritz, came over to my spot and moved my music stand back along the wall behind us. I remember this happening in silence and slow motion, as if in an overcranked scene from a Martin Scorsese film, and in my memory everyone at the party stared at me and laughed, still in slow motion. "The Monkees don't read music," Tootie snapped at me. We had not yet learned that the Monkees did not play much of the music on their early records, either.

I quit the band after that, as I recall, though I might actually have been kicked out. Over the years, I have always thought of the precipitating incident as a conflict over the values of notation and ear playing, the traditions of musical literacy and vernacularism, though I think it really had more to do with the low value of my guitar playing. I was an amateur, and the band was playing a job. We weren't in the drummer's living room anymore.

2

THE RISE OF RECORDS

WHISPERING

The art on the cover of the sheet music to "I'm from New Jersey," published in 1961, is a pink-tinted photograph of Frank Sinatra in his ring-a-ding-ding glory. He has a tweed, narrow-brimmed fedora cocked low on his brow, and he is leaning forward toward the photographer, grinning a wide, toothy grin as he winks at the lens. With his right hand, in a movement frozen by the camera, he is toggling his pointer finger back and forth in the universal gesture for "Come to Papa, sweetheart." Just as a nineteenth-century sheet music buyer would know from the etching of J. Aldrich Libbey on the cover of "After the Ball" that Libbey must have performed the song in a show, anyone who saw the picture of Frank Sinatra on the music to "I'm from New Jersey" would know that Sinatra must have recorded it, and the fact of such a recording, in 1961, would have been impressive evidence of the song's success. Unfortunately for Red Mascara, such a recording was not a fact but one of his almost-plausible fantasies. Unless one were to take the cover to indicate merely that Frank Sinatra was from New Jersey, as he was, being the most celebrated expatriate of Hoboken, the use of Sinatra's photograph can be understood only as a harmless act of small-time fraud.

What's interesting about it, I think, is its implied assertion of the value of recording as a mid-century pop music ideal—an ideal of value so great that it was worth the risk of incurring the displeasure of Frank Sinatra. In a much earlier phase of commercial popular music, before recordings came into prominence, performances by stage and vaudeville acts had been recognized as useful in helping to establish a song with the public so the song could become a hit through sales of sheet music for performance at home. With the advent of recording, the form of the hit became a single performance, captured on disc and sold for listening to—or dancing to—at home. At one time, a serious-minded critic such as Sigmund Spaeth, writing in one of the early histories of American popular music, could sneeringly describe the vaudeville star Nora Bayes as a song "plugger" for having made a recording of the pseudo-Oriental ballad "The Japanese Sandman" (by the composer Richard Whiting and the lyricist Raymond Egan). The song was still considered the commodity, and Bayes's recording was conceived of as a plug for its sales in the sheet music market. With the phenomenal explosion in recording—the medium that would make the career of a subtle, quiet singer such as Frank Sinatra possible—the performance on a disc became established as the commodity, and in time even the falsified suggestion of the existence of a record by Sinatra could make a song look good.

Among the recordings Sinatra actually made in 1961 was his final album for Capitol Records in the big-band style, *Come Swing with Me!* It was orchestrated and conducted by one of Sinatra's longtime collaborators, Billy May, a veteran of the swing era whom I interviewed a couple of times in the early 1990s. May talked avidly about his work with Sinatra, and he remembered the sessions for *Come Swing with Me!* with special fondness. "Rock was starting to be the big craze, and everybody was in a panic about it," May recalled. "That record, we planned out as a showcase for stereo [and] the long-playing record [format]. Hi-fi was the thing for music nuts. We set up the orchestra in the studio to show off the stereo effect—the brass on one side and reeds on the other side, and so forth. We went through a lot of trouble figuring out how the ears work."

In the nineteenth century, the success of the camera as a mechanical means of not simply emulating sight but transcending it—by freezing images in tangible, storable, marketable form—spurred efforts to do the same with sound. The gods of the machine age, the wizard-tinkerers still venerated today in fifth-grade American history lessons, went through a lot of trouble to figure out how the ears worked, as a starting point.

As early as 1874, Alexander Graham Bell came up with a resourceful, though disgusting, proposition. He built a machine for documenting sound waves that incorporated, among its parts, a human ear surgically removed from a corpse. Surviving drawings of the device show how it functioned: The user would speak or sing into a metal cone, which was connected to the ear of the deceased. The sound would cause vibrations in the eardrum, which had a stick of straw attached to it, and the straw would etch the pattern of the waveform on a moving plate of glass coated with charcoal. The device functioned as a rudimentary way to document sound waves, though it had no sound-playback capability and might not have been practical to put into mass production until the period of World War I, when the supply of corpses multiplied exponentially.

The first song ever recorded, by all accounts, was a folk tune sung into an entirely mechanical device developed by a Parisian bookseller, printer, and inventor named Édouard-Léon Scott de Martinville. Much like the Bell machine, Scott's "phonautograph" was designed not to reproduce sound but only to document sound waves in graphic form, for the purpose of auditory study. In April 1850, Scott used the device to make a record of the sound of someone—probably the inventor himself—singing a few bars of the lilting little French song "Au clair de la lune," and in 2008 scientists at the Lawrence Berkeley National Laboratory, a U.S. Department of Energy lab at the University of California, Berkeley, figured out how to decode this obscure curio, digitally, and play it. The song, incomplete on the recording, foreshadows the whole history of recorded popular music in thematic content. It's about sex.

The song tells the tale of a young man, Lubin, who knocks on the door of strangers' houses in search of a pen, for some reason. He ends up at the home of a dark-haired girl, and she fulfills his search. In translation, the song concludes,

> The pen was looked for, the light was looked for
> With all that looking, I don't know what was found
> But I do know that door will shut behind them.

Although "Au clair de la lune" was often sung to children as a lullaby, as it is to this day, the song tells a grown-up kind of bedtime story.

Thomas Edison—the prototype for iconship in the industries of technical innovation, the precursor to Walt Disney and Steve Jobs as an avatar of both creativity and the lordly stewardship of intellectual property rights—held, among his 1,093 patents, one for the cylinder recording-and-playback system that established the recorded-music trade in America. Initially, Edison had another purpose in mind. He imagined the cylinder primarily as a format for businessmen to record dictation, in order to cut down the amount of time spent talking to secretaries. Cylinders, metal tubes slightly smaller than toilet paper rolls, contained their audio information in markings embedded into their interior surface, and their reproduction quality was adequate for sounds of limited complexity in the range we associate with the tenor voice. A cylinder recording of a vaudeville performer such as Lonnie Johnson would have sounded about as much like he sounded onstage as a black-and-white daguerreotype portrait of him would have looked like he looked in action under the footlights. The mind would have had some work to do, filling in the gaps of the sounds or the colors lost in the flawed and limited processes of recording and reproduction, just as the mind does in the reconstruction of memories of felt experience, and this fact acts counterintuitively to the benefit of the experience of listening to recordings made with any technology. The mind tends to like having a little work to do.

The cylinder, as a recording format, had a quality in common with every technology to follow it: mortality. After a few good years, cylinders were supplanted in the marketplace by flat discs made from a compound of secretions from insect shells (shellac). Developed mainly by Emile Berliner, a German-born American, and put into mass production in the United States by the Victor company in the early twentieth century, shellac discs sounded about as good as cylinders and proved more durable and more practical to produce, to ship, to market, and to use and shelve or stack in the parlor. The name of the first major institution of the record business, the Victor Talking Machine Company, nodded to Edison's notion of recording's applicability to speech, although Victor and other early disc makers documented performers making sounds of many kinds. Victor, in its initial years of operation, released patriotic speeches by politicians such as William Jennings Bryan, dramatic recitations by actors such as the British Shakespeare star Ellen Terry, sermons by spiritual leaders such as the African American minister J. M. Gates, hokum by comedians such as the rapid-fire monologuist Murry K. Hill, and music in half a dozen traditions: musical theater, vaudeville, opera, instrumental classical music, minstrel tunes, and other ethnic specialties.

The Victor Talking Machine Company was a monolithic, vertically integrated producer and marketer of entertainment hardware and software. It scouted talent, made recordings in its own studios, pressed and packaged the discs, and manufactured the equipment people needed to play them—machinery whose brand name, the Victrola, reinforced the parent brand (as the iMac and MacBook later would) and fell quickly into common usage as the generic term for a windup record player. Victor created the medium and named it for itself. All the company's operations took place in a grand, decoratively towered factory building in Camden, New Jersey, the once robust and long since busted city about an hour's drive from my hometown, going south along the Delaware River.

When the Victor company was thriving, setting the foundational terms for the young record business and dominating it, it was one of two major manufacturing operations in Camden, the other being the Campbell Soup Company. Sixty-some years later, when I was in elementary school, the teachers would sponsor annual class trips to the Campbell's factory, and the tour would always include a lecture on Camden's industrial history; the speaker would invariably mention the early importance of RCA Victor in the city, and that would be the only part of the talk that I would retain. After a merger in 1929, Victor became RCA Victor, a brand familiar to every adolescent I respected in the 1960s, from the labels on the Jefferson Airplane records.

I remember thinking as a boy that there was something funny in the fact that both soup and music had been packaged within the space of a few blocks in the same grim old New Jersey city. Cans and records were both vessels of preservation and storage designed for mass production and mass marketing. In fact, I eventually realized, the dual operations of canning sustenance for the body and the spirit were of a piece, two manifestations of a utopian ideal of industrial age capitalism: to produce easily digestible, contaminant-free, efficiently manufacturable, and profitable goods to satisfy the appetites of the masses. Mass-produced pop entertainment and Campbell's soup were connected by Camden zoning half a century before Andy Warhol brought them together in art.

Through a third young industry of the early twentieth century, advertising, both Victor and Campbell's stimulated tastes that the consuming public had not previously realized that it had. Who had a clamoring for condensed split-pea soup before becoming indoctrinated in the benefits of its convenience and its alleged equivalence to home cooking? Who had craved tinny two-and-a-half-minute reproductions of musical performances before becoming educated in the gratifications of their convenience and their supposed equivalence to the concert experience?

Advertisements for early Victor records and record players conjured an image of the parlor Victrola as a magic cabinet, an instrument of transformation. In one full-page, two-color magazine ad from 1915, we see a group of five splendidly rich white people gathered in a home appointed with signifiers of prosperity and taste, along with a Victrola. A crystal chandelier hangs from a high ceiling, and a bearskin rug lies on the floor. On one side of the room there is a marble nude on a pedestal, and on the other there is a floor-standing Victrola in dark-wood cabinetry. A man and a woman are coupled off in the foreground—we're in their home—and a man with two women, all in evening wear, has just entered, in the background. (A man with *two* women. This was a post-Victorian image of modern progress.) In the caption, the man with the two women says, "What a coincidence! That Caruso record you just played on the Victrola was the same aria we heard him sing at the opera tonight!"

From the standard narrative of recorded-music history, we know, correctly, that records helped democratize American musical culture. Enrico Caruso, the revered Italian tenor, went to Camden to record for Victor, and through the arias and excerpts from arias (and other pieces) that he recorded, opera entered the homes of millions of Americans of every class. (The short playing time of the records necessitated the excerpting, the condensing, of the material.) In a real way, this demonstrated the democratizing capacity of records; recordings brought professional performances of many kinds of music—formal and informal, high-toned and low-down, portions of arias and faux-Oriental exotica—to all those who could afford the playing equipment and the records. (A low-end Victrola cost about fifteen dollars, the price of a wardrobe trunk in 1915, and records typically cost one dollar apiece, the price of a pair of fabric gloves. Some stores catering to working-class customers, such as Woolworth's, sometimes rented records by the week, for five cents.) But this was a limited democratization. Victrolas were marketed and purchased, in part, on the grounds of their power to elevate—to provide the lower orders with a mechanism (or at the very least a symbol) of upward mobility. The new specialty stores devoted to selling records and record-playing equipment, such as the Landay's chain in the Northeast, were designed as sedate showrooms befitting luxury goods, prohibited by the chain owners from the exercise of "gaudiness and show."

I inherited five or six old shellac records that my grandmother saved in her basement—to be honest, I snuck them out of her house one afternoon after school, while she was cutting dandelion greens out of her yard, to fry for dinner—and nearly all the discs were by Caruso. This fact was not simply evidence of my grandparents' Italian blood. Enrico Caruso made some 260 recordings for Victor between 1904 and 1920. If nine out of ten Caruso records had shattered over the span of fifty or sixty years, there would still have been at least five million Carusos in American grandparents' basements in the 1960s, and every family was not Italian. Late in my mother's life, when I was starting this book, I asked her if her parents really listened to opera records, and she screamed at me, "What do you think? They had no *class*?"

As the body copy of that ad for Victor records proclaimed, "Hearing the world's greatest artists sing the arias you like best is an everyday pleasure with Victrola. Just as real, just as enjoyable, in your own home as though you were hearing them in the great opera houses and theatres of the world." The record industry laid claim to making the "greatest" something "everyday." It promised to deliver fine things to working people like my grandparents, by means of acquisition and consumption—fine things, that is to say, that qualified as such by the standards of the higher orders. That the everyday could also have a kind a greatness, a fineness—that the music and the other arts popular among the broad public could excel by standards of their own (or, for that matter, by traditional formal standards)—was a proposition not unheard of, even in the early twentieth century, but not relevant to the marketing purposes of the new mass medium. The record business, which for a while was essentially the Victor company, sought to appeal to the broad public by promising to fulfill dreams of social aspiration it helped to create.

If sheet music industrialized the production of popular music, records professionalized the experience of it. At a glance, the revolution records enacted might seem like one primarily of domestication. Records brought the arias of Caruso—and the ragtime piano of Eubie Blake, the Irish songs of Billy Murray, the comic numbers of Fanny Brice, the fox-trot dance music of Paul Whiteman, the bawdy blues of Ida Cox and Bessie Smith, and a great deal more—into the American living room, whether or not the room also had a marble nude on a pedestal. Yet the living room is precisely where popular hits had been performed by the millions of amateurs who had purchased sheet music to plink out and warble for one another. Professional and semiprofessional performances took place on vaudeville stages, in legitimate theaters, in tent shows, and on the town squares where regional acts and touring companies routinely played. Now the performance taking place in the living room was a professional one. The reproductive quality of records was surely limited—shellac 78 rpm records hissed and crackled, and they played too slow or too fast, slurring or whinnying, if the Victrola wasn't properly cranked and adjusted—but the performance quality of someone such as Enrico Caruso or Eubie Blake was likely to be better than that of one's cousin Theodora or oneself.

At the same time, records made the taking in of a professional performance something private and intimate, conducted somewhat on one's own terms—at whatever hour one wanted (within the limits of family life in a house with one parlor and one Victrola in it), as often as one wanted (with the same restrictions in force). As the Victor ad with the tony operagoers pointed out, "The Victrola has these advantages: You can make your choice of artists and selections, and have as many encores as you desire." Two women *and* all the encores you desire! Records took a music that had been industrialized and professionalized, and they personalized it. Music, now recorded and made playable, could be replayed and replayed again and again—at no further cost, other than the progressive deterioration of the disc and the growing annoyance of one's housemates. Records provided the listener with a sense of individual control over the musical experience in the home, in exchange for the loss of creative control over the material that came with the turn away from amateur performance in favor of listening.

Before record producers and recording artists learned to manipulate audio technologies for creative effect, and long before the aural fingerprints of recording and playback technologies came to be seen as having aesthetic value of their own, any audible evidence of recording technology at work was considered a failing of the technology. A record was still conceived strictly as a document of a performance, and playing a record was supposed to be about sound reproduction rather than production—the re-creation of existing sound, without the creation of anything that might diminish, add to, or otherwise change that sound. As recording was understood, its first duty was the faithful replication of reality. (Its second duty was to enable mass duplication of that reality for sale at retail.) All the aesthetic value in a recording was thought to be in the music as it was created, prior to the intervention of recording apparatuses. In the original and only there was what Walter Benjamin, in his famous early critique of mechanical reproduction, imagined as the "aura" of creative work.

Music recording, like photography before it, helped crystallize distinctions between the original and the copy, the unreal and the real in popular art. Indeed, it helped create these distinctions, in order to blur them. To make possible the glorification of the unreal, the real needed to be glorified first.

Victor, in one of its ads, showed two photographs, side by side: one of Caruso as Radamès in Verdi's *Aida*, resplendent in a caped Egyptian costume; the other of the Victor record of Caruso singing "Celeste Aida," the *romanza* from the opera. "Both are Caruso," said the ad. "The Victor record of Caruso's voice is just as truly Caruso as Caruso himself." The Barnumesque syllogism hangs neatly on the idea that veracity—*truly*-ness—is something fluid. For a record to be "just as" real as a person, realness has to be relative. What was more real, a concert performance or a record? The question established technology as the determinant factor and tabled the issue of the elemental theatricality of all performance, live or recorded. By implication, moreover, the question provided its own answer: If records were legitimate by virtue of their equality to live performances, the two were not equal at all.

Caruso was a superstar in the Victrola age, a romantic figure with dark European good looks who sang weepy and melodramatic material with voluptuous emotionality, and had the first million-selling hit in record history with "Vesti la giubba," the deliciously overwrought first-act finale of Leoncavallo's *Pagliacci*, which he sang for Victor in 1907, when there were probably only about half a million record players in the country. He was a popular sensation on record in part because the strengths of his singing—its vigor, its brightness, its clarity—compensated for the weaknesses of early records and windup record players. Caruso made records sound good. Just as significantly, perhaps, the high theatricality of his work enlarged the experience of record listening; Caruso carried into the home something of the splendor of an evening at the opera house, a sense of participation in a grand occasion. His presence on record relocated his listeners. His music was not suited to the living room, and that's what made it work so well there.

When I moved to Greenwich Village to go to New York University, my mother exhorted me to protect my belongings, including the writing I was beginning to do in earnest. She told me she learned about the risks of theft in New York during an adventure she had toward the end of World War II, before she dropped out of high school, while my father was overseas in the navy. Without telling anyone, she snuck into the city one day, on the bus, and met a handsome composer. He was Italian and was working on a symphony he hummed into her ear as they sat by the pond in Washington Square Park. He took her that night to a smoky little nightclub where he was shocked to hear his own music, stolen by someone and turned into wild jazz. When I heard this story, I did not yet know there is no pond in Washington Square. Nor did I realize my mother had fancifully inserted herself into the plot of a B movie from the 1940s called *Greenwich Village*. And why not? All people who go to New York are, broadly speaking, editing themselves into their fantasies.

Greenwich Village, the film, was a minor piece of nostalgic Technicolor sentiment geared to soothe home-front audiences weary from four years of war. It was set in the 1920s—or, more precisely, in the Roaring Twenties of sleeve garters and speakeasies we know from movies made years after the fact. Don Ameche played my mother's suitor, a suave highbrow musician who finds the melodic ideas of his lovely but pretentious music pilfered and adapted in vulgar but fun vaudeville entertainment. (Ameche, a doe-eyed journeyman of mixed Anglo-Mediterranean heritage, projected a bland, essentially white, but almost vaguely ethnic near otherness and was cast in several pseudo-historical Hollywood fairy tales about America's racially complicated popular music, including *Swanee River*, in which he starred as Stephen Foster, and *Alexander's Ragtime Band*, in which he played the pianist and songwriter for the movie's titular group.)

Greenwich Village used as its musical theme (and one of its plot devices) a dance tune from the early history of records: "Whispering," by the composers Vincent Rose and John Schoenberger, with words by Richard Coburn. An instrumental record of "Whispering" (on one side) and "The Japanese Sandman" (on the other) by the ballroom-orchestra leader Paul Whiteman was one of the biggest hits of the Victrola age, selling some two million shellac discs. With its sprightly melody and circular harmonic structure, "Whispering" was nicely suited to the dance fad of the day, the fox-trot—a dance just cozy enough and so easy to do that it became a craze, and not only in the ballrooms where young people gathered to meet, but in the homes where they had their record players.

Paul Whiteman, whose surname was a comic descriptor worthy of Dickens, had been a classical viola player and leader of a navy orchestra before he put together a dance band. Whiteman's music was nothing if not beautiful. Raucous, it was not; nor was it shocking or earthy or vitally original. It was consistently lovely, however, and often irrepressibly, unoppressively clever. Whiteman had high professional standards and an ear for talent, as he demonstrated in his development of important young jazz musicians such as the cornetist Bix Beiderbecke, the violinist Joe Venuti, and the saxophonist Frankie Trumbauer, the last of whom became a primary influence on the elegiac swing-era saxophonist Lester Young. It was Whiteman who, in 1924, commissioned George Gershwin to compose *Rhapsody in Blue* (with orchestration support from Whiteman's staff arranger and pianist, Ferde Grofé) for Whiteman to perform with an edition of his group expanded to mirror the symphony orchestras whose stature Whiteman seemed to envy desperately. He is perhaps most influential as the first celebrity in popular music to orient his work to his craving for acceptance as a serious artist. Whiteman outsold Caruso and coveted his standing in the culture.

When the Whiteman record of "Whispering" and "The Japanese Sandman" was released in November 1921, there were no fewer than six versions of "Whispering" on disc, from various musicians (Harry A. Yerkes's Dance Orchestra, the Van Eps Specialty Four, and others) on multiple labels (Aeolian, Pathé, Brunswick, and more); and there were at least three versions of "The Japanese Sandman" on record, including the vocal rendition by Nora Bayes. The

Whiteman orchestra's record was the one that sold two million copies, and it takes nothing away from the affecting proficiency of the group's performance to factor in that Whiteman's record label, Victor, was the one with the broadest distribution and the most aggressive marketing. Whiteman's performance of "Whispering" might or might not have been the best one on record—the Van Eps Specialty Four rendition was pungent and bright, stronger to my ears—but of the record labels Victor was surely the best performing.

To hear Whiteman's record of "Whispering" today is to be reminded of the documentary function of early recorded music. With its chunk-a-chunk banjo rhythm and corny slide-whistle solo, the music is wholly an artifact of its time. The record captured three minutes and seventeen seconds of playing by nine musicians in 1920, and however fresh it might have sounded when it was recorded, it would forever after sound like nothing other than a moment in 1920. Canned goods are no longer fresh.

If we think of recorded music as the opposite of "live" music, we could be tempted to think of it as dead. Once documented, the music on the record is, in a way, entombed—unchanging but for the effects of wear and decay. This way of conceiving of recording is nearly as old as recording itself. When the Victor Talking Machine Company began, it used, as the image on its soon-to-be-iconic logo, an adaptation of a painting of a calico fox terrier peering into the sound cone of a windup Victrola. In the original artwork, rendered in the late nineteenth century by an English artist named Francis Barraud, the machine was a cylinder player, and it was sitting on what looked like the top of a coffin. Nipper, with his head tilted, his nose in the cone, was fixed on the presence of his late master's voice, the sound of the dead.

If recording represents a death, though, a record itself fosters a life—the ongoing existence of the music after it has been made reproducible, storable, and sharable, as well as sellable. The case of "Whispering" is a good example.

After those six records of the song in 1920, "Whispering" was recorded another dozen or so times—as instrumentals by Benny Goodman and Erroll Garner and in vocal renditions by Bing Crosby, Frank Sinatra, and Lena Horne. One of the people who heard and admired the Goodman version was the guitarist and recording innovator Les Paul, who would record the song as a smoothly swinging ballad with his partner and wife, Mary Ford, in 1951. One of the people who heard the Les Paul version was Chet Atkins, who would record the tune as a fingerpicking chamber-hoedown showpiece, in 1961. One of the people who heard at least one version of it was the jazz composer and trumpeter Dizzy Gillespie, and he reinvented the tune, writing an angular new bebop melody over an adaptation of the chord changes, naming the new work "Groovin' High." Gillespie wrote the piece for a recording session conducted on February 9, 1945, two days after the opening of the movie *Greenwich Village*, and he always said he first heard "Whispering" in a movie. He once recalled the film as a western serial featuring the stunt rider Yakima Canutt, though I have not been able to find a Canutt movie that included "Whispering."

When I was a freshman in high school, in 1970, I bought a vinyl LP bootleg of the Beatles' "Get Back" sessions in the underground-record bin at the Upper Story, the only head shop within ride-grubbing distance of my house, across the Delaware River in Easton, Pennsylvania. Unofficial releases of live concerts and studio outtakes still had the illicit cachet of black-market goods, and countless numbers of bootleg-collecting teenagers like me imagined themselves as members of a secret league of music-nerd bandits, a Resistance to the tyranny of the record companies. With the "Get Back" sessions, recorded at the Apple studios throughout January 1969, the Beatles had attempted to escape from their self-imposed exile from live recording and prove—to themselves, as much as to their audience— that they could make a record the old way, as four members of a band playing together, without the use of the studio technology that had become essential to their music.

As George Martin said of this period, "They felt like prisoners of the studio—and prisoners of mine—and they were attempting to break free by behaving as if they were still merely a dance band." Jamming in the studio, the Beatles pulled out songs they had learned when they were kids, and one of them was "Whispering," which George Harrison played very much like Chet Atkins played it on the record he made after hearing the way Les Paul recorded it after hearing the record of it by Benny Goodman.

3

THE COTTON CLUB

JUNGLE NIGHTS IN HARLEM

Hearing is only a part of what we are doing when we experience music, popular or otherwise. We take in the sounds, and then our mind starts working with them. We make connections and associations, relate what we hear to what we know or think we know, tap memories, make mental pictures, and submit to feelings of all sorts. What are we hearing when we listen to music? We might just as fruitfully ask, what are we *seeing* in our mind's eye? *Who* are we thinking about? *Where* do we imagine ourselves?

Late one afternoon in the fall of 1974, during my first semester at NYU, I arrogantly walked into the English Department office and asked if I could meet with Ralph Ellison, who was teaching a course in American literature that I had missed out on, because I had neglected to register for it in time. Ellison, with his courtly good grace, gave me ten or fifteen minutes of his time. I was so panic-stricken, having not prepared for the possibility that Ellison would really be there and be willing to talk to me, that nothing of what Ellison said that day got through to me. All I retained was how he looked behind his desk: flawlessly dignified in a dark suit and tie, his pencil mustache trimmed with precision. Ellison, politely, invited me to come back another time, and I, in my unwavering arrogance, returned a couple of weeks later, after rereading *Invisible Man* and looking up some of Ellison's magazine pieces on music. In this second visit, Ellison said some things that have stuck with me ever since, one of which led me to think about the power of music to conjure images and stir associations in ways that effectively (and sometimes problematically) transport listeners to other places, including those constructed largely, if not solely, for that purpose. Ellison got me thinking about the Cotton Club.

First, he told me a little parable about a man he had seen fishing a copy of *The New York Times* out of a garbage bin in Riverside Park. If I were serious about writing, Ellison said, I should think of that man as my ideal reader. I took that as a lesson in the importance of not making presumptions on the basis of social or economic status or racial identity, a point Ellison also made memorably in his essay "The Little Man at Chehaw Station." Ellison then brought up Duke Ellington. Picking up the theme of demeaning presumptions, Ellison told me how white society had undervalued Ellington, early in his career, and painted his work as "jungle music"—that is to say, by the colonialist idea of the jungle: primitive, barbaric, animalistic. Uncivilized, uneducated, *unwhite*. Ellington, Ellison said, exploited these conceptions at the same time he upended them. If I wanted to understand American music, Ellison said, I needed to study the Cotton Club, and I needed to understand it not as a physical location but as a place in the cultural imagination. As Ellison explained, in a pithy phrase, America "went there on the radio."

The Cotton Club, I soon began to see, was elemental to the story of American popular music as a nexus of blackness expressed, imagined, demeaned, and exalted. It was not only a celebrated hub of nightlife during the Harlem Renaissance but, as Ralph Ellison stressed, a phenomenon of broader reach—and somewhat different consequence—on the airwaves.

Jack Johnson, the fearless and charismatic boxer who was the first African American heavyweight champion of the world, ran the venue briefly, as the Club DeLuxe, in a vast ballroom on the second floor of a neo-Georgian-style building on the corner of Lenox Avenue and West 142nd Street. An all-around sports-and-entertainment celebrity and catalyst for controversy, Johnson would be an utterly familiar kind of figure a century later. In his time, however, he was unprecedented and unacceptable to white society. He exploited his extraordinary success in the ring with paying endorsements for products such as the White Steam Touring Car and held interests in multiple entertainment businesses, including nightclubs in both Chicago and New York. The white public could not tolerate his accomplishments or his failure to apologize for having achieved them as a black man or, worse yet, for having enjoyed them.

In 1920, Johnson was traveling the world with his wife while a warrant awaited him for arrest on a charge of violating U.S. law against "white slavery," a loaded charge that amounted to his being a black man with a white woman. On July 20 of that year, Johnson surrendered to federal authorities at the Mexican border, and by September he was in Leavenworth. He apparently operated the Club DeLuxe from prison until his release in July 1921. By 1922, Johnson lost control of the club and relinquished his interest to the Irish gangster Owney "the Killer" Madden, a fearsome little Hell's Kitchen rat who, at the time he took over the Cotton Club, was in Sing Sing on a conviction for the murder of one of his rivals, Little Patsy Doyle. Prohibition brought early bloom to the racketeering trade, and Madden was looking for an outlet to sell his bootleg beer, known as Madden's No. 1. I don't know if the name was intended as a urine joke.

Madden, through his front men George "Big Frenchy" DeMange and Walter Brooks (who had experience in entertainment as part of the Mob-connected organization that brought Eubie Blake and Noble Sissle's all-black musical *Shuffle Along* to Broadway in 1921), revamped the venue and reopened it with a new name: the Cotton Club, suggesting nothing other than an exclusive nightspot on a plantation. The president of the corporation that owned the club was someone named Sam Sellis, whose previous position had been as a pickpocket. The club's unspoken but broadly whispered connections to gangland, functioning in concert with the exoticized mode of negritude that it presented, made the Cotton Club seem glamorously taboo to white audiences. With both Prohibition and the Harlem Renaissance at their peaks, gangster chic conjoined with an expanding interest in the African American arts to produce a vogue for black entertainment that seemed to represent something more than minstrelsy.

"White people began to come to Harlem in droves," recalled Langston Hughes in his autobiography, *The Big Sea*.

> For several years they packed the expensive Cotton Club on Lenox Avenue. But I was never there, because the Cotton Club was a Jim Crow club for gangsters and monied whites. They were not cordial to Negro patronage, unless you were a celebrity like Bojangles. So Harlem Negroes did not like the Cotton Club and never appreciated its Jim Crow policy in the very heart of their dark community. Nor did ordinary Negroes like the growing influx of whites toward Harlem after sundown, flooding the little cabarets and bars where formerly only colored people laughed and sang, and where now the strangers were given the best ringside tables to sit and stare at the Negro customers—like amusing animals in a zoo.

The interior of the Cotton Club was decorated by the Viennese architect and designer Joseph Urban, an aesthete with a showbiz flair who worked also for the Ziegfeld Follies and the Metropolitan Opera, and he did the club up as a dream pastiche of Art Nouveau opulence and safari-movie kitsch. There were chandeliers and potted palm trees, trompe l'oeil foliage and bush creatures on the fascia, and movable panels painted with images of devilishly grinning tribal masks. Cab Calloway, the singer and bandleader, played extensively with his orchestra in the Cotton Club and described it as "a white man's fantasy"—one that he subverted with the outré modernity of his act. Bedazzlingly attired in a white tuxedo cut in measurements of outlandish extremes—his coattails and bow tie and the brim of his hat all extravagantly huge—Calloway dressed, sang, and moved in the modes of hepcat high fashion. "They tried to make us out like cavemen," he recalled in an interview in the 1980s. "We walked out, and they saw for themselves. We were the modernest thing in town. We weren't any gangster's monkey."

The Cotton Club presented a series of lavish floor shows, each featuring a judiciously balanced hodgepodge of acts: a dance orchestra of twelve pieces or so (Ellington and his ensemble, from December 1927 to June 1931, with Calloway filling in at least once during those years and playing regularly after 1931), singers (Ethel Waters, Adelaide Hall, Aida Ward), a comedian (Flournoy Miller), a dance specialty act (Bill "Bojangles" Robinson, Earl "Snakehips" Tucker), and a chorus of dancers (including, briefly, a teenage Lena Horne). A fresh show opened in the fall and in the spring, with new music and arrangements written specially for each one, along with some interpolations of current popular material or music associated with the featured performers. The Cotton Club, in essence, presented a new Broadway-style revue, in an idiom all its own, two times a year.

To create the music for these shows, the club employed teams of young songwriters and arrangers, most of whom were not African American themselves. The writers had, if no black blood, an affinity for African American popular music or a knack for faking one to the satisfaction of its almost exclusively white audience. (Negro celebrities popular with whites, such as Bill "Bojangles" Robinson, might be allowed to sit in the club—at the tables by the kitchen—for the titillation their presence provided the Anglo patrons.) "The boys behind the music were white—so the white boys owned it," said Calloway. "But they had to sound like colored boys to the people. If they couldn't write black, no good—no money—but the people [in the audience] were white. You have to see, this was show business."

Talented musical journeymen such as the songwriters Jimmy McHugh and Rube Bloom considered themselves jobbing at the Cotton Club, exploiting an opportunity to reach a sizable paying audience and to establish reputations as reliable writers for hire. McHugh would say that he thought of the tunes he wrote for African American performers (in the Cotton Club as well as in the all-black Broadway revue *Blackbirds of 1928*) as "genre" songs, like lullabies, hillbilly songs, or "mother" songs. After all, he was working in an industrial-age model of production and conceived of his job as one of satisfying his customers rather than his id. The best of the McHugh songs that were performed at the Cotton Club (though not necessarily composed originally *for* it)—"I Can't Give You Anything but Love" and "Exactly Like You," both written with the lyricist Dorothy Fields and performed by Ellington—are gently swinging and unforced. (Dorothy Fields, the daughter of Lew Fields of Weber and Fields, the old Bowery team famous for its "Dutch" act of ethnic parody, understood caricature as a gimmick of her father's era and avoided "cooning" or crudeness of any kind in her wry, urbane lyrics.)

Along with the music Ellington wrote for the Cotton Club, the most substantive and durable songs produced for the club's shows were composed by Harold Arlen, the son of a cantor, born Chaim (or Hyman) Arluck, whom Ethel Waters called "the Negro-est white man I know." Among the major popular-song composers of the first half of the twentieth century who were not African American, Arlen sounded the most black. Heavily influenced by the blues and the adaptations of it that he heard from white composers such as George Gershwin—as well as by Jewish folk music and the Caruso records his parents played—Arlen wrote a polygenetic music most definable by its affinity with black expression.

Arlen would recall being swept away in his youth by Gershwin and Irving Caesar's "Swanee," a catchy and harmonically advanced, though lyrically unenlightened, variation on Stephen Foster minstrelsy made popular by Al Jolson in cork. Before he became associated with the Cotton Club (through McHugh, who had done some work with Arlen's lyric-writing partner at the time, Ted Koehler), Arlen had already written "Get Happy," in which the cantor's son (with his lyricist) conjures the exaltation of a camp-revival meeting in thirty-two bars. For the Cotton Club shows, beginning with one titled "Brown Sugar—Sweet but Unrefined," Arlen and Koehler wrote a songbook of future standards indebted to the blues, to the music of the black church, and to jazz: among them, "Stormy Weather," "Ill Wind," "Between the Devil and the Deep Blue Sea," "I've Got the World on a String," and "As Long as I Live," along with specialties for Cab Calloway such as "Minnie the Moocher's Wedding Day" and the delirious marijuana-scare confessional "The Wail of the Reefer Man."

Alec Wilder, the art song composer and occasional author, gushed about what he called the "American-ness" of Arlen's music in his book *American Popular Song*, a critical study of the music of the first half of the twentieth century, published in 1972. "Of all the better song writers," Wilder wrote, Arlen had the deepest "emotional kinship with the jazz musician and his bittersweet, witty, lonely, intense world." Wilder, in his twelve-thousand-word chapter on Arlen, never explicitly noted African American music or culture but referred only to "American-ness" and, in code for blackness, to Arlen's connection to jazz. Wilder's image of jazz artists as tortured and isolated but clever people is a long-standing stereotype of jazz musicians of all races, and to the extent that it was meant to imply a characterization of African Americans, it was a stereotype that songs such as "Stormy Weather" and "Ill Wind," moaning laments of victimhood, helped to codify in American culture.

Ethel Waters, who introduced "Stormy Weather" at the Cotton Club in 1934, was having romance trouble at the time and sang the song as a message of personalized anguish. Because Waters and her man, Clyde Matthews, weren't together, it seemed to be raining all the time. "That song was the perfect expression of my mood. I was working my heart out at that time and getting no happiness," Waters recalled in her memoir *His Eye Is on the Sparrow*. "I found release in singing it each evening. Only those who have been deeply hurt can understand what pain is, or humiliation."

Lena Horne, a sixteen-year-old chorus girl in that show, later took up "Stormy Weather" as her signature song, and when she performed it, she considered a broader anguish. She thought of the gloom and misery everywhere. "I loved that beautiful, haunting song. You can hum it, and all the sadness is still there," said Horne, in one of a series of interviews I did with her over several years' time in the early 1990s. "Harold was a dear man [with] a great feeling for my people. He was Jewish, and that's as good as black." (Decades after Horne and Arlen's shared apprenticeship at the Cotton Club, the two of them worked together on the Broadway musical *Jamaica*, which Arlen wrote with Yip Harburg.)

"I never did 'Stormy Weather' as a love song—you know, 'Oh, boo hoo for little old me the sad-assed colored girl,'" Horne said. "I could take care of myself. I thought about the stormy weather for my people" in the era of Jim Crow. "Everybody at the Cotton Club had a story. There was only one ladies' room in the whole place, and the girls in the chorus weren't allowed to use it. The girls were all expected to entertain the customers after hours—you know what I'm talking about. The only reason I got out of that was my age. The gangsters didn't want to get shut down [on a morals charge]. My costume was precisely three feathers. That was my outfit. That was supposed to be realistic jungle wear. I shimmied like a fan dancer. The trumpet players were all growling like animals. That was supposed to be realistic jungle music. The whole thing was practically pornography." Rationalized as a kind of floor-show anthropology.

Duke Ellington, who served as the house arranger and bandleader, orchestrating the songs contributed by McHugh and Fields, Arlen and Koehler, and others, composed extensively for the Cotton Club himself, and he was encouraged by the management to write in a "jungle" style to match the venue's visual motif. He did this, as he did everything, with sly intelligence and panache. Ellington's drummer, Sonny Greer—a gifted showman who had a sensationally elaborate drum setup, complete with enormous gongs, a timpani, and a floor-standing set of chimes that he never needed to learn to play— would lay an insistent rhythm on the tom-toms, and the horn players (most notably the trumpeter Bubber Miley) would produce musical wails and growls, simulated animal sounds, with the rubber heads of toilet plungers. Ellington changed the name of his group from the Washingtonians (after his hometown, the District of Columbia) to the Jungle Band (after an imaginary version of Africa) and presented such pieces as "Jungle Jamboree," "Jungle Blues," "Jungle Nights in Harlem," and "Echoes of the Jungle."

In surviving recordings of broadcasts from the Cotton Club, the master of ceremonies, Dan Healy, can be heard introducing Ellington and his ensemble like a circus ringleader: "I'd like to have the pleasure of introducing the greatest living master of jungle music, the rip-roaring harmony hound, none other than Duke Ellington! Take your bow, Dukey!"

Ellington, in his memoir, *Music Is My Mistress*, described the music he made at the Cotton Club as work of scholarly yeomanship. "At the Cotton Club," Ellington wrote, "much attention was paid to acts with an African setting, and to accompany these we developed what was termed 'jungle style' jazz. As a student of Negro history I had, in any case, a natural inclination in this direction. This kind of theatrical experience, and the demands it made upon us, was both educative and enriching, and it brought about a further broadening of the music's scope."

Students of culture and history other than Ellington were just beginning to look closely at the African element in American music—this, before the principle of African Americanism was broadly established. Scholars such as William Morrison Patterson, a professor of English at Columbia, and historically inclined journalists such as Lafcadio Hearn had, by the second decade of the twentieth century, published a handful of serious articles attempting to connect what they called the "jass" or jazz strain in American music to Africa, with some esteem for that provenance. Among the white masses at the time, however, any argument for an African influence in American music was taken as a case for the music's savagery, and few people were talking about savagery as a worthy value in music. (That would change in the rock era.) A nationally circulated wire-service report was published in the *San Francisco Chronicle* with the headline "How 'JAZZ' MUSIC Originated in the JUNGLE" (with that capitalization), and it said, "Music has charms to soothe the savage beast, but on the other hand, one touch of 'jazz' may make savages of us all."

At the same time, in the sphere of the fine arts, primitivism was thought to be aligned with abstraction and intellectualism among the alienating decadences of modernism. *Le sacre du printemps*, with Nijinsky's angular, anticlassical choreography and Stravinsky's eruptive, dissonant score, was set to a pagan ritual, entwining the primitive and the avant-garde, and it was already seven years old when the Cotton Club opened, in 1920. Picasso painted his Cubist pastiche *Three Musicians* in 1921, and nobody needed to be told that the music the abstracted trio was playing had to be jazz. It was not entirely to its advantage that the jungle music of the Cotton Club could be considered as decadent as modernism. In 1925, *The Christian Science Monitor* reported Aldous Huxley as having said, "Barbarism has entered popular music from two sources—from the music of barbarous people, like the Negroes, and from serious music which has drawn from barbarism for its inspiration. The only music a civilized man can take unfailing pleasure in is civilized music."

The Cotton Club disproved this statement in two ways (and I'm not going to bother with the period gender bias in the reference to "civilized man"): For one, the scale of the club's popularity, at first as a New York nightspot and later as a national radio phenomenon, vividly demonstrated the pleasure that civilized men (and women) took in "barbaric" popular music. For another, the insistent and unique artfulness of that music, as composed by Arlen, Ellington, and others, and orchestrated (in most cases) by Ellington for performance by his musicians, showed that popular art can be sophisticated in nontraditional ways and potent in ways not as simple as sophistication.

After Ralph Ellison's death in 1994, I was writing about Ellington and Billy Strayhorn (with whom Ellington, in the late 1930s, began his long association), and I turned for help to Albert Murray, the cultural critic and novelist who was Ellison's lifelong friend. I told Murray about Ellison's having sent me off to study the Cotton Cub, and he nodded. "I suspect I suggested that postulation to Ralph," he said. Then again, he added, "My own thinking was greatly indebted to Nathan Huggins," the historian of African American culture.

"Huggins tells us that Harlem served the purposes of white America by providing, through avenues like the Cotton Club, a manner for whites to indulge and realize aspects of humanity that society had made forbidden to them. In a manner of speaking, the white customers were wearing black masks at the Cotton Club. However, the so-called Negro artists in the stage shows, and I include Ellington among them, were also wearing black masks. Each individual was performing, because his true identity was neither purely black nor purely white." Like Alec Wilder, Albert Murray saw and heard a complicated Americanness—or, in Murray's phrase, an omni-Americanism—instead of simple black and white.

By 1925, the New York radio station WFBH, a midsized, 500-watt station with a reach to some three hundred thousand listeners, began regular weekly broadcasts from the Cotton Club, with a wire hookup to a couple of additional stations in outlying areas. It is not clear today how many listeners received these broadcasts—thousands, maybe fewer. Yet the broadcasts were immeasurably important by virtue of their having made a vein of black entertainment available to people in neighborhoods of every kind, for no charge—other than the cost of a radio set, which many Americans did not yet own, because commercial broadcasts had begun in the United States only in 1920. "The Cotton Club enjoys the distinction of drawing hundreds who would not otherwise know of the place and the opportunity to witness the work of the colored artists [who] will never visit the Cotton Club," reported the *New York Amsterdam News*, the black paper, in 1925. Later that year, the Hotel Majestic, which housed WFBH on the Upper West Side, shut off the radio station's signal, concerned that listeners would associate the sounds coming from the Cotton Club with the hotel.

As Ellington would recall, in his memoir, "So far as we were concerned, the engagement at the Cotton Club was of the utmost significance, because as a result of its radio wire we were heard nationally and internationally." (Some of the club's broadcasts were recorded on metal discs for sale to radio stations in Europe, and copies of those discs survive today.)

If the Cotton Club had always been a fictive space—a phantasm of trompe l'oeil vines, tactically positioned feathers, and imitation animal sounds where whites and blacks could come together in inequitable complicity to exploit an imaginary blackness—it was even better suited to the airwaves than it was to a ballroom on Lenox Avenue in Harlem. The phenomenon of free commercial radio was no less democratizing than records. It dissolved barriers of race, class, age, and gender to allow into any home any sounds that station programmers and their sponsors thought of as companionable with advertising messages. As Ellison said, listeners went to the Cotton Club on their radios; in other words, they went somewhere they could only imagine, a place where the vines could crawl and the feathers fall away.

"With the technology of radio, those Cotton Club broadcasts cut the whole of America to its core," Albert Murray said. "Ellington conspired with the contrivances of 'primitivism' in the stage shows to produce a music that used and disallowed the proposition that the so-called primitive was regressive or inferior. The listener at home had no minimum to pay and no front to put on for his friends at the table. If he was Anglo, he could listen without patronizing or accountability, and if he was Negro, he could listen, period—and possibly with pride. That is something the Cotton Club in Harlem would never abide."

In 1974, when I moved to Manhattan, it was a glorious time to be young, broke, and hungry for music in New York. The city was bankrupt and dangerous, available to everyone. I was living alone as a student in a one-room sixth-floor walk-up on Macdougal Street, above Panchito's, a Mexican restaurant that helped sustain the building's robust population of mice. I had a shower in the kitchen, and I shared a toilet in the hall with two floor mates and a few homeless people. I bought a five-octave Wurlitzer electric piano, the old kind with mechanical hammers and a chime for each note—I was studying music fairly seriously now—and a mouse lived inside the piano for a while; I had started learning about John Cage, and as I lay in bed listening to the mouse crawling around on the Wurlitzer chimes, I thought, now *this* is living.

To cover my rent, I finagled to do the cleaning in the building, collecting the garbage and mopping the floors twice a week. For entertainment, the girl in the apartment below me worked the coat check at Max's Kansas City and got me in for free, and for pocket money I worked part-time as a scooper at a trendy ice cream parlor on Sheridan Square called Mother Bucka's.

In the building I lived in, there were a couple of other music geeks, including a guy from New Jersey about ten years older than me who shared my interests in both Tin Pan Alley pop and rock and roll, Lenny Kaye. He was writing a music column for *Cavalier*, a knockoff of *Penthouse*, while he was working in a record shop and playing guitar for a writer-singer whose music I had not yet heard, Patti Smith. I wanted to be Lenny Kaye, and I suspect he could tell that when I started up conversations about Gene Austin or the Squires if he came out of his apartment while I was cleaning the hall.

The rising cult of rock criticism was such that, somehow, thirty years before Facebook, I could recognize Jon Landau by face. Landau, writing for the rock magazine *Crawdaddy* and *The Real Paper* (the alternative in Boston to the alternative *Boston Phoenix*), was, along with Robert Christgau, Ellen Willis, Paul Nelson, and Greil Marcus, among the smartest and most ambitious writers in an emerging school of young critics who seemed to be making rock more serious by taking it more seriously. On an evening in the spring of 1975, I served Landau a cone at Mother Bucka's—I cannot remember the flavor— and brought up Bruce Springsteen.

Springsteen, in this early period of his career, was making a rangy and mercurial music, a jazzy sort of folk-pop, with rambling, verbose, and cleverly pretentious lyrics. When I first saw him play, in a show in the cafeteria of the student center at Seton Hall University in New Jersey, where I took courses for a year between high school and starting at NYU, Springsteen's band had the charismatic African American saxophonist Clarence Clemons; a jazz pianist, David Sancious; a female Israeli violinist with a warm classical tone, Suki Lahav; and a drummer who had a bit of a Latin feel, Vini "Mad Dog" Lopez. Springsteen was drawing freely from multiple cultural traditions, trying to find his place as an artist. A great many of his songs had to do with growing up, including the one called "Growing Up." Springsteen used the idea of traveling from our mutual home state to New York as a metaphor for coming of age—how could I resist a music that so literally reflected the way I saw my own life?—and he portrayed the city in romantic clichés of shadowy intrigue, easy sex, and looming violence. Springsteen's New York was a noir-movie montage of street gangs, runaways, deals gone bad, "wolfman fairies" dressed in drag, Puerto Rican girls, and black boys: the urban jungle.

The trope of the jungle as a lurid paradise of unbridled thrills and dangers had survived for forty years, transplanted from the Cotton Club and transmuted by the noir movies, comics, and 1950s rock and roll that the kids of Springsteen's generation had grown up on. In many people's minds, rock and roll itself, like jazz, had been born in the jungle—*Blackboard Jungle*, the MGM studio paean to teen rebellion that began, notoriously, with the sound of Bill Haley and His Comets playing "Rock Around the Clock." (More on this in a later chapter.)

When I saw Jon Landau in Mother Bucka's, I knew of him as the critic who had proclaimed Springsteen as "the future of rock and roll," and I told him I was studying music and writing and that I would love to interview Springsteen. He asked me a few things to test me and then told me that Springsteen happened to be in New York, recording a new album. If I wanted to talk to him, I should go the following evening to the Record Plant, a well known rock recording studio in midtown, and tell the receptionist that Landau sent me and that I was there to see Bruce Springsteen. (Landau did not mention, and I did not realize, that he was producing the album.) When I followed his advice the next night, the man at the reception desk rang a number on the house phone and handed the receiver to me. "This is Bruce," Springsteen said.

He was busy recording, he told me, and couldn't talk. He said I should give him a few months to finish the album, then call him to arrange to get together for an interview. He gave me his home number, which I put down in the *S* section of my address book and called at the end of that summer, by which point the album he had been recording, *Born to Run*, was released, and the number was disconnected.

The hard-driving title track of the record took Springsteen out of the quirky genre mingling of his early music and positioned him as a rock-and-roll star. The closing song, a nine-minute melodrama about a tragic misadventure in Manhattan, begins with violin: Suki Lahav, playing a spare, foreboding solo. Then piano: Roy Bittan, a pop-oriented player whom Landau had brought in, laying out the two-chord harmony of the verse. Then Springsteen: talk-singing, in a stage whisper, "The Rangers had a homecoming in Harlem late last night . . ." The story in the song is a racially and narratively ambiguous sketch of a playlet about kids living in shadows and streets on fire and all that, ending with the hero, the Magic Rat, getting gunned down in a subway tunnel uptown—"tonight . . . in . . . Jun-gle-*laaaaand*." Springsteen howled a sequence of long, sustained notes in full voice, and the album faded out.

With *Born to Run* on the whole and "Jungleland" in particular, Springsteen lost me. Its grandiosity and determination to impress felt oppressive to me, and the urban jungle of Springsteen's imagination had, to me, come to seem cartoonish. This was the "future of rock and roll"?

That summer, the Top 40 radio stations were playing hits of irresistible and sonically complex pop-funk—"Lady Marmalade" by Labelle and "Shining Star" by Earth, Wind, and Fire—along with goofy pap like "Sister Golden Hair" by America. But many of the most widely read rock critics, nearly all of whom were white (and male, with the notable exception of Willis), were not paying much attention to the music of acts like Labelle; Earth, Wind, and Fire; and the Ohio Players. The music was musically dense, complicated, and fun but collaborative and not lyric oriented or ponderous and, hence, not well suited to the lit-class approach to criticism that most rock writers were applying in their mission to elevate rock and perhaps, in the process, themselves. Where was the future of rock and roll? One could speculate only with the hubris of a critic, the audacity of my own aspirations.

Early one morning around then, when I was coming home from work, I bumped into Lenny Kaye, and he told me he had just been playing in a club on the Bowery called CBGB, and he said I had to check it out. I didn't write down what he said, but the point was that a new kind of music was being made, and it was primitive and savage.

4

THE CHARTS

MAKE-BELIEVE ISLAND

Commercial success does not necessarily follow commercial intent. The writer of a hit song might have created it without the marketplace in mind, and producing for the market does not guarantee good sales performance. Even under the production-line scheme of Tin Pan Alley, songwriters sometimes wrote tunes mainly for personal, rather than professional, reasons. Irving Berlin composed his mournful ballad "When I Lost You" upon the death of his first wife, Dorothy, after she contracted typhoid fever during their honeymoon in Havana, and he wrote "Always," his irreducibly plain expression of devotion, as a wedding present to his second wife, Ellin. Then, as if to prove that self-expression and good business are neither mutually exclusive nor interdependent, Berlin included in this marital gift the royalties to "Always." *I love you*, Berlin was saying, *even more than I love a copyright*. The bride had to have been moved.

In the early days of the swing era, the singer Ina Ray Hutton, a vivacious performer with pinup-girl looks, led one of the dozen or so all-female orchestras in operation around the country: among them, the International Sweethearts of Rhythm, the Darlings of Rhythm, the Dixie Sweethearts, and, with their start in 1934, Ina Ray Hutton and Her Melodears. Now commonly misconstrued to have been a secondary effect of wartime conscription, like the All-American Girls Professional Baseball League, the phenomenon of all-female swing bands actually arose several years before Pearl Harbor. In fact, many of the exclusively female groups had disbanded before the United States entered World War II. The orchestras were usually (but not always) packaged as sexy novelty attractions, much to the frustration of the musicians called upon to play demanding dance-band orchestrations and to improvise inventively while looking alluring in skin-squishing gowns and cut-glass baubles. Male audiences ogled, and male critics shrugged. As the jazz writer George T. Simon scoffed in his biographical history *The Big Bands*, "Only God can make a tree, and only men can play good jazz."

Ina Ray Hutton, the older half sister of the jazz-pop singer June Hutton, is known now to have been of mixed heritage; researchers have found that she was registered in at least one census as "mulatto." But with her platinum hair set in a soft wave, Ina Ray Hutton projected a white-goddess Jean Harlow image—promoters called her the "Blonde Bombshell of Rhythm"—and she leveraged her sex appeal to claim the leadership of an assemblage of first-rate dance-band musicians. The most conspicuously gifted among them was Hutton's pianist, Ruth Lowe, an occasional composer who, like Irving Berlin, lost a spouse not long after getting married—Lowe's groom died in surgery—and found herself, in mourning, moved to write a song.

Lowe, twenty-five at the time, in 1939, wrote a softly aching melody and set it to a few short stanzas of generic words about loss—the end of a romance, according to one phrase in the lyric, though the general ambiguity of the words and the melancholy in the music made possible a deeper implication. Lowe passed the music on to one of her colleagues, Vida Guthrie, a woman who was serving as the musical director for Percy Faith, an orchestra leader who specialized in sweet and romantic mood music, and Guthrie made an arrangement of it for Faith to play on his CBC radio show. Talented female musicians of the big-band era such as Lowe and Guthrie were being hired almost exclusively to play either with other women or with men like Faith, who made music that was gentle, polite, and easy on the ears—music conceived of as girly. A copy of the music to "I'll Never Smile Again" made its way to Tommy Dorsey, the "sentimental gentleman" with a soft spot for soft music.

Dorsey, a virtuoso of checkbook musicianship, had recently taken expensive steps to provide his band with both more musical vigor and more star appeal. He hired away the brilliant African American arranger Sy Oliver, who had been working for Jimmie Lunceford, the leader of one of the hardest-swinging black bands, and he bought out the contract of the boy singer for the Harry James Orchestra who had begun to become a sensation with teenage fans, especially young women: Frank Sinatra. Oliver gave Dorsey a Lindy Hop dance-floor hit with his rearrangement of Jimmy McHugh and Dorothy Fields's "Sunny Side of the Street," once a staple at the Cotton Club, and Sinatra gave Dorsey the bestselling record of his career with his brooding, delicate reading of Ruth Lowe's "I'll Never Smile Again."

Dorsey assigned the song to a small ensemble, a subgroup of his group called the Sentimentalists, and they justified their name on the record made in April 1940 for Bluebird Records. Axel Stordahl, who would later become known for his grand, lush string orchestrations for Sinatra and others (including Ina Ray Hutton's sister June, whom Stordahl would marry), crafted a pretty arrangement of the tune. Joe Bushkin, the pianist, tinkled an accompaniment on the celesta straight out of a dry-ice heaven scene in a movie like *Here Comes Mr. Jordan*; and the Pied Pipers, Dorsey's in-house vocal group, crooned the melody in sugar-syrup harmony. The singers sounded as if they were wearing costume gowns and wire halos. All this gave the record an otherworldly feeling suitable to the notion of the song as a message to a loved one sent across the great divide. As such, "I'll

Never Smile Again" was a swing-era variation on a tradition that dated back to the turn of the twentieth century, when parlor musicians were singing and playing things like Charles K. Harris's morbid novelty tune "Hello Central, Give Me Heaven," in which a child rings up her late mother on the phone.

In the 1990s, Lena Horne came out of a decade-long semiretirement from music to make an album dedicated to her departed friends, including Billy Strayhorn, and I gave her a hand with the repertoire. She was torn between two choices for the project's title song: "I'll Never Smile Again" and "We'll Be Together Again," the latter composed by Carl T. Fischer with lyrics by the singer Frankie Laine and introduced by the Pied Pipers. Both songs by then had come to be closely associated with World War II, although the first tune was released on record a year before America entered the war, the second one a year after the war was over. Horne ended up choosing "We'll Be Together Again," partly because she thought Sinatra's youthful rendition of "I'll Never Smile Again" was definitive. Joking, with a big wink implied, she called the young Sinatra "a better woman" than she.

Lena Horne had a point. Frank Sinatra sang "I'll Never Smile Again" quietly, softly, with precise but delicate articulation. As he would always say, the microphone was his instrument, and his early style can most readily be grasped as a masterly realization of the potential of electronic recording and delivery technology. The microphone, since it had come into use in the late 1920s, had made feasible a new kind of singing—indeed, a new definition of what it meant to sing. When Al Jolson was the biggest star on Broadway, in the era before records and radio, much of the force of his appeal came from his ability to project from the footlights to the balcony. That skill became less of an asset—in fact, it became something of a liability—with the rise of the microphone and the relocation of popular entertainment from the public sphere to the home. The first vocalists to exploit the potential of the microphone—Rudy Vallee and Bing

Crosby early among them—were once considered incompetent for their failure to project, with gusto, from the diaphragm. In a movie called *Crooner*, made in 1932, a critic of the leading man snaps, "He can't sing. He only *croons*."

With microphones, singers learned to work more conversationally, sensually, and subtly, and Sinatra mastered these possibilities to sing with such warmth and gentleness that his early music was scandalous. This is not easy to fathom today, knowing as we do that Sinatra turned out to be a swaggering emblem of masculine bravura, but Sinatra made his name, with "I'll Never Smile Again" and its follow-ups, as an artist whose delicacy and sensitivity were seen as shockingly, even dangerously transgressive. In a three-part series of profiles of Sinatra published in *The New Yorker* in 1946, E. J. Kahn Jr., one of the smart generalists who made the magazine's reputation in the mid-twentieth century, quotes a critic of Sinatra's "who thinks much about these things" as finding Sinatra's "style very dangerous to our morale, for it is passive, luxurious, and ends up not with a bang but with a whimper." The implication was that Sinatra, as a singer, was not enough of a man.

Rudy Vallee, who in the late 1920s had been an early idol of the microphone age, murmured his songs more quietly than Sinatra and had vocal limitations that made his music sound tenuous and thin. He was commonly derided as effete, though he exploited that fact as part of his comically bookish college-boy image. Vallee used the sexual ambiguity of his singing as a joke.

Bing Crosby, the great innovator of jazz-pop singing whom Sinatra idolized and emulated in many ways, was more musically sophisticated than Vallee and sang with a coolness, an evident casualness, that made his singing sound confidently, almost diffidently offhanded. He parceled his emotions in his music—a discreetly placed glissando, an occasional trill—from a distance. The low-key naturalism of his delivery came across accurately as restraint rather than weakness.

Sinatra added unabashed sentimentality and profound vulnerability to the conversational naturalism and coolness that Vallee and Crosby had introduced to mainstream popular music in the microphone age. Sinatra's phrasing had a precious lyricism, his tone a rare loveliness. These qualities, working in conjunction with aspects of Sinatra's extra-musical image at the time, conspired to make him awfully suspicious to parents of his young fans (and other protectors of what no one had yet started calling heteronormativity). The gossip columnists and co-medians who helped shape public opinion defined Sinatra as much by his skinniness as by his singing. (In a Looney Tunes short from the mid-1940s, *Swooner Crooner*, a character based on Sinatra is so thin he disappears behind his microphone stand, and in another cartoon from the same period the Sinatra figure is so frail he needs to be pushed around in a wheelchair by an orderly.) After America entered the war, Sinatra's exemption from military service (4-F for a perfo-rated eardrum, diagnosed in Sinatra's second visit to the draft board, after he was initially classified as 1-A) only fed his reputation for unmanliness—or, at best, a funny new kind of manhood. In the early 1940s, a song *about* him was published, and the lyrics said, "Dear Mr. Sinatra, you're so tender and sweet and so fine."

I once interviewed Joe Bushkin, who played with Sinatra dozens of times after their apprenticeship with Tommy Dorsey, and we talked about the codes of machismo in pop music of the 1940s. "They didn't know what to make of him [Sinatra]," Bushkin said. "They thought you were light on your feet if you gave half a shit about beauty."

On July 27, 1940, *Billboard* magazine, the trade journal for the music business, started publishing a weekly list of the bestselling records across the country, under the heading "The Billboard Music Popularity Chart." Prior to that issue, *Billboard* had published other music lists—one, as early as 1913, for "Popular Songs Heard in Vaude-ville Theaters Last Week," and others, after that, for "Sheet Music Best Sellers," "Songs with the Most Radio Plugs," and "Records Most Popular on Music Machines" (jukeboxes). The magazine had reported on record sales in articles and columns but had not yet attempted to produce an ongoing, systematic tabulation of the sales of 78 rpm singles. (Long-playing records had not been invented, though the term "album" was beginning to be used for booklets packaging three or four 78s by theme, such as "Songs from Hawaii," much like a photo album.) The "Music Popularity Chart" was presented as a "trade service feature," intended to provide market information for the benefit of wholesalers and retailers trying to decide what to stock, radio programmers trying to figure out what to play on the air, and songwriters and producers looking for cues on styles to mimic and trends to exploit. The chart in that issue in 1940 listed ten records, nearly all of them ballads, and most of them sad.

At the bottom of the list, at number ten, was "Make Believe Island," a limpid quasi-tropical ballad recorded by a group named in recognition of the voguishness in popular music and the importance of the female audience: Mitchell Ayres and His Fashions in Music. Listed above "Make Believe Island" were songs nearly all striking for their musical languidness and lyrical melancholy: "Sierra Sue," a poky, vaguely western ballad with Bing Crosby whispering about being "sad and lonely" over wistful strings; "The Breeze and I"; and a semi-exotic English-language adaptation of the Spanish ballad "Andalucia," in which both the singer and the air currents "sigh that you no longer care"—a lament of self-pity with echoes of "After the Ball," performed by Charlie Barnet and His Orchestra. At the top of the list, at number one, was "I'll Never Smile Again," recorded by Tommy Dorsey and His Orchestra, with a vocal refrain by Frank Sinatra and the Pied Pipers.

When we think of the pop charts, we tend to conceive of hit songs as bouncy and cheery puff. We imagine hits as having a self-defining airiness, a lightness of spirit that critics of pop sometimes project upon the music's audience and conflate with dimness of mind. Hit songs, as we generally think of them, are resolutely, simplistically upbeat expressions of romantic bliss—and so a great many hits have been. Long before Paul McCartney and Wings, there were deeply silly love songs such as "You Are My Sunshine," which was published in the same year that "I'll Never Smile Again" became a hit. Yet the musical and lyrical sunniness of "You Are My Sunshine" has never been a requisite of success for a pop tune, and love songs have always been more likely to deal with the yearning for love, the complications of love, love's betrayal, or the loss of love (or even, sometimes, the loss of life) than the fancied bliss of love fulfilled. As the songs on the first *Billboard* chart remind us, a strain of sadness has long been laced through the popular songbook. Music listeners' likes have never been restricted to things that make them happy.

Not that anyone should have expected to find hard evidence of any song's popularity in the early *Billboard* charts—or in any of the various lists of song hits to have preceded them in the magazine or elsewhere. *Billboard* had begun, in the last decade of the nineteenth century, as a magazine of the promotion industry, and through the long life of the publication hype has remained essential to its purpose. Under its original name, *Billboard Advertising*, the magazine had as its initial subject matter the business of outdoor ad signage—mainly, the printed poster bills that were pasted onto the power-line and telephone poles sprouting up everywhere as the country electrified, as well as the giant murals for branded products and businesses that were hand painted onto the sides of buildings as urban landscapes bloomed. (The large roadside billboards we know today did not yet exist, because automobiles were still fairly new and car trips were not yet common.) Because those poster bills could be plastered quickly anywhere and plastered over easily, they were widely favored by itinerant and seasonal entertainment businesses—circuses, carnivals, Wild West shows, amusement parks, and county fairs. Soon, as *The Billboard*, the magazine was covering developments in all the most robustly populist and aesthetically unruly areas of American entertainment. The magazine reported on the enticements of Pallenberg's Famous Exhibition of the Bears That Dance, along with the music sung and played in traveling tent shows, and its coverage of music expanded with the growth of the popular music business. By 1940, *Billboard* was focusing mainly on various dimensions of the music industry: publishing, live performance, radio, film scores, and records.

Itinerancy and seasonality are elemental to pop hitdom—songs come and go with the calendar—and *Billboard* understood the way that worked. Before *Billboard* started ranking record sales in each issue, it had laid out the rough terms of a vector for hit activity under two subcategories in its charts for "music machine" songs: "Going Strong" and "Coming Up." The flow of coins in the jukeboxes kept a hit going, and the imperative of change in the passing of time ensured that a new one would always be coming.

In and out of the music profession, people of mid-century America talked about the body of songs that were currently popular as "the hit parade," a phrase that vividly captured the fleeting nature of hits. They pass by, one after another. To experience hits is very much like watching a parade, and our impression of a song is like a moment impressed on the eyelids during a blink. Open your eyes, and a new part of the parade is in front of you. The thing that caught your attention for one moment—the twirl of a baton, the turn of a melody— is gone, and something else—a decorated float, a pounding dance tune—has replaced it. By 1940, town parades were already corny throwbacks to the era before radio, records, and the movies brought mass entertainment to America. The parade as a phenomenon had passed by the public consciousness, and the hit parade had come along to replace it.

Since 1935, the phrase "hit parade" had become closely associated with an hour-long weekly radio program, one officially titled *Your Hit Parade* and sometimes referred to as "The Lucky Strike Hit Parade," after its cigarette company sponsor. Broadcast for a while by both the NBC and the CBS radio networks, the show featured a regular group of singers (Buddy Clark, Kay Thompson, Lanny Ross, and other versatile journeymen, as well as Frank Sinatra, briefly in 1943) performing fifteen songs that the program established to be the top hits of the week, as identified through an impressive-sounding method explained on the air: "[A] *Your Hit Parade* survey checks the best sellers on sheet music and phonograph records, the songs most heard on the air and most played on the automatic coin machines—an accurate, authentic tabulation of America's taste in popular music." Exactly how the tabulation got to be so accurate and authentic, the producers did not say.

Billboard was a bit more specific about the process by which it produced its record chart. As the editors explained in a block of text printed above the list, the magazine surveyed several dozen record dealers in major cities, and the store names were listed. Danny Goldberg, a late twentieth-century record company executive (and, most famously, manager for Nirvana) who started out in music at *Billboard* in the 1970s, told me that the lore he heard in-house at the magazine was that the first *Billboard* charts had been put together through a combination of those retail surveys, conducted by mail and also through stringers hired to visit the shops, and "divining rods and hoopla." Each of the surveyed stores provided the magazine with a ranked list of the records it said had sold best over the previous week; the ranking was relative, supported by no sales figures. The chart editors processed that information, which was something other than data by the standards of a later era; it was a distillation of memories, impressions, assertions, and wishes, really. The editors then factored in the talk they picked up from promoters, press-relations people, the magazine's advertisers, and other trade insiders, and they made their best estimates of how the records ought to rank.

By this almost-scientific method, the *Billboard* record chart purported to assess "popularity" through the measurement of sales. The underlying principle was taken as a given: that the purchase of a record was an exercise of aesthetic will, a statement of personal taste—*I like that song, and here's the proof: I paid money for it.* On the radio, meanwhile, the "Your" in *Your Hit Parade* served to reinforce the proposition that buying a record was an assertion of individual judgment—a democratic act. That is to say, it was disc purchasers who made songs into hits; the privilege of hit making was *theirs*. The charts just documented the results.

Yet the acquisition of anything is never purely a matter of personal will. Nor, for that matter, is the sheer desire for ownership. The urges to buy, to have, to use, or otherwise to be connected to goods— cultural products, among them—are informed by innumerable factors, including marketing and social forces. Tastes and judgments are never formed independently, in a cultural vacuum. As every citizen of the twenty-first century understands from the pervasive use of social media, and as social scientists were just figuring out in the mid-twentieth century, people's "likes" emerge in the context of what they believe other people to favor. Personal tastes are socialized tastes, and the first *Billboard* chart measured the popularity of songs at the same time it helped enhance and enforce that popularity by formalizing it and institutionalizing it through a process that qualified as quantification. In Danny Goldberg's words, "A song is on the chart because it's popular, and it's not just double-talk to say that it's popular, to some extent, because it's on the chart."

Social scientists would categorize phenomena such as the charts as social proof—testimony of popular opinion that acts to expand the popularity of that opinion. In 1940, the era of phenomenological road travel metaphors such as the hit parade, the idea would have been referred to as jumping on the bandwagon, and the first *Billboard* record chart demonstrated it well. After the rendition of "I'll Never Smile Again" by Dorsey and Sinatra became known as a number one hit, more than a dozen other musical acts, popular or hoping to be, recorded the song. The rush to capitalize on the success of the record was such that less than two weeks after the publication date of the *Billboard* chart, the music writer Bill Gottlieb would report in his nationally syndicated newspaper column, "Russ Morgan is the latest to supply an insatiable public with 'I'll Never Smile Again.'" Gottlieb, a good writer, generally, had momentarily forgotten that the public's appetite for any song will inevitably be sated, only to be supplanted with a hunger for a new tune.

Donald Clarke, in his judicious study of Sinatra and his work, *All or Nothing at All*, quoted his mother on the omnipresence of "I'll Never Smile Again" on the radio. "It was all you *heard*," she said. I relay the quotation in part to show how the song was perceived by the public of its day and in part to show that I am not the only writer on music who quotes his mother in a book.

As "I'll Never Smile Again" subsided in popularity, it became, as all major hits would become, an instrument for the measurement of the success of other songs. Gottlieb, by November 1940, described a new hit, the boogie-woogie tune "Beat Me, Daddy, Eight to the Bar" by Will Bradley and His Orchestra, as "the biggest thing since 'I'll Never Smile Again.'"

For the pop music audience, following a song's progress on the charts became a form of entertainment in itself. The way the pop charts influenced consumer thinking did not go down well with Jean-Paul Sartre. In the *Critique of Dialectical Reason*, first published in 1960, Sartre described the culture of hits as a kind of social tyranny—a threat to individuality, rather than a mechanism for the exercise of aesthetic will. "If he listens to the radio every Saturday and if he can afford to buy every week's No. 1 record, he will end up with the record collection of the Other, that is to say, the collection of no one," Sartre argued. "Ultimately, the record collection which is no one's becomes indistinguishable from everyone's collection—though without ceasing to be no one's."

The pop charts elevated their own status, as well as the status they conferred upon songs and song makers, and prompted the making of more charts—more accurate charts, more extensive charts, more specialized charts, and more, more, more charts. By the late 1950s, *Billboard* had devised a formula for factoring information about radio play into its song rankings, a refinement that only reinforced the circularity of the charts. The chart position of a song helped determine how much a song was played on the radio, and airplay helped determine the chart position. The system seemed inscrutably hermetic, while it was also highly susceptible to corruption. Record executives knew how to rig the charts and "buy position" by influencing DJs and retailers, as well as the magazine itself, through the weight of advertising dollars.

With the widespread adoption of bar codes and scanning during the 1980s came a way to document purchases accurately, at the retail level, and in 1991 *Billboard* replaced its system of surveys, divining rods, and arm-twisting machinery with a less corruptible electronic system, SoundScan. This briefly rattled the record industry, by showing that more people were buying country music and black music than the old charts had suggested and that fewer people were buying records by the big-hair guitar-rock acts that male record executives liked to be associated with and that male store clerks liked to say that they were selling. SoundScan was precise but incomplete, failing to account for independent record stores that weren't wired for the technology.

As evidence of the popularity of songs, all sales statistics are inherently limited, anyway. The decision to divest oneself of some of one's capital—even fifty cents, the typical price of a 78 rpm single in the early 1940s—is indisputable proof of one's interest in possessing something, even if the thing one wants to possess is the social status of being known among one's friends for having it. (For teenagers and young adults in the mid-twentieth century, fifty cents was not an insignificant sum. My father, in his after-school job as a delivery boy for a butcher shop in a Hungarian neighborhood in New Jersey, made sixty-seven cents per hour.) Still, commercial transactions tell only part of the story of a song's popularity. All that occurs after the purchase (or, for that matter, what does not happen) may be as telling as the fact of the sale.

A record has been sold. Then: what? How often is the song played?

When and why and where? Is it played for comfort, by one listener alone in a room, or for dancing at a Friday night party? What thoughts, if any, does the record provoke? What feelings does it stir—or relieve? How do other people in the record buyer's house feel about the song? How long has the record remained in active use? Has it been traded for another record or passed down to a younger brother?

When I was a kid, one of my favorite records was "Cool Jerk," a boogaloo single by a one-hit group called the Capitols. (Years later, I heard that the indelible groove track might have been recorded clandestinely by the Motown house band, the Funk Brothers.) The copy of the record my mother got from the Gateway jukebox guy was too scratched to play. My sister, Barbara Ann, who was six years older than I, had a copy that she had borrowed from one of our cousins, and I snatched it out of her room. A few years after that, when I was in high school, I dubbed the song onto an audio cassette mix by placing my shoe box Radio Shack cassette recorder next to the speakers for my stereo. That mixtape became the primary source of music in my car, a profoundly used 1963 Chevrolet that seated seven comfortably, thirteen for short hauls. Without aggrandizing my teen years, which were eventful only by the standards of a teenager, I can say that "Cool Jerk" was part of the soundtrack of multiple occasions memorable to my high-school friends and me. How could I capture the place that the song held in our lives? Certainly not by recounting the fact of the sale of a copy of the record to the cousin of mine who loaned it to my sister before I stole it from her. When I think of the song, I hear the jiggy-jaggy opening piano figure, and my memory drifts. I don't hear *cha-ching*.

"Cool Jerk" never made number one. It peaked at number two on the *Billboard* R&B chart, and at number seven on the magazine's "Hot 100," in July 1966. By the ostensibly quantitative and plainly mercantile terms of the pop charts, "Cool Jerk" was never as successful as any number one song, from "I'll Never Smile Again" to "Hello," the piano ballad by Adele about a failed romance that was the first song to sell a million copies as a digital download in a week's time, in 2015. The numbers simply do not compare, in a realm where numbers have been established as the only terms of comparison. Once a song is ranked and assigned a numerical value, the number replaces every other value—aesthetic value, social value, personal value. Identified as number one, a song is one number superior to the song that's number two, and ninety-eight numbers better than the song that's number ninety-nine. This line of thinking has become a tautology in the age of digital aggregation and data mining, an era that the early *Billboard* charts and *Your Hit Parade* foreshadowed and began to make possible.

However memorable "Cool Jerk" may be to me, the pop charts have established that it will never be as big a hit as "Hello." Memorability and hit status are essentially different matters. A hit does not need lasting power to be a hit. Indeed, it cannot last long—not *as* a hit. There are only so many people available to buy or stream a song, to share one in digital form, or to share one's interest in one through social media. The life of any song on the pop charts is intrinsically limited, like that of one of those species of insects that exist only long enough to spawn and then die. Impermanence is a necessity of the pop culture ecosystem. The charts mark birth and growth as new songs appear and rise in popularity, and they require the decline and disappearance of others. To follow a song as it ascends the chart and inevitably falls, then, is a kind of death watch. It may be only fitting that the first number one on the first *Billboard* record chart was a song inspired by a death.

≡5≡

GOING WEST

HOLLYWOOD BARN DANCE

In the late 1980s and early 1990s, Johnny Cash, Waylon Jennings, Willie Nelson, and Kris Kristofferson worked on and off as a country supergroup called the Highwaymen. The name branded all four of them with the outlaw image that Cash and Jennings had cultivated throughout their careers and that Nelson acquired relatively late through his middle-age transformation from a clean-scrubbed Nashville songwriter into a ponytailed, pot-smoking exotic. Kristofferson, the Rhodes Scholar / movie star / liberal activist who wrote gems of commercial country music like "Help Me Make It Through the Night," was something of an outlier in the group. The Highwaymen played a show at the Nassau Coliseum on Long Island in 1990, when I was doing music writing for *The Hollywood Reporter*, and I was granted twenty minutes with them backstage. Kristofferson wasn't there. Cash and Nelson sat in steel folding chairs next to each other, and Jennings stood about ten feet away, by the catering table, drinking a beer.

I asked all three of the musicians to tell me about their earliest influences—a boilerplate question that I thought of as an icebreaker. Without a beat, Johnny Cash answered, "Gene Autry."

Not sure if he was serious, I rephrased the question to make clear that I wanted to know about artists who affected them most deeply when they were starting out in music. I expected Cash to talk about one of the iconic pioneers of vernacular music in America—Jimmie Rodgers or, perhaps, the Carter Family, from whom his wife, June Carter Cash, was directly descended. Cash seemed to be pondering the matter for a moment, then he nodded his head as he said, "It all started with ol' Gene for me."

I turned to Willie Nelson and asked him the same question, expecting to hear about Django Reinhardt, the gypsy jazz guitarist whose influence on Nelson's guitar work is well known. Nelson said, "Ol' Gene for me, too. And don't forget Roy!"

Cash and Nelson used nearly all of the twenty minutes we had together educating me on the importance of Gene Autry and Roy Rogers in the history of American music, while Waylon Jennings inched his way toward us, silently. I was dubious about what I was hearing, suspicious that Cash and Nelson might be playing a prank on the Yankee writer, until Jennings joined the conversation.

"Listen," he said, plopping his empty beer bottle on the table. "Jimmie Rodgers was a genius—okay? But how many people really knew that in his lifetime? Every kid in this country went to Autry pictures, and half of them went out the next day and bought a guitar."

Nelson chimed in, "We're the sons of the Sons of the Pioneers," and he started to sing: "I'm a roaming cowboy riding all day long, tumbleweeds around me sing their lonely song."

About a hundred years before social scientists began studying the role of the herd mentality in the dissemination of music, the folklorist John A. Lomax dealt with the subject in literal terms. He assembled the ur-text of American folk music scholarship, *Cowboy Songs and Other Frontier Ballads*, which was first published in 1910 with an epigraph taken from one of the songs in the book, "The Jolly Cowboy":

> What keeps the herd from running,
> Stampeding far and wide?
> The cowboy's long, low whistle,
> And singing by their side.

There has never been much evidence that cattle drivers on horseback calmed their steers by crooning to them. To the extent that cowboys sang, they were most likely singing for themselves or for one another rather than for their herds, and the songs *about* cowboys that Lomax collected were not necessarily sung *by* cowboys. Still, the image of the cowboy as a heroic figure with a free spirit, two good fists, and a song in his heart was a weirdly enchanting one, and Lomax's work helped to fix it in the public consciousness.

Lomax's intent was to elevate the status of the vernacular songs of the American West, songs that he was personally attached to, and the time was ripe for his purpose. Having grown up on a ranch in Texas, Lomax took up research into American folk music during the early bloom of American folklore studies in the first decades of the twentieth century. This was the period when the United States was just emerging as a world economic power, thanks to the complicit benefits of industrialization, the seeming inexhaustibility of our natural resources, and the plentifulness of labor provided by expanded immigration from China and eastern Europe. What America needed in order to achieve closer parity with the Old World powers was higher cultural standing, and folklore studies helped by showing that this still-young country had indigenous artistic traditions with parallels and links to European arts, as well as qualities distinctively, natively its own. Lomax, like other American folklorists of his day, was engaged in the practice of recovered history.

With the industrial boom and urbanization, the conservation movement came, and Lomax's work contributed to the necessary idealization of the endangered frontier. *Cowboy Songs* was dedicated to Theodore Roosevelt, the cowboy president, and included an introduction by Roosevelt in a facsimile of his handwriting. Roosevelt lauded the book as "a work of real importance to preserve permanently the unwritten ballad literature of the back country." As the president was saying, *Cowboy Songs* was an act of preservationism.

Lomax's model was the late nineteenth-century song scholarship of Francis James Child, the Harvard professor of literature who had produced anthologies of English poetry before he turned to folk materials. Child collected several hundred Anglo-Saxon folk songs and their American variants in his book, *The English and Scottish Popular Ballads*, transferring the status of written literature to a body of vernacular songs—material that, like the captives of serfdom who had once sung those songs, came to be known by the surname of their benefactor as the Child Ballads. His book was a meta-canonical text, a work that almost single-handedly established a canon and became a model for canon making.

Lomax, with his collection, linked cowboy songs explicitly to the Child Ballad legacy, while he framed his material in the rhetoric of the established mythos of the American West. "Out in the wild, far-away places of the big and still unpeopled west . . . yet survives the Anglo-Saxon ballad spirit that was active in secluded districts in England and Scotland even after the coming of Tennyson and Browning," Lomax wrote.

> The broad sky under which [the cowboy] slept, the limitless plains over which he rode, the big, open, free life he lived near to Nature's breast, taught him simplicity, calm, directness. He spoke out plainly the impulses of his heart. But as yet so-called polite society is not quite willing to hear.

Lomax, his contemporaries in folk song collecting (among them N. Howard Thorp, a cattleman-poet who in 1908 published the slim but important collection *Songs of the Cowboys*), and Lomax's son Alan, who became his father's collaborator and successor (and in time surpassed the elder Lomax in fame as an advocate of vernacular music), advanced a conception of the music of the West framed in opposition to the commercial pop of the Northeast. Folk music in general and western songs in particular seemed like clear alternatives to, if not direct arguments against, music made by a professional class for mass consumption.

As John Lomax described them, cowboy songs represented the ideals of freedom, independence, plain speaking, and personal strength, enlaced with a sympathy for outlawry. The songs were created and sung by nonprofessionals (or people whose profession was cowpoking rather than music making) for the singers to share among themselves (and their livestock)—untainted by the pursuit of capital or by catering to the marketplace. The provenance of the work was rural, not urban—natural, not man-made: pure. The songs were simple and direct—unspoiled by bourgeois fanciness, uncorrupted by the effects of education. And the heroes of the songs were often antiheroes—outcasts, mystery men, or bad men like Jesse James. As Lomax wrote, "The songs represent the operation of instinct and tradition"—not learning, formal or otherwise, or contemporaneity, but gut feeling and fealty to past practice.

And yet folk art and commercial culture were much more tightly entwined than either John or Alan Lomax was disposed to admit. The very word "cowboy," along with the image of rough-hewn gallantry associated with it, had come into widespread usage during the late nineteenth century through showbiz hoopla rather than field reports from the plains. Before that, it had been the frontiersman—an explorer or scout, a homegrown American descendant of Columbus and the other European expeditioners who valorized the origin myth of the New World—who had personified the West in the popular imagination, thanks primarily to the celebrity of Buffalo Bill Cody. A former cavalry scout and rifleman, Cody earned his nickname by killing bison in shooting contests; he won a championship by shooting 69 animals in one competition and, over the course of his career, claimed to have killed 4,280 bison. He parlayed this peculiar glory into a career as a stage marksman and showman in the touring circus spectacle called "Buffalo Bill's Wild West and Congress of Rough Riders of the World." The shows presented reenactments of stagecoach robberies, Indian attacks, and Pony Express rides, as well as sharpshooting demonstrations, all with costumes wilder than the West. Cody gave noisy, gaudy theatrical form to all the tropes of the West, and cross-merchandised them with pulp novels written by his advance man, Prentiss Ingraham.

In 1887, Ingraham promoted a new addition to Cody's show, Buck Taylor, who was being presented as a gunslinging prairie man, and in the books Ingraham wrote to hype him, he referred to Taylor by a fairly little-known term, "cowboy." In *Buck Taylor, King of the Cowboys* and four follow-up books published by 1891, Ingraham abandoned the existing conception of the herdsman as an ill-bred, amoral roughneck, and he replaced it with a portrayal of the cowboy as a gristly but valiant do-gooder, a knight with a six-gun. It would not be long before he got a guitar. From Wild West shows and junk literature, the cowboy moseyed the short stretch to vaudeville and, from there, to records, radio, and the movies.

Tin Pan Alley tunesmiths, ever eager for a new trend to exploit, picked up on the popularity that cowboys had in tent show entertainment and pulp literature and began producing tunes in a semblance of the western style several years before John Lomax's *Cowboy Songs* was published. They did not need the Lomax book to crib from, though it might have helped them. There were a dozen or so minor hits with western themes in sheet music during the first decade of the twentieth century—"Cheyenne" and "In the Land of the Buffalo," both by the composer Egbert Van Alstyne and the lyricist Harry Williams, and "Pride of the Prairie," by George Botsford and Harry Breen, as well as others—and they vaguely conjured a generic West with *clippity-clop* melodies and lyrics about ponies and cacti and starry skies.

Some of the better Tin Pan Alley cowboy songs—"Pride of the Prairie," "The Utah Trail," "Sierra Sue"—were sung by mainstream stars of the day, such as Ada Jones and Billy Murray, and later taken up by mid-century country-and-western singers such as Patsy Montana (the "Cowboy's Sweetheart" of records and radio) and Tex Ritter, who mixed the songs up with traditional material in their repertoires. Country-and-western artists were also doing older tunes from the prime years of sheet music publishing—the homey, sentimental, and morbid songs of the Sunday musicale days. The material had, over time, came to be conflated with traditional music. The song sheets for those tunes had been sold all over the country, absorbed by parlor singers in communities everywhere, and passed on from mother to child, neighbor to neighbor. In the process, the songs had lost all association with their original identity as hits of the day. They ended up being thought of simply as old songs, and in their sensibility they were surely of another time—old-timey.

In a scene recounted by the country music historian Bill C. Malone in his smart book *Singing Cowboys and Musical Mountaineers*, the late ballad singer Doug Wallin gave a presentation on the songs of Appalachia at an academic conference on traditional music in 1989. Wallin, then seventy years old, talked about an old-time mountain tune that his mother had taught him, and when Wallin sang the song, Malone recognized it as "After the Ball."

The fact is that the appropriation of commercial music is one of the great traditions of traditional music. The people who have sung, played, passed on, listened to, and danced to vernacular music have never been as fussy about musical categorization as the people who have collected folk songs for books, institutional archives, and university classes like the ones I teach. Strains of commercial pop have always been present in country-and-western music, campfire songs, the blues, and the innumerable regional varieties of informal music in America. Just as folk styles of many kinds have nourished popular music, folk styles have been fed by pop. By the twenty-first century, traditional rural music would be most commonly known not as folk but as Americana, and what is more American than commercialism?

When I want to hear some classic country songs, the first thing I usually play is the music of the Carter Family, the trio of two sisters-in-law—Sara Carter, who sang lead and played the autoharp, and Maybelle Carter (June Carter Cash's mother), who played the guitar and held up the trio, musically—and Sara's husband, A. P. Carter, who sang harmony and managed the group. The Carters' music, well preserved through the recordings they began making for Victor in 1927, was judiciously austere: music planed flat and clean. Sara Carter's singing was unfussy but highly controlled—reedy and bare, with no vibrato or showiness, a sound that suggested Puritan humility and discipline—and Maybelle Carter's guitar accompaniment was propulsive, subtly emotive, and exacting. The group's repertoire, put together by A. P. Carter (and mostly copyrighted in his name, whatever the source of the material), mainly comprised songs that honored the values of hearth and family, songs of mourning or hardship, and songs that dealt specifically with southern or rural life—tunes such as "'Mid the Green Fields of Virginia," "Little Log Hut in the Lane" (the Carters' variation on an earlier song, "Little Old Log Cabin in the Lane"), and "Wildwood Flower."

The Carters drew from the body of tunes they had learned when they had been young, in Virginia, and A. P. Carter would also bring in material that he would find during song-hunting trips. He would drive around the countryside in the new-model Chevrolet that he had purchased with recording royalties, asking folks he met to share old songs with him, and he would sometimes return with piles of sheet music for popular ditties dating back to the previous century. The Carters had no bias against a song like "'Mid the Green Fields of Virginia" because it had been written by Charles K. Harris, who confessed that he did not know if corn was grown in Virginia or if the Carolinas had hills; nor would they reject something like "Little Old Log Cabin in the Lane" because it had been written by the commercial writer William Shakespeare Hays for a minstrel show. (Hays, who worked in a music store in Louisville, published more than 350 songs said to have accumulatively sold some twenty million copies.) "Wildwood Flower" and "Keep on the Sunny Side of Life," the latter of which became the Carter Family's theme, were both also popular songs published in the nineteenth century, and so were other tunes in the Carter Family songbook.

Many of the group's songs had lyrics written by the Carters or words adapted from found sources, including traditional ballads, news reports, gossip, and hymns. One of Maybelle Carter's original songs, "You Are My Flower," was based on a poem she clipped out of a magazine, with a melody derived from a Mexican tune she had heard on a border radio station. Much of the trio's work was deeply personal—A. P. and Sara Carter, both of whom had affairs and who split up only to reunite for the opportunity that reconciliation offered, wrote lucidly about betrayal and heartbreak. Still, they wrote the songs in order to record them, in order to be paid. There seemed to be no conflict in their multiple intentions.

The music of the Carter Family spoke with knowing eloquence about human suffering, the comfort and hope that faith provides, and the mysteries of the natural world. The life this music reflected and vindicated, with no (or little) romanticizing gloss, was a tough but good life of hard work and precious few rewards, none of them monetary. There is no disservice to the music's veracity and potency in the fact that the Carters were unapologetic professionals, working for profit and finding it through use of the latest technologies of mass delivery, records and radio. They were never rich; money was a problem as persistent in the Carter family as romance trouble. But neither were they amateurs or social outsiders, folk musicians by the terms folklorists tended to prefer; the Carters took pride in being paid for making their music.

In the first week of August 1927, the Carter Family made six recordings in two short sessions at a studio in Bristol, Tennessee, under the producer Ralph Peer, whom Victor Records had hired to expand its offerings in "hillbilly" music. Nearly all the songs were grim—tragedy ballads about orphaned and homeless children, storms upon the sea, and scorned lovers praying to die. One of the tunes, an adaptation of a mountain ballad called "Single Girl, Married Girl," was a critique of female subjugation under marriage, and the Carters performed it as a duo between Sara and Maybelle. A. P. Carter was silent as his wife sang of the unmarried woman who "goes to the store and buys" and the married one who "rocks the cradle and cries."

The song was released by Victor as a single and made available for mail order through the Montgomery Ward department stores in 1928, and it sold so well throughout the South that the Carter Family was offered a deal to travel to Camden to record in bulk for Victor. "Single Girl, Married Girl," an unwithering assertion of feminine discontent—sung and played by a duo of women related by both talent and marriage, decades before the feminist movement took form up north—set the Carters, and with them country music, on their course. The stark, gray sound of the Carter Family, sustained by the singing of Sara Carter and the guitar work of Maybelle, defied the clownish yokel image of vaudeville hillbillies and established that commercially produced country music could be radically artful and serious, not just entertainingly hokey. The early Carter Family recordings have often been called "the big bang of country music," though they hardly burst from a vacuum. (No sales figures for the early Carter Family records exist. As described by the Carter Family biographers Mark Zwonitzer and Charles Hirshberg in their book, *Will You Miss Me When I'm Gone?*, the single 78 rpm record with two songs, "Single Girl, Married Girl" and "The Storms Are on the

Ocean," "sold and kept selling," and "suddenly the Carters were making money.")

Like many people my age or younger, I first heard "Single Girl, Married Girl" on one of the records in the three sets of double albums packaged as the *Anthology of American Folk Music* in 1952. The collection itself was about twenty-five years old by the time I heard about it, when I was living on Macdougal Street in the mid-1970s. The *Anthology* was then older than most of its individual recordings had been at the time their collector, Harry Smith, assembled them for the LPs. Smith was still living in the Village in the 1970s—he did not die until 1991, after a heart attack in the Chelsea Hotel—and was a figure of cult prominence among the old Beats, avant-gardists, espresso house regulars, budding punks, and would-be bohemians from New Jersey like me. Smith, an experimental filmmaker and poet as well as a master curator of musical arcana, had a wild-haired, thick-lensed look to match his reputation as an underground genius. He was the promise of Joe Gould fulfilled—a bohemian cartoon with a real and meaningful body of work.

Everyone thought of his anthology as *his*, "the Harry Smith collection." The music within it carried the mystique of its curator. The selections were all drawn from Smith's personal stock of records produced in the late 1920s and the 1930s, and the material was mostly traditional or traditional sounding and sung and played by musicians who either were or seemed to be rural, southern, or black. To listeners who came to this music through the *Anthology of American Folk Music* at any point after 1952, the songs and their makers would invariably seem bafflingly, thrillingly ancient and strange. They seemed to capture what Greil Marcus has memorably called the "old, weird America." The aura of the material was only magnified by the fact that the Smith collection was underdistributed and never a big seller, a work known—or known *of*—through a reputation that expanded as the discs were passed among connoisseurs of vernacular music and studied like sacred objects. The status of the collection as unpopular among the broad public helped to make it beloved among the connoisseur class.

Lost under layers of fetishization was the fact that every selection in the Smith anthology had originally been produced for sale by a commercial record company. These were not field recordings made with a battery-powered disc cutter on a flatbed in the Delta. Just as "Single Girl, Married Girl" was recorded in a studio by the Carter Family for Victor Records, "See That My Grave Is Kept Clean," a sublime original composition by Blind Lemon Jefferson, was recorded by Jefferson for Paramount; "Shine on Me," a gospel favorite, was recorded by Ernest Phipps and His Holiness Singers for Bluebird; "Way Down the Old Plank Road," a stage-show staple for the serio-comic "rube" performer Uncle Dave Macon, was recorded by Macon for Vocalion. One track, "The Lone Star Trail," by Ken Maynard, was a song from one of his singing-cowboy movies, *The Wagon Master.* Not that the commercial nature of the recordings made them less legitimate or authentic. Rather, it mainly proved that since the early history of the recording medium record companies were willing to experiment with any music that might have had enough of a market to have made it profitable to stamp, package, and ship the goods.

A couple of years after I moved to the Village, when I was still a student, I started conducting interviews with veteran folk musicians, and nearly everyone I talked to brought up the Smith collection. (These interviews eventually led me to write a book about the 1960s folk scene.) "The anthology was a revelation to us," said Dave Van Ronk, the gruffly urbane blues singer and guitarist whose collegiality and authority on pretty much everything earned him the nickname the Mayor of Macdougal Street. "We had been living with the records of Teresa Brewer—who was a damn good singer, by the way, though you could never tell that from her records. She recorded utter piffle. We learned everything we knew about old-time music from the *Anthology.* It was our Talmud. It was our Bible, and that is a strange thing to say about it, because I think Harry Smith was a Satanist.

"We ate up the songs, even if we hated them. We thought they were all terribly exotic. We thought they were all antediluvian, and, you realize, quite a few of the singers were alive and well. It didn't quite sink in to us that everything on the recording was a commercial recording. Some of them were quite popular in their day. We couldn't have fathomed such a thing."

As country-and-western music took shape as a popular art in the first half of the twentieth century, the "country" in it gave way to the "western." Singers and instrumentalists alike adopted the persona of the cowboy—and the cowgirl—as a way to perform in rural and traditional musical styles without playing into the jokey stereotype of the slow-talking, tobaccy-chawing hayseed. Both the cowboy and the hayseed were caricatures, of course. The cowboy was just a more flattering one. In moving symbolically out of the South and into the West, musicians escaped the racially complicated character of the space below the Mason-Dixon Line, too; they could remain rural without associations with the South.

Jimmie Rodgers, the "Singing Brakeman" who was one of the primary voices in country music, had never been a cowboy; before he started performing professionally, he really had been a railroad brakeman, and he fell back on rail work at least once during slow spells in show business. But he was willing to pose as a cowboy for publicity, he wore ranch duds onstage sometimes, and he took up writing prairie songs (such as "The Cowhand's Last Ride" and "When the Cactus Is in Bloom"). A onetime blackface minstrel performer, Rodgers was a skillful mimic as well as a bold and original artist. He picked up yodeling from a Swiss act he caught on an American tour, and he brilliantly recombined the blues and yodeling with a plaintive rural feeling in a record he called "Blue Yodel," which became one of the first major hits in a style we would recognize today as country music. (The song came to be known as "Blue Yodel No. 1" or "T for Texas" after Rodgers recorded a dozen follow-ups, from "Blue Yodel No. 2" and "Blue Yodel No. 3" to "Jimmie Rodgers' Last Blue Yodel," which was released in 1933, several months after his death from tuberculosis at age thirty-five.)

To promote his records and shows, Rodgers dressed for the camera in exquisite western regalia: white wide-brimmed hat, scarf knotted around at his neck, buffed leather chaps with feathery fringe along the sides, a studded hip holster, and Cuban-heeled riding boots with etched spurs. He had a flattop guitar on his knee, his left arm rested on the body of the instrument, and the long fingers of his right hand pressed lightly on the handle of the six-shooter in his holster, as if he were just about to draw.

Western wear had become standard-issue outfitting for entertainers with a rural orientation. Unlike the farmer clothes of vaudeville hillbilly acts—raggy overalls and clodhoppers with the soles flapping—cowboy gear communicated rugged prowess and expertise rather than pauperism and backwardness. Cowboy garb was the uniform of a skilled class: riders and ropers and shooters—and strummers; and their accessories were the equipment for the doing of manly things. With their lassos, cowboys caught steers and wrestled them to the ground. Farmers milked cows. With their spurs, cowboys prodded their horses and galloped along the plains. Farmers chased chickens. Singing and playing their guitars round the campfire, the men in cowboy camps entertained each other on the long, lonesome nights on the trail, and the fringe on those leather chaps made sure they looked snazzy while they did it. (There has always been sexual fluidity within the hypermasculinity of the cowboy mythology.) To this day, cowboy clothes are the costume of country musicianship, reduced to the visual shorthand of a Stetson hat and needle-nosed boots.

Jimmie Rodgers, a showbiz pro who generally preferred to dress in a bow tie and a straw hat, was attuned to public tastes—after all, he released twelve records with the same title as the hit that had made him famous—and cowboy music was a popular vogue in the 1930s. Radio stations in nearly all the major cities, and most of the midsized ones, were broadcasting "barn dance" or "jamboree" shows of country-and-western music, homespun banter, and comedy. More than 160 such programs were broadcast before World War II. New York had the *WHN Barn Dance*, starring the singers Ray Whitley and Tex Ritter, both of whom would end up going west to become singing cowboys in the movies; Los Angeles had the *Hollywood Barn Dance* on the NBC affiliate KNX; and Chicago had the most successful of these programs, the *National Barn Dance*, which featured a corral full of future screen cowboys—Gene Autry, Smiley Burnette, Pat Buttram, and Eddie Dean—as well as a couple of juvenile acts featuring children who would grow up to be fixtures of non-cowboy entertainment in mid-century television's period of high blandness: Andy Williams and George Gobel. (The call letters for the Chicago station, WLS, stood for the slogan of its founding owner, Sears, Roebuck: "The World's Largest Store.")

Dozens of musical cowboys and cowgirls and cow groups—John White, the "Lonesome Cowboy"; John Crockett, the "Cowboy Singer"; Johnny Marvin, the "Lonesome Singer of the Air"; Cowboy Sam Nichols; Red River Dave; Doc Schneider and His Yodeling Texas Cowboys; Louise Massey and the Westerners; the Girls of the Golden West—were surfacing all over the country, as well as in shows coming from outside, if just barely outside, American territory. In fact, one of the stations involved most significantly in the early populariza-tion of country-and-western music was situated immediately across the southern border in Villa Acuña, Mexico. Broadcasting under the Mexican call letters XER-AM, the station was owned and op-erated by John R. Brinkley, a conscienceless American who brought medicine-show dupery into the radio age, using cowboy music to help sell bogus treatments to enhance male virility.

After the launch of talking pictures, in 1929, the movie studios found themselves stuck with a backlog of unreleased silent movies that were suddenly outdated and unreleasable in the form in which they had been made. So, producers would shoot a few new scenes with sound and edit them into the silent footage—a practice that came to be known in Hollywood as "goat glanding." The phrase was derived from a medical technique made infamous by Brinkley, a crank doctor with a mail-order degree who promised to cure impotence by transplanting slices of the testicles of billy goats into a man's scrotum. The process had a high rate of success at inducing illness and death.

Brinkley, a charismatic speaker who once nearly won election to the governorship of Kansas, grasped the power of radio and connived a way to shill his various sham medical treatments and placebo elixirs through broadcasts out of Mexico, where FCC regulations regarding the allocation of frequencies and signal strength were not yet enforceable. (The U.S. and Mexican governments would later come to agree on common standards, largely in response to the abuses of Brinkley's station and the "border blasters" that followed it in the 1930s.) XER-AM was the most powerful station in the Americas and probably the strongest ever in world history. Brinkley amped up the transmission power until it reached one million watts, twice the strength of the most powerful station licensed in the United States during the 1930s. XER-AM could be heard throughout most of the United States, across the country to both coasts and north into Canada, not to mention Mexico. People reported picking up the station on the metal fencing in their yards. It bled into telephone service, running in the background of people's conversations. It played over the fillings in people's teeth.

Brinkley designed the station's programming as an aural environment for his pitches for male potency treatments. Hence, he played mostly country-and-western music, blasting the music of Jimmie Rodgers, Gene Autry, Red Foley, Cowboy Sam Nichols, and Doc Schneider into the homes (and the dental work) of tens of millions of people across the United States. Brinkley would give a lecture about the miracle effects of his procedures and mail-order preparations to improve sexual function and follow it with a song to plant the image of a cowboy, singing with a horse between his legs.

Alan Lomax did not think well of the form cowboy music took in the decades after his father published *Cowboy Songs*. As he defended the values of raw and simple expression, he criticized sophistication and polish, and he saw commercialization as corruption. "The worst thing that ever happened to cowboy music," Lomax once said, was a western group called the Sons of the Pioneers.

Assembled in Los Angeles in the early 1930s, the Sons of the Pioneers were a quartet of clear-voiced singers, three of whom were also deft instrumentalists: Len Slye, a tenor who played swing guitar and exuded neighborly high spirits; Bob Nolan, a baritone who played upright bass and wrote most of the songs in the group's repertoire; Hugh Farr, a bass singer and expert fiddler; and Tim (sometimes billed as Verne or Vernon, his given first name) Spencer, a solid journeyman who could sing tenor or light baritone and who took up management of the group. (The membership changed over the years, and the group expanded to a quintet.) The Sons of the Pioneers recorded for Decca Records, the label of the popular singers Bing Crosby and Judy Garland and the jazz artists Billie Holiday, Jimmie Lunceford, and Earl Hines. They dressed in unmatching but spiffy dude-ranch clothes and made elegiac western-style music in warm and fastidious four-part harmony.

The songs by Nolan (with occasional contributions from the others)—"Tumbling Tumbleweeds," "Cool Water," "Moonlight on the Prairie," "I Follow the Stream," "The Hills of Old Wyoming," "On a Mountain High"—broke from the traditions of both popular love songs and cowboy ballads and focused on the natural beauty of the western landscape. Nolan took the cowboy out of the western song and left only the West—or a prettified, neatly framed image of it. The art of the Sons of the Pioneers was a string-band parallel to the glorifying, lush, and textured landscape photography Ansel Adams was doing at the same time. The Pioneers, in their songs, conveyed a picture-perfect West. They made beautiful music about the beauty of nature, and they leveraged it beautifully. Under Spencer's business direction, the Sons of the Pioneers signed up with a syndication service that circulated programs to radio stations around the country by recording them on long-playing discs.

Being popular and wholesomely attractive in both sound and appearance, the Sons of the Pioneers were offered movie spots, playing themselves in the B features and short subjects that Hollywood was manufacturing to capitalize on the fad for singing cowboys. By 1936, two years after the Pioneers had made their first recordings for Decca, they had appeared in nine pictures, from matinee program filler like *Radio Scout* to the almost-big-budget western musical *Rhythm on the Range*, starring Bing Crosby. (For the latter film, Johnny Mercer wrote the cheeky "I'm an Old Cowhand from the Rio Grande," which Crosby and the Pioneers performed together as a western-style jazz jam, with Louis Prima taking a verse.) Two of the movies the Pioneers made in 1936, *The Big Show* and *The Old Corral*, put them on-screen with the only movie cowboy more popular than Bing Crosby: Gene Autry.

Autry had started as a Jimmie Rodgers soundalike. He yodeled in Rodgers's way and sang Rodgers's signature tunes, including several of the "Blue Yodel" numbers and "T.B. Blues," about the disease that took Rodgers's life, tuberculosis. After a few years of experimenting—singing ballads, country blues, hillbilly novelties, and cowboy tunes—Autry had a hit with an original number (co-written with his early duo partner Jimmy Long) that pulled a gender switch on the sentimental songs of mother love popular in the previous century: "That Silver Haired Daddy of Mine." It sold five million copies.

Autry's voice was high-pitched, tight, and dry. His singing was unexceptional, but endearingly so. He hit all the notes, if not straight on, and he had some twang left from growing up in Texas. Autry did not sound like a professional singer by the standards that Crosby had set. He came across like the most talented amateur in town, the kind of person one might actually find singing at an actual barn dance. Working from the imaginary barn in a studio on the sixth floor of the Sherman Hotel in downtown Chicago, Autry became a radio star, and his popularity on records and on the air led him to Hollywood.

Autry's very unexceptionalism, working in odd conjunction with the fame he achieved as an exemplar of ordinariness, made him a quintessential figure of the singing-cowboy movies. Unlike the western stars who had sung on-screen before him, such as Bob Steele and Ken Maynard (whose singing voice was dubbed in at least one film by Bob Nolan of the Sons of the Pioneers), Autry was not particularly good-looking, at least not in the conventional leading-man way. He was thickset and soft all around. He had a large, rectangular head and a carrot nose, and his smile was broad and toothy and frozen in place. He looked quite a bit like the Tin Woodsman in W. W. Denslow's original illustrations for the *Wizard of Oz* books. On-screen, Autry seemed uncomfortable, and when he read his lines, there was never doubt that he was reading lines.

Between 1934 and 1953, Gene Autry made more than ninety movies as a singing-cowboy star, and he was almost always cast in the role of Gene Autry, singing-cowboy star. In the credits for *In Old Santa Fe*—a movie set in no such place but, rather, on a dude ranch in the present day of 1934—he was listed as "Gene Autry, Cowboy Idol of the Air." He got his first starring role the following year, in *The Phantom Empire*—a no-budget western sci-fi cliff-hanger about a "scientific" society of beings called Muranians who live secretly underground, conveniently below the Radio Ranch, where Gene Autry is broadcasting his radio program. Much of the serial's suspense hung on the drama of whether or not Autry would make it out of the subterranean city in time to do his show.

Autry became a movie star by playing a movie star with no star quality. Homely, awkward, asexual, and unglamorous, Autry defied almost every convention of the celebrity culture. Kids loved him. His movies were like backyard playtime fantasies—loopy romps of the juvenile imagination, where wagon trains and pickup trucks, six-guns and telephones, existed together in delirious irrationality.

The bad guys in Gene Autry pictures were generally bankers, radio station owners, land speculators, and others in the ranks of powerful businessmen whom Autry would join, more benignly, by the late 1950s, when he retired from performing to run his varied holdings in broadcasting, real estate, and sports. He had learned quite a bit about business by watching himself be underpaid and overworked at Republic Pictures. In 1936, he was earning only two thousand dollars per film and being called upon to shoot six or seven features per year. The following year, Autry walked out on Republic, temporarily, and the studio head, Herbert Yates, started auditioning actors to replace him. Yates hired one of the members of the Sons of the Pioneers, the tenor singer and guitarist Len Slye. To avoid any connotations of wiliness implied by his last name, the studio renamed him—first as Dick Weston and then as Roy Rogers.

Cute and cheery, athletic and good with a horse, Rogers would make more than eighty westerns for Republic and other studios, as well as TV shows in the vein of his movies. Rogers's films and TV episodes were essentially Gene Autry pictures with a new star: childish, wholesome, and unyieldingly predictable mishmashes of chase scenes, shoot-outs, fistfights, and songs, with occasional moments of sexless romance, thanks to the introduction of a love interest, Dale Evans, in Rogers's movies in 1944. (Evans, a former big-band singer, was a more commanding vocalist than Rogers, as well as a gifted songwriter; she wrote the tune that would become Rogers and Evans's theme, "Happy Trails." After the death of Rogers's first wife, Arline, Rogers and Evans married but withheld from their screen fans any hint of an interest in the union's consummation.) *Box Office,* the film industry trade journal, ranked Rogers as the number one box-office attraction in western movies for ten consecutive years, from 1943 to 1952.

Rogers's surpassing act was one of self-merchandising. Like Autry, Rogers made films and TV programs that simulated child's play. Rogers's innovation—indeed, his unique contribution to American pop culture—was to bring material form to that play. He turned himself into a toy—or, rather, a whole store full of licensed products for kids. With the help of a sharp agent, a former record company executive named Art Rush, Rogers retained from Republic the right to exploit his name and likeness in merchandised products, in lieu of a high salary, and he set up a company to produce and market a mammoth line of goods spun off his screen image: Roy Rogers guitars, Roy Rogers cap guns, Roy Rogers watches, Roy Rogers hobbyhorses, Roy Rogers lunch boxes, Roy Rogers paper dolls, Roy Rogers checkers sets, Roy Rogers playhouse dinnerware, Roy Rogers binoculars, Roy Rogers saddlebags, Roy Rogers wallets, Roy Rogers shirts and pants, Roy Rogers bolo ties, Roy Rogers belts, Roy Rogers slippers, Roy Rogers gloves, and Roy Rogers more.

Rogers essentially inverted the business power dynamic of the studio system. Traditionally, film companies exploited actors' celebrity to promote movie product. Rogers used his movies to promote products based on his celebrity. In a two-page-spread advertisement to toy and clothing retailers in the 1950s, his company touted Rogers as not just the "King of the Cowboys" but the "Monarch of Merchandising." The pressed-pattern boots and bright snap-button shirts and beaded holsters that were marketed in Rogers's name were close enough facsimiles of his screen wardrobing, and with each film his movie costumes looked more like his product line. Rogers appeared increasingly like a boy dressed up like Roy Rogers. There's an easy pun in the fact that cowboys had previously been engaged in a different sort of branding, and there I've used it. By packaging himself as a toy, Rogers made himself something that was not only marketable and collectible but discardable, easy for his fans to give up and leave behind with their skates when they grew up and moved out of their childhood rooms.

A boy of a man, a singer and action hero, a movie star and playtime fantasy, an emblem of the Old West and marketing mogul, Roy Rogers carried on and built upon Gene Autry's multiple legacies for the children of the shopping-center age. Between them, Gene Autry and Roy Rogers made more than 150 movies in the 1930s, 1940s, and 1950s, as well as TV series episodes, and when they made them, not much else in popular entertainment had a comparable grip on young people. No fewer than one hundred million people, most of them kids at the time, watched Autry and Rogers on-screen or heard them on records and the radio, and through Autry and Rogers they developed an affection for simple, rural music sung in natural voices and played on the guitar. This was music that seemed wholly different from the urban, piano-based, swing-oriented songs that their parents were listening to. It was music parents looked down on, while young people took it as something preciously their own.

6

ROCK AND ROLL

THEY WENT CA-RAAAAAZY FOR IT!

The observer effect, by which things change in the process of being experienced, applies to music as well as to subatomic phenomena. With pop songs, who's listening sometimes matters as much as who's making the music, and proof of this lay in the rise of rock and roll in the decade after World War II.

This story, being a tale of American music in the modern era, begins with the blues. As Albert Murray, the great scholar of blues theory, explained to me in a conversation/impromptu lecture on the prehistory of rock, "No Bessie, no Basie, no Beatles."

Murray referred first in that alliterative syllogism to Bessie Smith, the singer and cyclonic force who embodied the blues in the mind of the public when the music surfaced as a popular phenomenon in the decade after World War I. The blues, having begun to coalesce as a musical form around the Mississippi Delta in the late nineteenth century, found a national audience in the early 1920s through recordings made by Bessie Smith, Mamie Smith (whose "Crazy Blues," recorded in 1920, was a blues grafted onto a vaudeville novelty song and became a million-selling hit), Ma Rainey (a primary figure in American music, billed during her own lifetime as the "Mother of the Blues," whose rowdy theatricality did not always translate well to record), Alberta Hunter (a witty lyricist and composer of blues for other singers, as well as a vocalist herself), Ethel Waters (who would later become a respected actress on Broadway and film), Ida Cox, Sippie Wallace, and other women. The blues they sang, with lyrics they often but not always wrote themselves, was hard-driving and tough-minded, rawly emotive, sometimes mournful or melancholy but just as often brassily joyful, with a lyrical sophistication that the tone of its back-alley talk belied; the blues was intricately coded, with multiple, sometimes contradictory meanings and allusions decipherable only to the informed. All the most successful blues singers of the music's first blossoming in the national consciousness, all African American and all women, projected, through both their music and their outsized stage personalities, a collective image of black womanhood as a prefeminist ideal of physical prepossession and independence of mind and body. Slinging double and triple entendres to punchy arrangements for small piano-based bands, the "blues queens," as they would come to be known, upended the Tin Pan Alley tropes of women as sweet little objects of male desire.

Bessie Smith was the biggest name among them—"the very sound of the blues to most Americans," in Albert Murray's words. Within a few years of her first recordings for Columbia Records, made in 1923, Smith became nationally famous as the "Empress of the Blues," outranking the mere queens around her. In the segregated South, she gave separate concerts for whites and blacks but played to full houses of both races. Her signature song, "Tain't Nobody's Bizness If I Do" (credited on her record to a pair of male pianists, Porter Grainger and Everett Robbins), was a manifesto of womanly self-rule:

If I go to church on Sunday
Then cabaret on Monday
'Taint nobody's business if I do.

The popularity of the blues queens had faded by the end of the 1920s, as if either the white male power structure of the entertainment business or the white male power structure of the world had had quite enough of black women acting as if they could be as clever and rough as men, black or white. Alberta Hunter, looking back on this period fifty years later, recalled it as a "dream that couldn't last." Rediscovered late in her life after decades away from the stage, Hunter was in the 1970s singing regularly at the Cookery, a midsized club in Greenwich Village run by the impresario Barney Josephson, who in the 1930s had broken racial barriers with a pair of mixed-race venues in Manhattan, both called Café Society. I interviewed Hunter for a journalism class at NYU, which was just a block south of the Cookery.

"I wrote 'Downhearted Blues' in 1920 or 1921," Hunter said. "I performed the song with King Oliver and recorded it in 1922, and my recording sold a thousand copies. I was in the big time. The next year, Bessie Smith made a record of it, and Bessie's record sold a million copies. She put me in my place." In fact, Bessie Smith's recording of "Downhearted Blues" sold more than *two* million copies and would eventually be named by the Rock and Roll Hall of Fame as one of the five hundred songs that shaped rock music.

If the dream of badass women subverting entertainment-industry conventions through bawdy, brawny, wildly transgressive blues couldn't last, the blues endured at the heart of American music, formal and informal, sweet and low-down, popular and otherwise. While I was interviewing Alberta Hunter at a table in the Cookery at lunchtime, an impeccably manicured gentleman not quite Hunter's age stopped by our table to pay his respects to her on his way out. Hunter introduced us, shaking me up momentarily by referring to me as a journalist rather than as a student. She acknowledged the man as "Mr. Wilson," and I hadn't the faintest idea who he was. *Mr. Wilson? Mr. Wilson?* All I could think of was Dennis the Menace's next-door neighbor.

"Now, you listen to this young lady," he said to me, eyeing the gigantic Radio Shack cassette recorder on the table. "This is the teacher of us all."

As he walked away, Hunter said, "Good afternoon, Teddy," and I scrawled down the name so I could look it up back in the school library.

The dapper and brilliant jazz pianist Teddy Wilson, I later learned, carried on and helped transmute the blues that Hunter, Bessie Smith, and the rest of their sorority had taught America. From the stages of vaudeville, the blues traveled fast and widely—north to the Cotton Club and other nightspots in the cities, west to the barn-dance shows where country and western caught on as a popular music, and all around the rural South, where singer-instrumentalists such as Charley Patton, Robert Johnson, and Blind Lemon Jefferson performed guitar-based blues in a form not far removed from that of its backwater provenance in earlier years. The ostensible jungle music that Ellington, Harold Arlen, Dorothy Fields, and their collaborators produced for the amusement of nightclubbing white voyeurs was essentially a feathered-up adaptation of the blues, and much of Ellington's early repertoire was stomping, wailing blues-jazz: "Down in Our Alley Blues," "The Blues I Love to Sing," "The Blues with a Feeling," "Tishomingo Blues," and more. Jimmie Rodgers, at the same time, was crooning and yodeling his own gently whitened-up adaptation of the blues, trading verses with Louis Armstrong, making records like "The Brakeman's Blues," "Never No Mo' Blues," and his long list of "Blue Yodel" variations, and earning the name the "Father of Country Music" for doing so. Even Gene Autry, during his apprenticeship as a Rodgers imitator, recorded a sizable catalog of blues numbers, including "Jailhouse Blues," "High Steppin' Mama Blues," and the Bessie Smith–influenced "Do Right Daddy Blues."

As Albert Murray said, Bessie Smith made possible Count Basie—and Teddy Wilson and the whole idiom of blues-based jazz for jive dancing called swing. Developed primarily by African American jazz musicians in the early 1930s, swing was played most often, early on, by large ensembles designed for the filling of ballrooms with high-volume, high-energy sound. Like jazz in general, swing could fairly be thought of as the blues citified, spruced up and pumped up, and like its historical predecessor, ragtime, swing was essentially a black invention taken up by whites.

Bing Crosby, on his radio show, once asked Louis Armstrong to explain swing to the audience, and Armstrong said, "Ah, swing, well—we used to call it syncopation. Then they called it ragtime, then blues, then jazz. Now, it's swing. White folks, y'all sho' is a mess!"

Before long, the idea of swing would take on a specific meaning pertaining to rhythmic flexibility. As Ralph Ellison wrote in *Invisible Man*, referencing Armstrong, "Invisibility, let me explain, gives one a slightly different sense of time, you're never quite on the beat. Sometimes you're ahead and sometimes behind. Instead of the swift and imperceptible flowing of time, you are aware of its nodes, those points where time stands still or from which it leaps ahead. And you slip into the breaks and look around. That's what you hear vaguely in Louis' music."

Fletcher Henderson, a key early innovator of swing, had started his career in blues, co-writing (in collaboration with the songwriter Henry Troy) "Gin House Blues" for Bessie Smith in 1925. The African American son of a school principal, Henderson had graduated from Atlanta University and moved to New York to study chemistry at Columbia but abandoned science to make music full-time. Henderson, along with the bandleaders Chick Webb, Jimmie Lunceford, and Benny Moten, the arrangers Don Redman, Edgar Sampson (who served as de facto musical director of Webb's band in its prime), and Sy Oliver (who orchestrated for Lunceford), and other musicians of jazz's second generation, worked up a big, fast, happy kind of dance music that clicked with the freethinking and free-spending young people of the period between the world wars.

Henderson sold dozens of his arrangements to a talented clarinetist, Benny Goodman, whose skill and charm as a soloist and bandleader, not to mention his whiteness, led him to be hired as the swing music act on a national radio show called *Let's Dance*, which first aired in December 1934 with sponsorship by the National Biscuit Company (Nabisco) to promote its brand-new product, Ritz crackers. (The program also featured two bandleaders with different styles: Kel Murray, who made soft music for slow dancing or napping, and Xavier Cugat, a Spanish-born, Cuban-bred self-caricature of Latin eccentricity who conducted while holding a baton in one hand and a Chihuahua in the other.) Goodman's segment, broadcast live from the Palomar Ballroom, a whites-only club for dinner and dancing in Los Angeles, brought what sounded clearly like black music—and was essentially that, despite the race of the bandleader—into the homes of some two million people of all colors.

My father, who was an adolescent when he discovered both Benny Goodman and swing on *Let's Dance*, was probably typical of white kids of the prewar era in his reaction to the sound of Goodman's performances of Henderson's arrangements of hard-swinging numbers such as "Stomping at the Savoy" and "Sing, Sing, Sing." He thought he was hearing "colored records," to use his language, and he could never fully process the truth when he learned that Goodman was Jewish. He was convinced that Goodman must have had some black blood in him, much as he would suspect, after seeing Elvis Presley on *The Ed Sullivan Show*, that he was part black. "There's a little woodshed in that boy," he would say pretty much every time he heard Elvis on the radio, and in cultural if not genetic terms he was right. Aesthetic miscegenation has provided American music with its lifeblood.

Goodman, to his credit, made a point to acknowledge Fletcher Henderson as the author of most of the arrangements in the Goodman band book. He thought of Henderson as a superior bandleader and said so to interviewers. Among the less enlightened members of the cultural establishment, the elementally black character of swing was accepted with a patronizing nod. *The New York Times*, pretending to explicate the music in an article titled "Swing: What Is It?," snorted, "Of its pioneers, most of whom were Negro, scarcely one could read music; the 'spots' [musical notes] meant nothing to them. They learned to play their instruments by intuition . . . In their blood was a seemingly limitless physical energy, a superlative rhythmic sense and an instinctively creative musicianship." *Intuition*, not training or practice. *In their blood*, not in their independent will. *Instinctively*, not learnedly. And all this, while echoing the early criticism of Tin Pan Alley music, passed for a defense of swing and its creators.

Goodman, radically for his time, made the integrated nature of his music visible by hiring Teddy Wilson to play with him and the white drummer Gene Krupa in the trio he formed as a subset of his big band. (I might have thought to ask Wilson about this, while he was standing in front of me, had I only realized who he was.) Goodman's good judgment and bravery were not universally applauded in the 1930s. A white writer for *Orchestra World* magazine, Lige McKelvy, objected to the very idea of having musicians of different races play together. "There is a distinct difference between white and colored musicians," McKelvy wrote. "Both are excellent, more or less, in their own elements. But mixed, the story is different."

Big-band swing—lively and fun, a social art meant for public use by teams of young men and women, produced mostly by large ensembles—was not sustainable in wartime. By the end of World War II, the big-band craze had faded, a victim of the decline in the dating population, the heavying of the national mood, and the resultant shutdown of dance halls and ballrooms (accelerated in 1944 by a battering federal excise tax of 30 percent, later lowered to 20 percent, on venues providing food, drink, and dancing). But a strain of swing survived in a musically stripped-down, lyrically juiced-up form called jump music or jump blues. Some people called it rhythm music or simply rhythm or used the broader term "rhythm and blues" in reference to it.

Performed by small groups, nearly all of them African American at first, jump blues was rawer than big-band swing, harder driving and more brazenly sexy. The music rarely ventured far from standard blues patterns, and the lyrics were mostly slangy celebrations of the pleasures of gin, reefer, and other sources of taboo kicks. Sex was never far from the lyrical content, even when the words were about dressing up or chowing down or finding a dance partner. After all, dancing, in popular music, is always code for sex—not that jump music had much patience for the genteel niceties of innuendo. It hardly took much poetic imagination to pick up the meaning in the image of "a one-eyed cat peepin' in a seafood store" in Big Joe Turner's record of "Shake, Rattle, and Roll." In jump blues, as in the blues historically, there was never any doubt that to slip and slide, to shake and rattle, to rock and roll, meant to have sex. And the music itself—insistent, ecstatic, throbbing, pounding—sounded, if not like sex in all the varied possibilities of eros, like the having of a good fuck. That the music was also elementally African American, suggesting nothing other than black sex—or, by vicarious extension to nonblack listeners, sex between blacks and whites—made it all the more titillating to the music's fans and terrifying to its detractors.

A gleefully exuberant, charismatic singer and alto saxophonist from the Chick Webb Orchestra, Louis Jordan, formed a small jump combo of his own, named the Tympany Five for the attention-grabbing drum that provided visual novelty and little else to the band, and recorded a succession of lighthearted but hard-swinging tunes that exalted in the having of good times: "Let the Good Times Roll," "Ain't Nobody Here but Us Chickens," "Choo Choo Ch'Boogie," and "Caldonia," a hit for both Jordan and the trumpeter/bandleader Erskine Hawkins (co-composer of "Tuxedo Junction") in 1945, which *Billboard* magazine described as "rock and roll." Jordan, in his prime as a jump blues star, was among the most popular entertainers in America. He recorded duets with the likes of Ella Fitzgerald, Louis Armstrong, and Bing Crosby and was a role model for young would-be musicians such as Chuck Berry, who learned the electric guitar riff that opened the Jordan record "Ain't That Just Like a Woman" and used it as the musical signature of "Johnny B. Goode," "Roll Over, Beethoven," and the many variations thereof that Berry recorded. "The first time I heard [that riff] was in one of [the guitarist] Carl Hogan's riffs in Louis Jordan's band. Ain't nothing new under the sun," Berry would later recall.

"To my recollection, Louis Jordan was the first [person] that I heard play rock and roll," Berry said. "I identify myself with Louis Jordan more than any other artist."

In the last years of World War II and the period immediately following the war's end, when the GIs who did not die returned home with the horrors of battle in their bones, jump music, in its exuberance and licentiousness, seemed at odds with the national narrative of sober maturity and self-sacrifice. It did not help the music's reputation for it to be closely associated with an emerging phenomenon that social scientists and the press were calling juvenile delinquency. That is to say, the music's bad reputation *boosted* its growing image as the sound of youth rebellion and nonconformity, the background score to the drive-in movie image of gangs of wayward teenagers rumbling in high-school parking lots.

To put this in perspective, we should return to the blues queens for a moment. Bear with me.

Ma Rainey, Bessie Smith, and Ida Cox all got their starts in show business as entertainers in a traveling tent show called the Rabbit's Foot Minstrels. It is not clear from the scant surviving documentation if any of the three of them corked up for the stage themselves, though other African American performers in "the Foots" worked in blackface. One of the male entertainers in the troupe was a singer-guitarist named Jim Jackson, who performed a mix of blues, jokey hokum numbers, and hybrids of the two. In the late 1920s, when record companies were targeting the African American market with lines of "race records," the Vocalion label signed Jackson, and he had one of the first hits in recorded black music with a two-part, double-sided record called "Jim Jackson's Kansas City Blues." A bright, fun number, it includes a line that many years later would be interpreted as quasi-prescient: "It takes a rocking chair to rock, a rubber ball to roll."

Following the folk and blues tradition of creation through adaptation and revision, by which untold numbers of songs have taken shape over time, through the accretion of contributions by many artists, the seminal Delta blues singer and guitarist Charley Patton took "Jim Jackson's Kansas City Blues," moved the setting seven hundred miles to the southeast, and made "Going to Move to Alabama," recorded in 1929 for Paramount Records (a "race" label run by a white Wisconsin manufacturer of record cabinets and other furniture, unrelated to the Hollywood movie studio). Ten years later, in the swing era, the Kansas City pianist and bandleader Count Basie took the musical essence of what Jackson and Patton had recorded, and he turned it into a spritely jitterbug dance number he called "Red Wagon." The title referred to the popular children's toy, and the phrase was also a slang term for vagina.

Eight years after Basie's record of "Red Wagon," when jump blues was all the rage, Hank Williams—then still a little-known young country singer and songwriter—took the meat of the tune and used it to make a swinging barn-dance number called "Move It On Over." The music of "Move It On Over" was essentially jump, countrified with a fiddle and steel guitar, and the lyrics told a story straight out of the Bessie Smith songbook, about a woman who sends her up-to-no-good man out to sleep in the doghouse. It became Williams's first hit record, number four on the Billboard country-and-western chart—the song that "changed everything" for Hank Williams, in the words of the Williams biographer Paul Hemphill.

In country music of the early postwar period, the jump sound was no anomaly. There was something of a craze for western swing— lively, jazzy, danceable music with a steady 4/4 beat played by small bands on stringed instruments—guitars, fiddles, and steel guitars, sometimes augmented with piano and a horn or two. Performed almost solely by white musicians and singers for white audiences, western swing embraced a form of African American expression— exuberantly, with no hint of parody or irony—and recombined it companionably with the tonalities and lyrical motifs of rural white music. For a few years in the mid- to late 1940s, there were dozens of western swing combos recording and performing around the country, especially in Texas, in the Southwest, and on the West Coast: groups led by Milton Brown (the "Father of Western Swing"), Bob Wills (the "King of Western Swing"), Donnell "Spade" Cooley (a rival "King of Western Swing"), Bob Wills's brother Billy Jack (whose band actually swung harder than his more celebrated brother's), and many others. Spade Cooley, by all accounts, wore his racist-slur nickname with more ease than a black man could ever have summoned. (Cooley's career ended when he murdered his wife after discovering that she had had an affair with Roy Rogers.)

Among the many minor bands playing countrified jump blues in the late 1940s were the Four Aces of Western Swing, an East Coast combo led by the singer-guitarist Bill Haley. A brawny guy born in the Midwest, Haley had a slight resemblance to Superman as he had been drawn in the 1940s, a fact that Haley accentuated by wearing his hair Kryptonian-style, with a lock of bangs curled and tonicked into an S form on his forehead. To young people, Haley had the look of a matinee fantasy, a singing cowboy superhero.

By the early 1950s, Haley was modestly successful in the Philadelphia area with a western-tinged jump band called Bill Haley and the Saddlemen. The group's repertoire was a mixed bag of country tunes such as "Deal Me a Hand," played with a pulse, and twanged-up renditions of rhythm numbers already recorded by black acts, such as "Rocket 88," the eight-cylinder juke-joint dance record made by Ike Turner and His Kings of Rhythm but released under the name of the singer Jackie Brenston in 1951. Haley and the Saddlemen followed Turner and Brenston with their version within months. A few months after that, Haley and the Saddlemen recorded another rhythm tune, "Rock the Joint," which was based on an earlier hit by a black group, Jimmy Preston and His Prestonians. I should add that Preston had gotten the idea for the song from a record called "Good Rockin' Tonight," by the black singer and bandleader Wynonie Harris, and Harris learned the song from a record by another black singer, Roy Brown, who claimed to have written it.

It was still 1952. Elvis Presley was a seventeen-year-old student at Humes High School in Memphis, and he wouldn't venture into a storefront studio to make his first recording, a birthday present for his mother, for another year. Chuck Berry had just bought a Nick Manoloff instruction book to teach himself guitar chords. Jerry Lee Lewis was seventeen and recently expelled from the Southwestern Bible Institute in Waxahachie, Texas, two years away from recording his first demo. Buddy Holly was sixteen and singing in the high-school choir in Lubbock, Texas. All of them were talented young people soaking in the pop of their day, and what they heard was the sound of rhythm music, a black invention already mixed up with country and western swing.

Jukeboxes in neighborhoods of every sort—or in every neighborhood that was of a sort to have jukeboxes—were filling with music that rocked and rolled, all in the name of jump blues, rhythm music, or rhythm and blues. Peter Guralnick, the fine historian of American vernacular music, would describe the sound as the "new hard-driving 'swing boogie' style." Increasingly, the imagery of "rocking" framed the way people talked about the music. Jimmy Preston, after "Rock the Joint," made "Rock with It, Baby" (1950) and "Roll, Roll, Roll" (in the same year). And the saxophonist Wild Bill Moore had hits with both "We're Gonna Rock, We're Gonna Roll" (1948) and "I

Want to Rock and Roll" (1949). Moore was especially popular around Cleveland, where the disc jockey Alan Freed, in 1951, started playing rhythm music on a station with an established audience of white listeners. One of the first records Freed played on his show, which he called *The Moon Dog House*, was "We're Gonna Rock, We're Gonna Roll."

Freed referred to the music he played by various names—"boogie," "the big beat," "rock and roll," and sometimes "bebop," a word that was not yet firmly established as the term of preference for the virtuosic and byzantine style of jazz that many musicians and critics were still calling "modern" music. But he favored the phrase "rock and roll," in part because it was not well known, especially to his white listeners. He could claim to have invented the term and, by extension, the music. Like Alan Lomax in the realm of American folk music, Freed had a keen sense of the value of astute curatorship in codifying and popularizing an art, and even more than Lomax, Freed was susceptible to conflating advocacy for creative work with the act of creation. He allowed himself to be billed as the "King of Rock and Roll," attempted to copyright the phrase "rock 'n' roll," and leveraged his influence as a song hypester to persuade novice songwriters like Chuck Berry to include Freed's name as co-author on songs such as "Maybellene." (For the music of "Maybellene," Berry drew heavily from Bob Wills's western swing record "Ida Red" and freely admitted so. In fact, Berry's original title for the tune was "Ida May.")

In 1952, Freed suggested that Bill Haley change the name of his band, from the Saddlemen to the Comets, to shake the cowboy association for something more pulpy and sci-fi-ish. (*Sputnik* and the dawn of the space age were still five years in the future.) Under the direction of their record producer, Milt Gabler, who also produced Louis Jordan, Bill Haley and the Comets focused on big-beat music and had their first top-twenty hit with a number credited to Haley, "Crazy Man Crazy," which laid hepcat lingo over a jump blues groove. Around the same time, a couple of journeymen music publishers out of Philadelphia, Max Freedman and James Myers, took note of the vogue for rhythm records and put together a song with music based on Hank Williams's "Move It On Over" that they called "(We're Gonna) Rock Around the Clock Tonight." Twenty-five years after "Jim Jackson's Kansas City Blues," the song was still being rewritten.

Haley's record of the tune, released in 1954 as a B side to a saucy, minor-key vamp, "Thirteen Women (and Only One Man in Town)," was a fizzle on the charts but found favor with a fifth grader in Beverly Hills named Peter Ford. His mother, the movie-musical star Eleanor Powell, had schooled him in swing, and his father, the actor Glenn Ford, was signed to star in the screen adaptation of *Blackboard Jungle*, a sensationalistic pseudo-social-realist novel about juvenile delinquency in an urban high school. Richard Brooks, the film's director, was visiting the Fords and asked the boy what kind of music kids these days were listening to, and Peter handed him his copy of Haley's "Rock Around the Clock."

The facts about juvenile delinquency were inconsistent and inconclusive at the time of the film's release in March 1955. In New York, reports of juvenile arrests had increased 20 percent in 1954. In Washington, D.C., court records showed a 30 percent *decline* in crime by minors. Statistics were inadequate at capturing the shift in attitudes that seemed to separate the generation of adults who had lived through World War II and kids reaching adolescence in the postwar climate. Young people were dressing and talking and acting differently than their parents did—as young people of every generation had long done for the precise purpose of alienating their elders and asserting their independent identities.

Meanwhile, the adult world almost dared them to act out. The complacency of returned veterans happy to be home, the industrial homogeneity of the fast-expanding suburbs, and the notorious blandness of the Eisenhower-era culture provided kids with big, easy targets of enmity, and pulp novels, magazines, movies, and comic books not only captured but glamorized and popularized—indeed, institutionalized—the terms of teen rebellion as a vogue and a social imperative. The rebels' causes, however plentiful, provable or not, became incidental to the appeal of acting out as a badge of belonging.

Blackboard Jungle taught a generation of teenagers who they were and established the music now commonly called rock and roll as the sound of teen kinship. The trailer for the film began as the movie does, with Bill Haley and His Comets playing on the background track. We see Glenn Ford, dressed in a suit and carrying a briefcase, glaring incredulously around the hectic street in front of a big-city school, like a white hunter entering the bush for the first time. Two pairs of boys behind the school-yard gates, one pair of them made up of a black boy and a white boy, do a swing dance, twirling each other around and flipping each other over their hips. "You are now listening to 'Rock Around the Clock,'" the narrator intones. "This is the theme music from MGM's sensational new picture, *Blackboard Jungle.*"

The scene cuts to a group of teenagers standing together silently, like a mob on the brink of something bad. A black kid stands next to a white boy sneaking a puff from a cigarette hidden in his cuffed palm. "Many people said the story could not, must not, dared not be shown," the narration continues. Then we see another set of boys—again, one black (a then-unknown young actor named Sidney Poitier), one white. "It is fiction, but fiction torn from big city, modern savagery," says the narrator. "It packs a brass-knuckled punch in its startling revelation of those teenage savages who turn big-city schools into a clawing jungle." Twenty years after the Cotton Club had shut down, the jungle still stood as a white fantasy of black horrors and temptations, set to an irresistible dance beat.

The full effect of these images and the role of "Rock Around the Clock" in relation to them can be understood only in the context of the racial upheaval that was just beginning to rattle America—an erupting set of events so fresh that the newspapers had not yet settled on calling it the civil rights movement. In January 1952, the Supreme Court announced that it would hear the case of *Brown v. Board of Education*. In the same period, Alan Freed was making headlines (his indisputable talent) for integrating pop music, presenting rhythm and blues records made by African Americans to a mixed-race audience of young people. In March 1952, Freed held the "Moondog Coronation Ball," a rhythm and blues concert that drew some twenty thousand young people—whites and blacks together, at the Cleveland Arena, to dance to black music—and the show was shut down after the first song, performed by Paul "Hucklebuck" Williams, out of fear that the music would lead to a riot. The music wasn't entirely new—it was still rhythm music and still elementally black—but the audience was changing, becoming more integrated as well as younger and more defiant, and that transformed the way it was taken.

The Supreme Court ruled on *Brown v. Board of Education*, outlawing segregation in the public schools, in May 1954, the same month "Rock Around the Clock" was released. The timing of the two events was a minor coincidence, of course; still, more broadly, racial integration was overlapping with musical integration, and each surely helped advance the other. By the time *Blackboard Jungle* opened, with its images of black and white kids smoking, jive dancing together, and otherwise acting "savage," the desegregation of the schools—and the larger movement to desegregate America—dominated the news and divided much of the country. *Blackboard Jungle* came across as a testament to the consequences of mixing the races—a nightmare of lawlessness or a dreamscape of overdue freedoms delivered, depending on one's point of view, race, or age. Rock and roll was not merely its soundtrack but its embodiment: black and white brought together with wild results.

"They called it voodoo music. They called it jungle music. They called it everything they could think up to tell the white kids that it was black and bad for you, so the white kids just went crazy for it—

they went *ca-raaaaazy* for it!" recalled Little Richard in an interview I did with him in 1991, forty years after he had started recording. Richard, who had begun singing and playing piano professionally in childhood, released a string of rhythm and blues singles with modest impact in the early 1950s and came into his own in 1955 with a manically hyperactive and sexually transgressive style of original music. On the only occasion we met, he was supposed to be promoting an album of children's songs that he had recorded, with his trademark mania, for the Disney record label. We met in a hotel suite in Manhattan, and Richard successfully discussed his interest in children for a solid two minutes before bursting into a splendiferous free-form monologue about his own loveliness and importance in American cultural history.

"They called Elvis Presley the King of Rock and Roll," he squealed, roaming around the room in a Day-Glo fuchsia jumpsuit. "Elvis was the King of Rock and Roll. But I was the *Queen*! *I was the Queen!*" I was reminded of the fear parents of the 1950s had in rock and roll's capacity to ingrain radical notions in the minds of kids.

In the mid-1950s, nobody seemed to like rock and roll except teenagers and the people who performed, presented, sold, and otherwise benefited from its production. Musicians associated with the Tin Pan Alley tradition, such as Frank Sinatra and Nat King Cole, were offended by the music's crudeness and vulgarity, qualities its fans took as virtues, counteragents to the slickness and politeness of the commercial pop of the day. As Sinatra said in 1957, "Rock and roll is the most brutal, ugly, desperately vicious form of expression it has been my displeasure to hear. Rock n' roll smells phony and false. It is sung, played and written for the most part by cretinous goons, and by means of its almost imbecilic reiteration, and sly, lewd—in plain fact, dirty—lyrics . . . it manages to be the martial music of every sideburned delinquent on the face of the earth."

Jazz buffs, much the same, dismissed rock and roll as dumb show.

"Rock 'n' roll bears the same relationship to jazz as wrestling bears to boxing," wrote the critic and record producer Leonard Feather in his *Encyclopedia Yearbook of Jazz*.

Civic leaders, PTA officers, members of the clergy, and other people concerned with youth welfare, in many (but hardly all) cases tended to fear rock and roll for its obvious ability to stir the body, ostensibly at the expense of the mind. As the Reverend Bernard Travaille said in September 1956 at Los Angeles's La Crescenta First Baptist Church, "Rock 'n' roll shows that morally we are not far removed from the Kenya tribesman. We have nailed a thin veneer of culture over our character and the rock 'n' roll has peeled off a portion to show what is underneath."

Even some advocates of traditional rhythm and blues criticized rock and roll as a diminishment of a music once made solely by African Americans. In the *New Journal and Guide*, an African American newspaper, the writer Phyllis Battelle chided the "torturous rhythm" and "bawling, squawling beat" of rock and roll as a "poor white trash version" of black rhythm and blues.

Once teenagers of all colors took up this music as their own, under the name that distinguished it as theirs, they craved singers who were their own age, or close enough to serve as objects of sexual fantasy without too much creepiness. Big Joe Turner, the blues shouter, had been born in 1911. In 1954, when he recorded "Shake, Rattle, and Roll" and it ended up as a hit on the *Billboard* pop chart, Turner was forty-three years old—robust and good-looking, but portly and visibly old enough to be the father of teenagers. (Early in 1955, Turner appeared in a low-budget music movie called *Rhythm and Blues Revue*; later the same year, a follow-up picture was made, also featuring Turner, and it was titled *Rock 'n' Roll Revue*.) Over the course of the mid-1950s, a wave of artists around Haley's age or younger, some black and some white, started performing and recording music geared increasingly to young ears, young hearts, and young libidos: Elvis Presley, who was nineteen when he released his first record;

Jerry Lee Lewis, who was twenty-one; Carl Perkins, twenty-four; Little Richard, twenty-three at the time of his breakthrough, "Tutti Frutti"; Fats Domino, twenty-seven at the time of "Ain't That a Shame"; and Chuck Berry, the oldest of the group at twenty-nine. Teen audiences went mad for them, with less and less interest in anyone like Joe Turner or Wynonie Harris and Memphis Slim (both born in 1915) or Wild Bill Moore (born in 1918).

Turner made an attempt to use his age to strategic advantage and released the unsubtly pedophilic single "The Chicken and the Hawk" in 1955. By then, Elvis Presley had arrived and had the chickens all to himself. Gorgeous, dreamy-eyed, transfixing, and white—and yet a child of the rural South, still something other, *almost black* in the mixed-up minds of white northerners—Elvis became the sexy symbol of a hypersexed music to millions of fans in the waiting, as well as an object of derision to the music's skeptics.

Within three months of the release of his first single for the Memphis-based label Sun Records, "That's Alright (Mama)," Elvis broke out to the southern audience through appearances on the *Louisiana Hayride* radio show, broadcast from the municipal auditorium in Shreveport, Louisiana. Before Elvis performed his second song, the host, Frank Page, asked his guest, with an audible smirk, "I'd like to know just how you derived that style, how you came about with that rhythm and blues style—that's all it is. That's all you can say about it."

Presley replied with the shy respectfulness that would disarm many of his early critics: "Well, sir, to be honest with you, we just stumbled upon it."

"Just stumbled upon it?" Page answered. "Well, you're mighty lucky, you know."

It goes without saying now that Elvis Presley had far more than luck. As talented and magnetic as he was good-looking and white, Elvis earned his fame and was at least as deserving of coronation as the "King of Rock and Roll" as Benny Goodman had been to be called the "King of Swing." Both were certainly much more qualified for their kingships than Irving Berlin had deserved to be promoted as the "Ragtime King." Presley made brilliant rock and roll, and Goodman played first-rate swing, and Berlin, despite having a sheet music hit with a popular song *about* the ragtime craze, "Alexander's Ragtime Band," never wrote a single ragtime composition.

While Elvis is thought of as an alpha source in rock history—and while he clearly dominated popular music in the second half of the 1950s, with thirteen number one records, from "Heartbreak Hotel" to "A Big Hunk o' Love"—he was in some ways a pre-rock figure. Elvis, very much like the white male pop idols before him—Rudy Vallee, Bing Crosby, and Frank Sinatra—was an interpretive artist, a singer of material created by a professional class of composers and lyricists, rather than a songwriter. (Both Crosby and Sinatra broke out of their usual way of working to write lyrics when they were so moved, and they both did so with distinction, Crosby co-writing the standard "I Don't Stand a Ghost of a Chance with You" with Victor Young and Ned Washington, and Sinatra co-writing "I'm a Fool to Want You" with Jack Wolf and Joel Herron. Vallee's name, like Presley's, appears on the writing credits of more than a few of the songs that he recorded, as a way to increase the singer's income.) Elvis, again like his predecessors, parlayed his early success as a pop singer to build a career as an all-around entertainer, acting in movies and mainstreaming his persona to appeal to a broad segment of the popular audience and not only teenagers. "They tell me I'm another Rudy Vallee," Elvis once said. "I guess that's good."

It was Chuck Berry, not Elvis Presley, who, in the 1950s, pointed to the near future of pop music, and not merely with the guitar conception he refined to snarling perfection from raw ingredients he found in some work by Carl Hogan and T-Bone Walker. Berry anticipated the approach of countless pop artists to come, writing original songs that both drew from his personal experience and dealt explicitly with the interests of his audience. His earliest songs were poetic mini-narratives taken from life: "You Can't Catch Me," about a race Berry had with state troopers on the New Jersey Turnpike; "Thirty Days," taken from one of his youthful run-ins with the law. While other early rockers—Fats Domino, Little Richard, Jerry Lee Lewis, Carl Perkins—were writing their own material, none were doing so with anything close to Berry's narrative sense and eye for detail. Only Berry was writing things like the lyrical, proto-hip-hop couplets in "Too Much Monkey Business," with its vivid descriptions of working in the "fillin' station," pumping "dollar gas."

Berry watched as rhythm music was taken up by teenagers of all colors, and he tailored his lyrics to his listeners. He wrote about the everyday concerns of ordinary kids in conversationally elevated language. He wrote about going to school and not liking it, about the thrill of driving a convertible and the greater thrill in parking—*cruising and playing the radio, with no particular place to go.*

After Berry, it would seem axiomatic that songs for young people should be about young life. Adolescents of the postwar era, the early baby boomers, exerted their influence as a market, and pop music adapted, becoming something not only accessible to them but all about them. Over many years of this kind of thing, the boomers would come to think that pretty much everything was their property and all about them. I say this with considerable embarrassment, being a mid-period boomer myself. I was born in March 1955, the same month *Blackboard Jungle* was released. I've always liked to think that I was born at the same time as rock and roll. If that's just boomer solipsism, Chuck Berry is to blame.

7

THE TRANSISTOR

MINE COMPLETELY

I have a soft spot for monaural sound, the single-speaker method of audio reproduction that predates stereo, and the way I feel about it cannot be wholly explained as the fetishistic glamorization of archaic technology that typically afflicts geeks like me. I don't wear "Back to Mono" T-shirts and don't believe, as some of the mono fundamentalists do, that Phil Spector should be pardoned from prison to produce more of his wall-of-sound records. My weakness for mono is physiological. I cannot process stereo sound well, because the hearing in my left side was damaged in childhood as a result of sleeping with my ear on top of my transistor radio.

When I was in fourth grade, my older brother was a senior in high school, and he gave me his beaten-up pocket transistor. It was a black-and-white Silvertone, from Sears, like nearly everything else in our house. At one point in the 1960s, my parents bought a top-lidded Sears freezer for food storage in the basement, and it came with a promotional package of frozen steaks. When my mother grilled them up for dinner, my father asked what kind of meat he was having, and she said, "Silvertone."

The radio I inherited from my brother was a heavyish plastic box a little larger than one of my mother's packages of Kent cigarettes. It had a silvery-toned finish that looked almost like the chrome on a car, worn at the edges to the beige plastic underneath, from my brother's manhandling. It had come equipped with a swivel handle that, when swung behind the device, doubled as a stand, but my brother had broken that off, because both a handle and a stand undermined the coolness of a transistor radio as something you can hold in your hand like a candy bar or slip into your pants pocket like a comb. On the face of the radio, below the Silvertone logo in streamlined script, was a symbol of an atom. This was the atomic age, after all, and transistor radios were thought of as a necessity in the event of a nuclear attack by the Soviets. (I'm not exaggerating this. Every educational film and instruction guide to nuclear readiness that I ever saw or read specified the need for powdered milk and a transistor radio.) There was one dial for volume and one for tuning in stations—AM only. I had no idea at the time that there was also such a thing as FM, let alone the specialized radio frequencies for weather, police communication, and such. On one side, there was a jack for an earplug—not a set of stereo buds for both ears, as we use today, but a single earplug. I would worm it into my left ear and turn the volume dial up to 10. To write this paragraph, I looked up the radio on a website for collectors of vintage electronics and found that my model was a Silvertone series 1205, marketed in 1961, three years before my brother handed his down to me. According to the Web description, the atom symbol was actually a stylized *S* and *R*, for Sears and Roebuck, interlocked, but I never noticed that. I saw only an atom and thought of the radio as a wonder of the space age.

I carried it with me nearly everywhere, playing WEEX, the Top 40 station out of Easton, Pennsylvania. I blasted it, relatively speaking—

even at 10, the volume of the radio could carry no more than fifteen yards or so—on my walk to school, and I jerry-rigged a holder for it on my bike, using one of the inside compartments from the box for my Monopoly game. In bed at night, I would hide the radio under my pillow, slip the earplug into my left ear, and sleep on that side, so my parents wouldn't see the plug if they peeked into my room. I found this setup unsatisfying, owing to the abysmal sound quality of the earplug, and worked up a technique of burrowing the radio into my pillow and covering the radio with my head. My ear was pressed tightly against the speaker. I would turn the volume up as loud as I thought I could get away with without my parents catching on and fell asleep to the sounds of 1964: the Kingsmen's "Louie, Louie," the Ventures' "Walk, Don't Run," the Shangri-Las' "Remember (Walking in the Sand)," which I loved for the eerie, noirish production by Shadow Morton, and, of course, all the Beatles' early hits, "She Loves You," "I Want to Hold Your Hand," "Please Please Me," "Can't Buy Me Love" . . . In the morning, many times, I would find the radio dead. It would have played through the night until the 9-volt battery was depleted, while my ear was smushed against the speaker. By the time I had my first hearing test, in eighth grade, my left ear was practically shot.

That seemed to me a fair price to pay for the benefits transistor ownership conferred. With a radio in your pocket, listening became something more personal and private than ever in the history of electronically reproduced sound, something anyone could do alone, anywhere, at any hour—or anywhere within reception range of an AM radio signal, at any hour a station was broadcasting. From our vantage point in the twenty-first century, it is hard to conceive of the personalized, private consumption of entertainment as anything exceptional. With handheld electronic devices now everywhere, on everyone, everyone now accepts as a given that we should hear most of the music we listen to, see most of the movies and TV shows we watch, and play most of the games we take part in on our own, on the fly. The drama in the transistor's impact is lost to the ubiquity of its legacy.

Before the transistor, in the era of vacuum tubes, the size, the expense, the high power requirements, and the delicacy of tubes, as well as their susceptibility to catching fire and burning things down, ensured that radios, electronic record players, and early TV sets were bulky objects best suited to use in the house, plugged into a wall, near a fire extinguisher. Tube radios had become commonplace in cars by the 1940s, but they drained auto batteries and broke down or overheated fairly often. The transistor, invented in the United States by a team of physicists (John Bardeen, Walter Houser Brattain, and William Bradford Shockley) at Bell Labs in 1947—or, more accurately, *discovered* by them, because they observed the transistor effect unexpectedly while looking for something else—replaced the vacuum tube with a solid object about the size of a pinkie fingernail. As usual in science, engineers in other countries uncovered the transistor effect and worked on its applications around the same time as the Bell team, though Bardeen and his collaborators were granted the U.S. patent for the technology and won the Nobel Prize in Physics for their work on the transistor. The Nobel committee awarded them the prize in 1956, nine years after they announced their work. At that point, the transformative potential of the transistor was clear in the form of the pocket radio.

Celebrated in engineering circles and discussed widely if vaguely in news reports, the transistor had been just another sciencey-sounding term of the science-obsessed postwar years until 1954, when a couple of preposterously ambitious and irrationally optimistic product developers—one at Texas Instruments, which had never made a consumer product before, and one at a small company in Indianapolis called I.D.E.A. (for Industrial Development Engineering Associates, a name rhetorically developed and engineered to produce the acronym), which had made only TV antennas for sale through Sears—arranged a joint venture to design and mass manufacture a battery-powered radio small enough to tote in a pocket. They made this decision in May 1954, figured how to produce the unprecedented set of tiny components, set up two manufacturing facilities and staffed them (mostly with women, who were found to be more adept at precision work than men), and had the radios in stores before November, in time for Christmas sales. Steve Jobs was conceived at roughly the same time as this product, and nothing he would do at Apple would be more outlandish or, historically, more influential.

Marketed under the unfamiliar Regency brand, the radio was priced at $49.95 (near the cost of assembling the devices for I.D.E.A. and less than the cost of producing the electronics for Texas Instruments, which was in this to claim the territory of transistor production) at a time when a man's suit cost around $40.00 and a monthly mortgage payment in Levittown, Long Island, was typically $63.00. After three years, some one hundred thousand Regency radios were sold—a number that was more than respectable but considerably short of I.D.E.A.'s sales projection of twenty million units. The company had based its sales estimates on an expectation that, by 1957, twenty million American families would buy transistor radios for their bomb shelters. The Regency radio was discontinued and replaced on store shelves by a thousand imitations, most of them made by Japanese manufacturers looking for a niche to build the country's industrial economy in the wake of World War II.

This was the moment when a group of young Japanese companies, targeting electronics as a growth industry, began to undo the image of goods made in Japan as rinky-dink trinkets—the birth of the Pacific electronics business that would come to dominate the field of home entertainment in the late twentieth century. Through the benefits of low-cost labor by high-performing workers (of both sexes), government support, grabby and fun designs, and cagey marketing, virtually unknown brands such as Sony, Toshiba, and Hitachi sold millions of transistor radios to Americans unmotivated by nuclear preparedness. They sold them primarily to young people at prices kids could afford with after-school-job money. The average cost of a transistor radio was about twenty-five dollars in 1960 and fell as low as fifteen dollars by the middle of the new decade. The salesmen for Sony had shirts custom made with oversized breast pockets so their radios would look smaller and more impressive to retailers. While all the major American manufacturers (General Electric, Motorola, and the like) offered their transistor products only through the licensed dealers whose main business was selling TV sets and living-room entertainment consoles to homeowners, the Japanese companies filled the racks of department stores and five-and-dimes where teenagers shopped. Several Japanese companies registered their radios as toys to get away with paying lower import tariffs, and the products ended up being merchandised to kids, alongside the Play-Doh and Etch a Sketches, in toy and hobby stores.

Adults, including college students, were for the most part listening to music thought of as worthy of adult attention: traditional, Tin Pan Alley–style pop sung by veterans of the big-band era such as Doris Day, Peggy Lee, and Frank Sinatra; Broadway musical scores; arty "cool jazz" such as Dave Brubeck's *Time Out*, the first jazz album to sell more than a million copies, in 1960; folk music, commercialized with sunny Ivy League earnestness by vocal-harmony groups such as the Kingston Trio and the Brothers Four; classical music, especially when performed by good-looking men such as Leonard Bernstein and Glenn Gould; and "mood music" records designed as an aural lubricant for sex, released by novelty artists such as Les Baxter and Jackie Gleason, the gifted TV comedian and musical dilettante.

Adults were doing this listening with records in a format that also seemed suitable to adult use: the long-playing 33⅓ rpm album, whose price of around $5.98 in 1960, compared with about $.98 for a 45 rpm single, was conceived of as too rich for teen blood and whose playing time of about twenty to twenty-five minutes per side was thought to overtax kids' attention spans. To listen to this grown-up music in a grown-up manner, adults were, in growing numbers, using fancy and expensive multicomponent hi-fi systems with LP turntables and separate receivers that pulled in FM radio broadcasts, whose wide bandwidth was notably superior to that of the AM stations playing the pop hits of the day. Albums, hi-fi, and FM were oriented to adults and marketed explicitly to "serious listeners." (More on albums in a later chapter.)

Single records, the AM radio stations that played them, and the transistor radios that picked up their signals were all, by contrast, generally thought of as unserious—kids' stuff. Sold alongside toys, transistor radios looked like playthings rather than the laboratory equipment that hi-fi gear emulated. (Nearly all hi-fi equipment sold in the United States was still being produced by American brands such as Fisher and Harman Kardon; Japanese producers were still working on little radios and would not move on to full-scale audio components for several years.) Japanese-made transistor radios, cased in brightly colored plastic and decorated with seemingly random elements— faux-chrome zigzags and curlicues and glued-plastic overlays in geometric shapes, all arranged with a sense of joyful abandon—looked more like study-hall doodles than products of industrial design. That is to say, they were expertly, inventively designed for the function of communicating the spirit of fun.

The AM radio music that came through transistor speakers, much the same, was created to appeal to young people, fitted to their interests and tastes—like Chuck Berry songs, though made by the methods of an era that predated Berry by half a century. For a period of about ten years, between the rise of rock and roll and the arrival of the Beatles, most popular music—or, more accurately, the music most popular—was made by a body of songwriters, producers, and performers who applied the old Tin Pan Alley model of production through specialization to make music for teens. A loose consortium of song sheet publishers and record companies centered on the Brill Building in midtown Manhattan, home base for the music business for decades, retrofitted its song-production machinery to make rock-and-roll records. Producers (such as Don Kirshner and his partner Al Nevins) hired young songwriters (such as Neil Diamond, Neil Sedaka, the team of Gerry Goffin and Carole King, and their rivals Barry Mann and Cynthia Weil) and arranged for the songs to be recorded by singers and vocal groups (such as Bobby Vee, Gene Pitney, the Shirelles, and the Drifters). The tunes were catchy, if simple, and the lyrics communicable, memorable, and oriented to teen life. They came across as less than serious, but only to adults who did not take adolescence seriously.

"Will You Love Me Tomorrow," composed by Carole King with lyrics by Goffin, typifies the proudly adolescent direction that AM pop began to take in the late 1950s and early 1960s. (King and Goffin, seventeen and twenty years old at the time they wrote the song, were a newly married couple with a baby; the consequences of sex were on their minds.) The tune was written as an "answer song" to a hit from 1960 called "Tonight's the Night," in which a young woman anticipates the event of losing her virginity with entwined feelings of anticipation and unease. Performed by the Shirelles, a four-member girl group with an unfussy school-yard-harmony sound, "Tonight's the Night" was written from a female point of view, with lyrics by the Shirelles' lead singer Shirley Owens that dared to have a girl expressing carnal yearning. "Will You Love Me Tomorrow," written expressly to pick up the girl's feelings after the big event, went further still, having the girl reveal the pleasure she took in sex: "Tonight you're mine completely, you give your love so sweetly." With words written by a man, the song hangs on the premise that the boy in the relationship holds the girl's self-worth in his hands. It is hardly as enlightened as a Bessie Smith song in its view of the sexes. Still, it deals fairly bluntly with sex as an adolescent at the cusp of the 1950s and the 1960s might have thought of it, and the very focus on *thinking* in the song tells us something about the impact of the transistor radio.

With the development of affordable pocket radios, parents had a way to purge teen-oriented pop from the family space in the home.

Instead of allowing the music to be played on the radio in the living room or the kitchen, adults could tell the kids to take their damn radios to their rooms, where their parents couldn't hear the music and kids could listen on their own. Transistor listeners often, though surely not always, listened alone or with a friend. To a significant extent, solitary listening replaced social listening—or at least augmented it— for a rising generation of young people, and many of the songs most popular in this period worked well this way, being ruminations on adolescent life, songs of the internal world. Geared to the audience that Brill Building producers saw as the primary market for teen pop, adolescent girls, pop hits became conspicuously intimate and reflective: "Only the Lonely" and "Crying" by Roy Orbison, "My Heart Has a Mind of Its Own" by Connie Francis, "Why" by Frankie Avalon, and "Sweet Nothin's" by Brenda Lee. Few of these tunes were particularly deep or complicated, but they were quieter and more ruminative than the hard-pumping, dance-oriented hits of early rock and roll. Just a few years after songs like "Shake, Rattle, and Roll" and "Whole Lotta Shakin' Goin' On" were saying, "Hey, let's fuck," tunes like "Will You Love Me Tomorrow" were saying, "Okay, but what does this *mean*?" The songs were nicely suited for listening alone, with your radio tucked inside your pillow in bed.

"Like any kid, I think, in my teens," remembered David Byrne, "you start to hear some stuff, in those cases on transistor radio, but it's the same as hearing something [today] on your phone or whatever. You realize it's coming from another world different than the little suburban place you are at. It's a world that sounds really exciting, that's directed towards where your head's going to be at in a few years. That's it—it's like, 'They're sending a signal, and it's directed towards me and everyone like me around the country. This is a direct thing.' Of course, it's coming through AM radio or something. But we think they've found us and we've found it and we've got a common link."

While making music feel more personal, transistors also make it more available. Now it was possible to listen to music anytime, wherever you went—in your room, in the backyard, in the park, at the beach, at the shopping center, whatever you were doing, wherever. Pop could be the soundtrack music for any scene in life. This was something radically new and, as such, incited some panic. As a guest editorial in the *Los Angeles Times* warned, in 1961, "Technological advances which have created the opportunities for home listening . . . have adversely affected our ability to appreciate music. Music is now readily available in the home, the auto . . . even via the transistor radio to the man in the street. We have become so accustomed to music as background sound that though we hear it we do not listen to it." The author of the piece, Elmer Bernstein, understood the effect of music as background, as a successful composer of film scores—music whose purpose is to be heard without being listened to.

Compared with hi-fi stereo, the sound of an AM transistor radio was atrocious. In fact, compared with the reproductive quality of a Victrola windup record player from 1922, the sound of an AM transistor radio was atrocious. AM waves, modulated to pick up more noise and interference than their FM counterparts, would reach the tiny radio's receiver, which, with its limited bandwidth, often cut off most of the bass and some of the treble tones in a song. Any music recorded for maximum fidelity—classical music, jazz, traditional pop, and nearly everything else that a record company would go through the effort to record—sounded scrunched and squeaky on a transistor radio, almost as if all the instruments had been physically squished into that little plastic box.

In the limits of AM sound, some pop producers saw possibilities. Phil Spector, overseeing production of girl-group records in New York, figured out ways to manipulate sound to suit the two-and-a-half-inch speaker in a transistor radio. He had his engineers push their limiters to their limits, compressing the sound of his recordings, and he played them back in the studio on a single, tiny monitor, to hear how the work would sound to kids listening in their rooms. At a young record company in Detroit at the same time, the studio founder, Berry Gordy, was using the same techniques for releases on his new Tamla and Motown labels.

One of the artists working under Gordy, the multitalented song-writer, singer, bandleader, and producer Smokey Robinson, bridled at first at a technique he saw as diminishing his music. "I had big dreams," Robinson said in an interview I did with him in 1989, when he published his memoir, *Smokey: Inside My Life*. "I had symphonies in my head. We were making 'My Girl,' and I told Berry that I wanted a string orchestra on the track. He really knew the market. The kids were listening in their cars [and] on their little radios on the street corner." After the session, Gordy gave Robinson a ride home, and Gordy flipped on the car radio. He turned the dial until he found a station playing classical music. As Robinson recalled, the two of them listened for a minute or so, and Gordy said, "Shiiiit."

A supposedly charmingly curmudgeonly old newspaper columnist named Joe Harrington summed up the attitude that I picked up from adults toward me and my friends and our radios. (This late Joe Harrington should not be confused with the gutsy and lyrical rock writer Joe S. Harrington.) "When we were growing up," Harrington wrote in 1958, opening his argument with his default setup, "no one provided us with a little machine to bring in popular music so we wouldn't get bored with life. We did have fun. But it was fun we arranged in our own gang, and we didn't depend on gadgets to provide entertainment."

In his misanthropic way, Harrington was almost a visionary. In the little transistor radio, he saw the cultural transformation it had begun, in which progressively littler and littler machines, from the boom box to the Walkman to the multimedia digital devices of the twenty-first century, have gotten us all dependent on gadgets to provide our entertainment.

By the early 1960s, carrying a radio had become a fashion statement; you could wear your taste in music as an accessory, a badge of belonging to a club for fans of music that adults were banishing from the home. Adults helped make the transistor radio a symbol of the cult of teen alienation by using it as a tool to enforce their distaste. I still remember my father and his brother, my uncle Bun (his name was not Bud, but Bun—I don't know why), laughing out loud when they saw me sitting alone by the shed in the backyard, listening to my transistor. Some time later, I almost mustered the guts to say no when my dad asked if he could borrow my radio to listen to a Yankee game while my mother was doing something or other in the house. I started to think my father was secretly envious of me and the listening freedom my transistor provided.

≡ 8 ≡

SINGERS AND SONGWRITERS

POTTY ABOUT DYLAN

Billy Eckstine, the jazz-pop balladeer with the huge vibrato and the even huger ego, was for several years one of the most popular singers in America, with twelve Top 10 hits on the charts from 1949 to 1952. By the time I got to see him perform, in the last set of a week's run at the Blue Note jazz club in New York, in April 1989, Eckstine had not worked in the heat of the cultural spotlight for decades, and he missed it. In his show that night, he gamely tackled a couple of lite-rock hits from the 1970s—Stephen Stills's "Love the One You're With" and Joe South's "Walk a Mile in My Shoes"— while Elvis Costello watched in the audience. At the end of the night, Eckstine gave me an interview in his dressing room for the book I was writing about Billy Strayhorn. We talked about Eckstine's growing up in Pittsburgh at the same time as Strayhorn—but in a much better neighborhood, Eckstine pointed out—and we wrapped up with some conversation about the plans that Eckstine, at age seventy-four, had for the future. He told me he had recently purchased an electric guitar and had started taking lessons. One of his sons had told him he ought to be writing songs, something Eckstine had not attempted since his earliest years as a performer, when he had tossed off a couple of blues riff tunes such as "Jelly, Jelly," a minor hit for him in 1940.

"It's not enough to be a great singer anymore," Eckstine said with a bite. Eckstine said everything he said to me with a bite. "Now you have to write the fuckin' songs."

As far as I know, Eckstine never published or performed any new original songs before his death in 1993. His final album would be one he had recorded in 1984, called *I Am a Singer*. Yet Eckstine was correct in his assessment of the terms of pop practice in the second half of the twentieth century. Between the time of Eckstine's glory and the era of "Love the One You're With"—between the early 1950s and the early 1970s—the functional definition of what it is that pop stars do changed radically, altering along with it the music they made. Singers came to be expected not only to sing but also to compose their own material and to accompany themselves on at least one instrument as well. Popular music, historically thought of as an interpretive art, was reconceived as an expressive one. Accordingly, the content of the music was now expected to deal not so much in the universal as in the personal.

Of the top ten singles at the midpoint of the 1950s—in 1955, when "Rock Around the Clock" was wedged in the year-end chart between a sultry mambo instrumental, "Cherry Pink (and Apple Blossom White)," recorded by the dance-band leader Pérez Prado (the "King of Mambo"), and Mitch Miller's sing-along rendition of "The Yellow Rose of Texas"—not one had been composed by the performer listed on the record label. Twenty years later—in 1975, when Elton John's anthem of disco Americana, "Philadelphia Freedom," sat on the chart alongside David Bowie's art-funk collaboration with John Lennon, "Fame," and the Eagles' "One of These Nights"—half the songs in the year-end Top 10 had been written by the people who recorded them. Something elemental had changed, and it was even more apparent in the domain of long-playing albums, which by the 1970s had become the dominant format of recorded music. A full nine of the ten bestselling albums of 1975 and the majority of the rest of the records on the list—albums by Elton John; Led Zeppelin; the Who; David Bowie; Earth, Wind, and Fire; and other notables of the mullet age—were made up mainly of songs composed or co-composed by their performers.

Authorship is a complicated thing, however, and it was so for years before Michel Foucault noticed. In art of all kinds, but acutely in popular music, the line dividing interpretation and expression has always been a spongy, leaking one.

Performers have personas—public images that are part of what they perform, along with the words and music of songs, lines of dialogue, dance steps, or other particulars of what we tend to think of when we think about an artist's work. A performer's image may be closely connected to the private reality of the person—or somewhat related to it, or only a part of the whole of the private self, or something entirely different from it, hard to reconcile with the person offstage, or perhaps even something more credible, more *real* to the audience, than the ostensibly real person. A great many things go into the making of a performer's image, including everything the audience knows or thinks it knows about the artist's private life. Still, the primary force behind the truth of a performance is usually performance itself. Great interpreters make their art feel as if it were expression—as a rule, though not always, because veracity isn't the point of every *kind* of performance. Traditionally, in popular music, the content and the style of the material the singer interprets have been central to the performer's image. It hasn't always mattered if he or she wrote the fuckin' songs.

This was the case as far back as the time of Eva Tanguay, the American singing star from the turn of the last century who was famous—no, famously infamous—for the radically sassy image she projected, a persona rooted squarely in the defiant lyrical content and musical snap of her songs, especially her signature tune, "I Don't Care":

> I don't care, I don't care
> What they may think of me
> I'm happy go lucky
> Men say I'm plucky
> So jolly and carefree
> I don't care, I don't care.

Tanguay's stage image conjoined with her material to define her as the "'I Don't Care' Girl." Tanguay was not only identified with the song but identified *by* it, and the fact that it was written not by her but by a pair of professional tunesmiths, the lyricist Jean Lenox and the composer Harry O. Sutton, was irrelevant.

Sophie Tucker didn't write any of the lusty, swaggering songs that came across, in her voice, like her own uncensored speech. Billie Holiday, while having co-composed several masterpieces, including "God Bless the Child" and "Don't Explain," wrote only a handful of the hundreds of songs she performed, yet through the power of her musical personality and the depth of her interpretive gifts she made nearly everything she sang seem deeply, openly, almost painfully personal. Sinatra had much the same effect when he sang "Ebb Tide" or "Angel Eyes"—or, working in another part of the emotional spectrum, "That's Life." So did George Jones when he sang "She Thinks I Still Care," and so did Ray Charles, no matter what he sang—"Hit the Road, Jack" or "Crying Time." Interpretation bled into expression, and singing another person's writing became a kind of authorship.

In the 1960s, popular singers, as a class, took up songwriting more literally. The Beatles, needless to say, are a big part—but not the totality—of the explanation. "I started writing songs because the Beatles wrote their own songs," said John Sebastian, a onetime teen-age jug-band musician who formed the Lovin' Spoonful, the pop-rock band with a strain of rackety jug-band jubilance, in 1964, the year of the Beatles' breakthrough in America. (The Beatles themselves had started as the British equivalent of a jug band—a skiffle group, complete with players on the tea-chest bass and the washboard—called the Quarrymen. The Grateful Dead had begun in the same mode, as Mother McCree's Uptown Jug Champions.)

"I grew up in Greenwich Village, and I went to prep school, so I was aware that there were such things as writers and composers," Sebastian recalled in an interview on a park bench in Woodstock, near his home. He picked idly on the guitar as we talked. "We named the band after a line from a song by Mississippi John Hurt [who employed the phrase 'lovin' spoonful' in a reference to semen], and I knew that musicians had always written songs. However, you have to understand, the Beatles were different. They were our age. They made our kind of music. They wrote hits. The girls loved them, and their music was very good. It sounded like nobody else but the Beatles could have made it. They *had* to have written those songs."

Sebastian decided that if the Beatles could be so "strange and unique" and get rich and famous and popular with the ladies in the process, there were possibilities for "other strange people" like Sebastian and his friend and partner in the Lovin' Spoonful, Zal Yanovsky. The Beatles sexualized and commodified creative ambition for a rising generation of musicians like Sebastian and Yanovsky, along with a zillion would-be musicians like my friends and me.

Mick Jagger and Keith Richards have both acknowledged the Beatles as the impetus for their having taken up songwriting. In the first days of the Rolling Stones, the band was primarily playing vintage blues numbers such as Muddy Waters's "I Want to Be Loved" and Bo Diddley's "Road Runner," peppered with a few rock-and-roll dance-party tunes such as Chuck Berry's "Come On," which the Stones released as their first single in 1963. John Lennon and Paul McCartney, not yet established as internationally fab, but hot in Britain as the new teen sensation, came to visit the Stones at a rehearsal and brought along a scrap of a tune that McCartney had started, "I Wanna Be Your Man." The Stones liked it. So Lennon and McCartney retreated to a corner of the room to finish the song while Jagger and Richards watched, in awe that turned quickly into a confidence that they could write songs, too, if that's all there was to it.

The Rolling Stones' manager, Andrew Loog Oldham, who had previously worked as a promoter for the Beatles, played a significant role here, too, by pressuring Jagger and Richards to write their own material for the dual benefits of developing the group's individual identity and building a source of revenue in songwriting royalties. According to Richards, Oldham locked Jagger and Richards in a kitchen and refused to let them out without a song. Jagger refutes the tale, but only its particulars. "Keith likes to tell the story about the kitchen, God bless him," Jagger said in an interview. "I think Andrew may have said something at some point along the lines of 'I should lock you in a room until you've written a song' and in that way he did mentally lock us in a room."

Lennon and McCartney's own chief inspiration as songwriters had been the Brill Building partners Gerry Goffin and Carole King, a few of whose songs were in the Beatles' band book in Liverpool. When Lennon sang "Will You Love Me Tomorrow," reversing the gender roles, girls in the audience crumbled. (The Beatles recorded one Goffin and King song, the mildly sadomasochistic "Chains," on their first album.) As Lennon recalled in an interview not long after the breakup of the Beatles, "When Paul and I first got together, we wanted to be the British Goffin and King."

That the songs might grow out of their personal experience or give voice to their inner thoughts or feelings was surely a welcome possibility, as it no doubt was for Goffin and King, but not a priority to any of them. Lennon and McCartney would write dozens of songs over their first several years as collaborators—"Love Me Do," "P.S. I Love You," "She Loves You," "I Want to Hold Your Hand," and all the rest—before they turned inward to a significant degree. This is not to say that Lennon and McCartney's early songs were wholly un-connected to their experience; Lennon is understood to have written "Please Please Me" as a plea to his girlfriend for oral sex. As a matter of songwriting philosophy, though, Lennon and McCartney were for some time concerned mainly with cleverness, novelty, and audience appeal rather than self-expression.

In January 1964, the Beatles played eighteen days of concerts, doing three fifteen-minute shows per day, at L'Olympia Bruno Coquatrix in Paris. They were one of nine acts on the roster and shared top billing with two solo singers: Sylvie Vartan, the girlie blond pop chanteuse who was well known at the time for her chirpy French-language record of Paul Anka's stalking apologia "I'm Watching You"; and Trini Lopez, the Mexican American singer and guitarist who had had an international hit with a bouncy, Latin-inflected record of Pete Seeger's sing-along antiwar ditty "If I Had a Hammer." The Beatles stayed in the George V Hotel. According to John Lennon, the main thing they did at the hotel was listen to *The Freewheelin' Bob Dylan*. "In Paris in 1964 was the first time I ever heard Dylan," John Lennon recalled in an interview. "Paul got the record from a French DJ. For three weeks in Paris, we didn't stop playing it. We all went potty about Dylan."

The second album Bob Dylan had recorded since moving to Greenwich Village from Minnesota in 1961, *The Freewheelin' Bob Dylan* was the first of his records to contain material that was almost entirely original—and vitally, strikingly poetic, serious, and mature, as we all know now and many listeners recognized immediately at the time. (The selections on Dylan's eponymous debut, released in 1962, had been mostly blues and grim traditional songs about death.) *Freewheelin'* was a radically idiosyncratic, hybrid work that drew liberally from varied sources—Anglo-Saxon folk songs, Negro spirituals, and songs that Dylan had heard his peers sing around the Village—and reconceived them and recombined them into something unmistakably Dylan's own. Several of the songs, such as "Masters of War" (its music derived from the medieval ballad "Nottamun Town") and "A Hard Rain's A-Gonna Fall" (its music based on a Child Ballad, "Lord Randall"), were songs with themes of political dissent but were not strident bromides like many protest songs of the 1960s. A couple of the tunes, "Girl from the North Country" (its music and some of its lyrics inspired by the English folksinger Martin Carthy's version of the traditional "Scarborough Fair") and "Don't Think Twice, It's All Right" (its music adapted from the folk tune "Who's Gonna Buy You Ribbons When I'm Gone?"), were melodically lovely and personal in their lyrical content. One song, "Blowin' in the Wind," was Dylan's first bona fide hit—number two on the pop charts in a smooth, pretty rendition by the commercial folk trio Peter, Paul, and Mary, released in the summer of 1962.

The now-famous album cover of *Freewheelin'* showed Dylan, scruffy and boyish, strolling past the tenements on Jones Street, arm in arm with his girlfriend, Suze Rotolo, after a snowfall. "There we were, this cute couple on the album cover—we looked so much in love, it could have been a Valentine's Day card picture," said Rotolo thirty-six years later, in an interview I did with her in the Manhattan loft where she painted and made three-dimensional art for decades before her death in 2011. "When Bobby and I were together, we talked a lot about politics. I gave him books to read. My family was very socialist and very politically conscious. The album cover communicated this message that he was a cute guy in love, and I think that's the reason people think of the record as personal. It's not really very personal at all. A couple of songs [had personal content]—that's all—and they weren't about me."

Over the first half of the 1960s, Bob Dylan would take so many turns as an artist that his changeability would become the great trope of the public myth he nurtured as conscientiously as he tended his music. I don't mean that as a swipe. As I've said, a public persona is one of the things that performing artists perform, and Dylan has been a master of many. After all, he started in music during high school as a rock-and-roll piano player, banging out Little Richard numbers in a pink shirt and bow tie under the stage name Elston Gunn. (The first name was a variation on Elvis, obviously, and the last name came from the soft-noir TV private-eye show *Peter Gunn,* famous for its jazzy theme song by Henry Mancini.) As Bob Dylan, writing and singing and accompanying himself on guitar—and occasionally, still, on piano—he simply evolved more quickly than his audience could follow, making it a matter of practicality for him to leave behind one entire fan base and pick up another.

After his first two albums, his third, *The Times They Are A-Changin'* (released early in 1964), was titled for an activist rallying cry that served to validate his standing as the voice of his generation's social conscience; with the following album, *Another Side of Bob Dylan* (released later in 1964), he inched away from politics with more personal songs such as "My Back Pages" and "It Ain't Me, Babe," tunes that veered musically in the direction of rock and rock-era pop. Then, after he heard the Beatles on the car radio on a drive up the California coast—"Did you hear that?" he blurted out to his car mate, Victor Maymudes, "Oh, man—fuck!"—Dylan turned in force to his early love, rock and roll, elevating the rock form with his cryptic, impressionistic lyrics. All this was several years before he would decide to abandon rock for country music, only to move on after that to gospel. In 2015, Dylan, at age seventy-three, made yet another zigzag and released an album of pre-rock pop standards associated with Frank Sinatra, crooning the tunes in a soft, grandfatherly croak.

Like Bob Dylan, John Lennon was a changeling artist. Referring to "You've Got to Hide Your Love Away" in the *Playboy* interview he did with Yoko Ono shortly before his death in 1980, Lennon said, "That's me in my Dylan period. I am like a chameleon, influenced by whatever is going on. If Elvis can do it, I can do it. If the Everly Brothers can do it, me and Paul can. Same with Dylan."

Lennon, the Beatle most directly affected by Dylan, absorbed Dylan's influence in several ways—by writing near-diatonic melodies in the vein of Anglo-Saxon folk tunes, by strumming along on his Gibson acoustic guitar as he sang in a conversational voice, and, above all, by making his songs more idiosyncratically personal. Lennon, by emulating Dylan, became more himself in his music. As he said to Jann Wenner in 1970,

> I started thinking about my own emotions—I don't know exactly when it started, like "I'm a Loser" or "Hide Your Love Away" or those kinds of things. Instead of projecting myself into a situation, I would try to express what I felt about myself, which I'd done in my books. I think it was Dylan that helped me realize that—not by any discussion or anything, but just by hearing his work—I had a professional songwriter's attitude toward songwriting. I was already a stylized songwriter on the first album. But to express myself, I would write [the books] *Spaniard in the Works* or *In His Own Write*, the personal stories which were expressive of my personal emotions. I'd have a separate songwriting John Lennon who wrote songs for the sort of meat market, and I didn't consider them—the lyrics or anything—to have any depth at all. They were just a joke. Then I started being me [in] the songs, not writing them objectively, but subjectively.

The Dylan-Beatles influence loop was not a closed system. Dylan inspired John Lennon, Paul McCartney, and George Harrison to work more internally and poetically; the Beatles inspired Dylan to rock out; and all of them inspired everybody else, while lots of others—country singers, pop acts, and avant-gardists—influenced Dylan and the Beatles. Steadily over the course of the 1960s, the received understanding of an artist's first purpose in popular music moved from performance to composition. The prospect of writing songs became less an option than something close to an imperative. The long-standing possibility that singers *could* write turned into a de facto rule that they *should* write. Before long, singers who did not generate their own material would start to seem like artists of a lesser stature—limited, substandard.

I remember watching one of the prime-time TV dance shows of the mod era—*Hullabaloo* or *Shindig!*—with my sister, Barbara Ann, when she was a teenager and I was a grade-schooler. Lesley Gore came on, and my sister told me to pay special attention. "She writes her own songs," Barbara Ann told me emphatically, leaving time for the information to sink in, as if she had said, "She's from another dimension," which is essentially what she was saying. Within a few years, when I was in high school myself, my sister and I would get into a squabble over Tom Jones, whom Barbara Ann liked but I dismissed, because he didn't write his own songs. I undervalued Jones, mainly because he was an interpretive artist rather than a writer and also because he was a sex symbol and wore a tux. He seemed inauthentic by my limited teenage conception of authenticity as something conferred through self-expression and noncommercialism.

As Joan Baez would point out, many artists of her generation who began their careers as singers rather than songwriters eventually felt an obligation to write. Baez felt Dylan's influence at close range. "Bob used to ask me, 'Why don't you write?'" Baez recalled. "I said, 'Why should I? That's what you do, and you don't make it look like very much fun.'"

Baez had recorded more than a hundred songs over nine years before she recorded her first original song, "Sweet Sir Galahad," in 1969. "I had something I wanted to say," she explained, "so I said it." At the time, Baez said, "I needed to prove that I could do that. I wanted to prove it to myself. It was important to me. I didn't like the idea that men did the building and women did the decorating. I wanted to show that I could build, too."

It is perhaps a testament to Tom Jones's comfort with his place in the musical world that he has been content to be an interpretive artist and a decorator. Countless others since the 1960s have either taken advantage of the freedom to write or succumbed to the pressure to write. Not all of them have found it necessary to have something earth-shatteringly pressing or profoundly original to say nor to have the ability to say it extraordinarily well, musically or lyrically; what tends to matter more, generally speaking, is that pop artists say something legitimately their own, in their own manner. There's something beautifully egalitarian and almost utopian in this, even when the music is less than exhilarating.

Joni Mitchell, the singer, composer, and guitarist (and sometime pianist) whose raw and delicate, elegiac songs elevated the art of personal songwriting, heard revelation in Dylan's "Positively 4th Street," a mordant verbal assault on a would-be friend. "Oh my God," Mitchell said to herself, as she later recalled, "you can write about anything in songs!"

In Mitchell's work, "anything" has meant any thought or any feeling—anything internal, from the thirst for love and lust she articulated in "My Old Man" and "Sex Kills" to the sense of futility she laid bare in "River" to the self-pity of "For the Roses." In the hands of songwriters less inclined to self-reflection or less adept at making art from the resource of the self, "anything" has meant just what it usually means: anything—an idea or an idle impression, a recollection, a catcall, a rant, a word that simply sounds good . . . Anything can mean everything, as it has in the great-sounding gibberish of R.E.M. and Guided by Voices, the cryptic hip-hop flow of Rakim, or the surreal non sequiturs of Tyler, the Creator, and it can mean nothing, as it did in most of the first ten years of Paul McCartney's output after the Beatles.

Carole King, after breaking up with her husband and lyricist, tried working with a couple of other collaborators until one of her musician friends, a rising singer-songwriter in the early-Dylan folkie mode named James Taylor, gave her some advice. As King explained from the stage of Madison Square Garden in a concert with Taylor in 2010, "It was James who convinced me that it was okay to write my own lyrics. I said, 'I don't know what to write about,' and he said,

'Just write about what's going on in your life. Write about the feelings you're feeling. What happened to you today? Write about that.'"

When I was just starting out in music writing, one of the first interviews I did was with Dave Van Ronk, the revered folk and blues singer whom I mentioned a few chapters back, in the context of Harry Smith's *Anthology of American Folk Music*. In the early 1960s, a decade before I met Van Ronk, he had been tight with Bob Dylan. Van Ronk's first wife, Terri Thal, had acted for a while as Dylan's manager, and Dylan—Van Ronk always called him Bobby—had slept on their couch. One afternoon in the early 1980s, Van Ronk and I were eating ice cream in his apartment—he poured Captain Morgan over his and made a kind of ice-cream-and-rum soup—and a James Taylor record came on the radio: It was something from Taylor's third album, *Mud Slide Slim and the Blue Horizon*—something quiet and reflective, like "Places in My Past" or "Isn't It Nice to Be Home Again." I was running a tape recorder, as I had gotten in the habit of doing when I was talking to the always quotable Van Ronk. He listened to the music on the radio for a minute and said, "Bobby has a lot to answer for."

I pointed out that Dylan's music generally had more fire than the gently ruminative things on *Mud Slide Slim*. Van Ronk coughed up a laugh. Van Ronk both laughed and coughed freely, and the sounds were indistinguishable. "It's hard to start a fire without the right equipment," he said. "Bobby makes it look too easy."

As songwriting became more personal and more assertively, conspicuously poetic, the lyrics of popular songs became more ambiguous— more impressionistic, more concerned with expression than direct communication, more challenging to the listener. Meaning became harder to parse and less important. The words of pop songs became more and more about the sound and the feeling of the words themselves, in much the same way that modernist (and postmodernist) literature and visual art have been concerned largely (though not solely) with the character of the expression itself. I'm speaking broadly and generally about popular songs since the mid-1960s, but I think the point I'm making is fair.

Let's consider two related songs: Chuck Berry's "You Can't Catch Me," from 1956, and John Lennon's "Come Together," from 1969. (As every Beatles fan knows, Lennon wrote the words and music to "Come Together" on his own, despite the joint credit to Lennon and McCartney, in accordance with their arrangement, just as McCartney wrote "Yesterday" without Lennon.) "You Can't Catch Me" is a story song about a highway chase, told with colorful and specific imagery, about riding the New Jersey Turnpike during the "wee hours." The driver spots a state trooper—"a flat-top"—closing in on him in his "suped-up jitney."

"Come Together" opens with an obvious, unapologetic lift from the Berry tune—"Here come old flat-top, he come groovin' up slowly"—and echoes "You Can't Catch Me" in its chanting rhythmic structure and simple rock-and-roll chords, with some interesting variations in the music added in the recording session by McCartney and the other Beatles. (Berry's publishing company sued Lennon and McCartney over "Come Together" and settled out of court, with Lennon agreeing to record three tunes the company owned, including "You Can't Catch Me.") But "Come Together" is a different species of creation from "You Can't Catch Me." It's an anti-story song, an intentionally formless collage of random, great-sounding words and phrases: "He Bag Production, he got walrus gumboot . . ." "He got joo-joo eyeball, he one holy roller . . ." There are plenty of allusions and seeming references to Lennon's life and work and lots of teasing wordplay that's fun to try to decode: Bag Productions was the name of John and Yoko's public-relations company. "Holy roller"—is that a reference to George Harrison? *Hmmm* . . . But most of the satisfaction in experiencing the song comes from the nonliteral pleasure that it provides the ear. As Lennon told the journalist David Sheff in one of his final interviews, "The thing was created in the studio. It's gobbledygook."

Popular songs are by no means all nonsense now, even if rational sense is not precisely what many songs now seek to convey. Nearly every song popular in the early twenty-first century is about *something*, even if the thing is obscure or implied, expressed through indirection, and, at the end of the song, unresolved. What is "Blurred Lines" about, exactly, with its chants of "Hey, hey, hey," its blurts of "Ooh!" and its ridiculous, leering taunts of "I know you want it"? It's about nothing other than the leering ridiculousness of its singer, Robin Thicke. That may not be much, but it's something.

It took a plagiarism suit brought by the estate of Marvin Gaye for Thicke to acknowledge, under oath, that he did not really write any of "Blurred Lines," despite the presence of his name on the copyright, alongside the names of the composer-lyricist Pharrell Williams and the rapper T.I. Thicke felt compelled to attach his name to the song because he "wanted some credit" in accord with the established practice for singers to be seen as the authors of their own material, even if they clearly stole it from Marvin Gaye. "This is what happens every day in our industry," Thicke testified in court.

In contemporary pop songwriting, a great many people contribute to the creation of work in a highly collaborative process in which composition, performance, and sound production all overlap. It is not at all uncommon now to see five or more names on the songwriting credit of a hit. Still, one of them is almost always the name of the performer, because performers still want the credibility of being seen as not just interpretive artists but creative ones. "You know," Thicke said in his testimony, "people are made to look like they have much more authorship in the situation than they actually do."

9

THE ALBUM

A PAIR OF TWENTY-MINUTE THINGS

My best buddy and garage-band mate, Harry Reilly, and I put together a scrappy, tepidly pseudo-radical underground newspaper when we were in high school. I wrote reviews of albums and concerts I saw at the Spectrum and the Tower Theater in Philadelphia, and the Main Point theater outside Philly, in Bryn Mawr— Joni Mitchell, still playing dulcimer, David Bowie on the Ziggy Stardust tour, John Lee Hooker, Mott the Hoople. Most of my writing for the paper would embarrass me now, with the exception of a piece about a theory I had that the musical *My Fair Lady* was an alien plot to infiltrate the minds of the earthling population. My evidence was the fact that a copy of the original cast recording of *My Fair Lady* had inexplicably appeared in every home, every school, and every library in America. My parents, in the course of their lifetimes, had no more than four or five long-playing records—two or three Christmas song collections they got for free as premiums for buying gas at the Arco station down the street, an album by Dean Martin that I remember by the cover photograph of Dino in a cowboy hat, and the cast album of *My Fair Lady*. If there was a cabinet of records in a house and I entered that house, I thumbed through the records, and I found *My Fair Lady* everywhere: in Harry's house, in my Waspy blond middle-class girlfriend's house, in my sister's boyfriend's apartment in the housing projects, in the home of my English teacher, Pete Tomaino, who invited the whole class over to watch *Fahrenheit 451* on TV—*everywhere*.

My theory was only tangentially related to the fact that the Lerner and Loewe score to *My Fair Lady*, as sung by Julie Andrews in her loverly bell tones and uttered by Rex Harrison in his haughty parlando, sounded alien to me as a rock-and-roll lover. What I had the most trouble grasping about *My Fair Lady* was the way that cast album had sold, almost fifteen years before I entered high school. Goddard Lieberson, the president of Columbia Records, had seen so much sales potential in *My Fair Lady* that he had arranged for CBS to fund the production of the musical on Broadway, at a cost of $360,000, in exchange for the album rights at a 40 percent royalty. The archive of *Billboard* charts for the years immediately after the album's release in 1956 show *My Fair Lady* to have been the best-selling album in America for eight weeks straight in 1956, and it bubbled right below the surface of the top for four years, popping up to number one again seven more times in 1957, 1958, and 1959. Released in the U.K. in 1958, it was the number one album there for nineteen weeks in a row. The album is understood to have sold some thirteen million copies on vinyl LP between 1956 and 1988, when it was re-released on CD.

By the time I was in high school, in the early 1970s, the 33⅓ rpm long-playing record had become the preeminent format of delivery for popular music, and most albums—certainly most bestselling albums—were of rock and funk music geared to teenagers and young adults. Singles, in the form of 45 rpm records, still sold by the millions, but mostly to preteens, though not exclusively to them. When acts of interest to rock fans of high-school and college age released a song only as a single, such as Crosby, Stills, Nash, and Young with their Vietnam protest song "Ohio," they would do so on the only single format available, the 45, and young adults would buy it. Much the same, veteran artists working in pre-rock styles were still releasing singles, such as Sammy Davis Jr. with his record of "The Candy Man," which was a Top 10 hit in 1972, in part because it was misconstrued as a drug song, and enough of these older acts' longtime fans (along with some young people who liked the music) would buy them for the songs to get onto the charts. Still, as a rule, Top 40 pop—fizzy junkfood music for middle-school ears, such as "Saturday in the Park" by Chicago or "Brandy (You're a Fine Girl)" by a one-hit band from New Jersey, Looking Glass—appeared on singles, and harder rock, funk, jazz, and other music intended for high-school and college-age audiences appeared on albums. Broadway cast albums fell somewhere in the "other" category in my mind as a high schooler. Nobody I knew bought them. The fact that every house had a copy of *My Fair Lady*, a Broadway score from two decades earlier, was an archaeological mystery to me. A *Chariots of the Gods* aliens-must-have-done-it explanation seemed as good as any.

I had no idea how important Broadway had been to popular music, including the music released on both singles and albums—and broadcast on the radio—for years before I started paying attention. Nor had I yet noticed how the musical theater had come to influence rock of my time or, more significantly, how rock had begun to transform Broadway. I watched David Bowie voguing in his glittery Ziggy magnificence without fully recognizing the many levels of theatrical allusion in the performance, and I listened to Yvonne Elliman bellowing "I Don't Know How to Love Him," from the album *Jesus Christ Superstar*, with no way of knowing that I was hearing, in Andrew Lloyd Webber's overbaked amalgam of operatic melodrama and rock-ballad schmaltz, the near future of the Broadway musical.

"It's the norm to compartmentalize popular music by the various ways it has been delivered over history—the tent show, the roadhouse, the radio, records, Broadway, the dance hall," David Sanjek, the music scholar and co-author of *American Popular Music and Its Business: The First Four Hundred Years*, warned me when I was starting this book. "But popular music has really always worked holistically. Records, as a medium, might appear intrinsically nontheatrical, and the Broadway stage might appear to exist [as something] separate from the pop charts and pop radio. But Broadway and pop music are not inseparable. Think about Cole Porter. Where did the songs on all those Frank Sinatra records come from?"

Porter, the urbane master of ascot-and-cigarette-holder wit and innuendo in song, personifies the much vaunted sophistication of American musical theater music in the period from the 1930s to the 1950s. As the lyricist and occasional composer Johnny Mercer told an interviewer, "Cole Porter is definitive of an era. He IS those years, you know? He is the style of all those shows, all that period."

Along with Jerome Kern, George Gershwin, Ira Gershwin, Richard Rodgers and Lorenz Hart (and Rodgers's second major songwriting partner, Oscar Hammerstein II), Harold Arlen and his primary collaborators, E. Y. "Yip" Harburg and Johnny Mercer, and a school of like-minded composers and lyricists who came up with them, Cole Porter applied high standards of craft and invention to a popular form, helping to produce a body of songs valorized since the second half of the twentieth century as the Great American Songbook. The work all these artists were engaged in was the writing of *shows*—musical comedies for the Broadway stage (and, in some cases, the movies). But what we remember the composers for are individual songs: Kern's "Smoke Gets in Your Eyes" (written with the lyricist Otto Harbach for the musical *Roberta*) and "All the Things You Are" (written with Oscar Hammerstein II for *Very Warm for May*); the Gershwins' "Man I Love" (written for *Strike Up the Band*) and "Someone to Watch Over Me" (written for *Oh, Kay!*); and Rodgers and Hart's "Manhattan" (written for *Garrick Gaieties*) and "My Funny Valentine" (written for *Babes in Arms*).

I have heard each of the songs I just listed well over a hundred times, if not hundreds of times, in performances and recordings by dozens of singers and instrumental musicians. Yet with the exception of *Very Warm for May*, which I caught in a short-run, abridged staged reading at Weill Recital Hall in New York in 1996, I have never seen any of the shows those songs were written for. The parts have outlived the wholes, and not simply because the songs are more entertaining and enduring than the shows they were written for, though some of them surely are. The songs of the Great American Songbook have lived on because they were built to survive outside the theater. They were written in hopes that they would be hits on their own.

This was not the way musical theater worked at first. At the turn of the twentieth century, most major American musical productions emulated the Victorian operetta model popularized in Britain by Gilbert and Sullivan. Victor Herbert—the American cousin of Arthur Sullivan, aesthetically speaking—stitched together colorful patchworks of musical elements to make his popular operettas *Babes in Toyland* (written with the librettist Glen MacDonough) and *Naughty Marietta* (written with the terrifically inventive but now forgotten librettist Rida Johnson Young). The shows were constructed in pieces, though the pieces were not precisely songs—not short, self-contained works that could stand outside the context of the characters and situations of the show, let alone be sung by the songs' fans, as popular songs generally can. With the rise of vaudeville and Tin Pan Alley in the first decades of the twentieth century, the operetta fell out of favor, and the musical revue—a patchwork of self-sufficient tunes strung together with the thin thread of a boy-meets-girl plot or no more than the stamp of the show's producer, as in the *Ziegfeld Follies* or *George White's Scandals*—now dominated the popular theater.

Most of the songs in these revues were sold first as sheet music and before long as shellac records. Stage shows and their songs became cross-merchandising vehicles, much as arena tours and albums would be in the rock era. Where a rising generation of Tin Pan

Alley–era composers—Kern, Gershwin, Porter, and the rest—found opportunity, suddenly passé composers such as Victor Herbert saw commercialism corrupting their art. "Songs from successful plays are printed in great numbers and are the source of great profits," groaned Herbert in a newspaper interview. "In order that these songs may sell, they must have words that are independent of the play—that is, on some general theme and attractive to the person who has not seen the play. I think that this may have had its effect in weaning us away from comic opera in which lyrics are woven into the plot and are part of it."

Cole Porter, like both Oscar Hammerstein II and Yip Harburg, had a youthful infatuation with Gilbert and Sullivan. "I was Gilbert and Sullivan crazy," Porter said. Harburg, engrossed as a boy with W. S. Gilbert's published verse, called Gilbert his "first great literary idol," though Harburg did not realize that Gilbert's words had been set to music and not only published in magazines until he was told so by another Gilbert buff in his elementary-school classroom, Ira Gershwin. From both Gilbert and Sullivan and their American imitators in operetta, the Tin Pan Alley tunesmiths developed an appreciation for winking humor and a respect for exacting craft, and they brought them to bear with a jazzy, street-smart attitude to make a body of distinctively modern and American musical theater songs.

Berlin, Kern, Gershwin, and Rodgers and Hart all started early enough in musical theater history to have done much of their early writing for the revues that supplanted operetta on American stages. Berlin wrote the bulk of the songs for the multiple editions of the *Music Box Revue*. Gershwin wrote "Stairway to Paradise" (with the lyricist Buddy DeSylva) for *George White's Scandals*, and Rodgers and Hart wrote the song that would become their first hit, "Manhattan," for the *Garrick Gaieties*. Yet all these songwriters came into their creative maturity as charter contributors to a new kind of musical theater: one of shows rooted in character and plot, like nonmusical drama, with songs that were elementally connected to the story of the show but also disconnectable. These integrated, narrative musicals—shows such as Kern and Hammerstein's *Show Boat*, Rodgers and Hart's *Connecticut Yankee*, and above all Rodgers and Hammerstein's *Oklahoma!*—came to define American musical theater in the twentieth century and established the form Lerner and Loewe followed in *My Fair Lady*.

If a show became a hit, running for months or longer on Broadway, its songs would be popular by virtue of their exposure on the stage. At the same time, the popularity of a musical was largely dependent on the appeal of its music. Producers, looking to do whatever they could to tip the odds for success in their favor, would often take a song written by one songwriter (or songwriting partners) that was already a hit through sheet music, records, or radio and insert it into a musical score written by a different writer (or writers). The script might be reworked to make the new song fit. Or it might not, as it wasn't when Al Jolson was starring in *Sinbad*, a musical by the composer Sigmund Romberg and the lyricist Harold R. Atteridge that had an *Arabian Nights* theme. George Gershwin and Irving Caesar's distinctly un-Arabian imitation Stephen Foster tune "Swanee" was added to provide Jolson with a number to do in the blackface shtick that always thrilled white theatergoers. *Sinbad* ran for over two years, and "Swanee" sold a million copies on sheet music and more than two million records. Through the same technique of cross-fertilizing hit quality, Irving Berlin's "Blue Skies" was interpolated into the Rodgers and Hart musical *Betsy*; and Harold Arlen and Johnny Mercer's "Blues in the Night," written for the film of the same title, was interpolated into the revue *Priorities of 1942*. Interpolation was Broadway's local method of goat glanding.

Even Charles K. Harris's ancient hit, "After the Ball," was interpolated into Kern and Hammerstein's *Show Boat*, though mainly for nineteenth-century flavor. It improved the show's score by contrast, demonstrating how superior "Why Do I Love You?" and "Ol' Man River" are to Harris's craggy old weeper.

Producers would also act preemptively to make hits of the songs composed for their musicals by arranging to have them recorded and performed on radio in advance of a show's opening. As the composer Jule Styne recalled in an interview, "At [one] time, I could walk into a record company and say, 'Here it is—so-and-so will record this number, and so-and-so will do that one.' And you'd have eight hit singles before the show opened." The plan worked to make pre-curtain hits of "Just in Time" and "The Party's Over," two (if not quite eight) of the songs from *Bells Are Ringing*, the musical Styne wrote with the lyricists Betty Comden and Adolph Green; it worked for "Hey There," from Richard Adler and Jerry Ross's *Pajama Game*; and it worked for "Hello, Dolly!," from Jerry Herman's show with that title.

Louis Armstrong's single of "Hello, Dolly!," released just before the opening of the musical in 1964, bumped the Beatles off the top of the pop charts, ending the group's run of three number one singles over more than three months. Armstrong had recorded the tune as a demonstration record for the music publisher's use, and Kapp Records decided to put the demo into commercial release. The extraordinary success of this deliciously unaffected performance of a catchy old-style showbiz trifle is clearly a testament to Armstrong's appeal across the generations. It helped, too, that the record, with its Disneyland Dixieland arrangement, had a novelty quality. It sounded almost like a children's record, but one that Mom and Dad and Grandma and Grandpa might like, too. It spoke to people of every generation except the adolescents who bought most singles. "Hello, Dolly!" is a fun and interesting pop-culture trivia-question anomaly. But its success should not be construed as evidence of the popularity of show tunes to the rock generation.

By 1964, nearly all the early masters of American theater music had retired, had settled into semiretirement, or had died. Cole Porter passed that very year. George Gershwin, of course, had died young, in 1937. Lorenz Hart had died in 1943; Jerome Kern, two years later.

Oscar Hammerstein II had died in 1960, though Richard Rodgers would plug along with a series of other collaborators (including Hammerstein's protégé Stephen Sondheim), writing shows of diminishing interest until his death in 1979. Irving Berlin had already written his last show, the creaky *Mr. President*, in 1962.

The old songs they had written for the musical theater and the movies were now being thought of as something new: the Great American Songbook. Popular songs that were no longer popular in the sense of being favored by the dominant audience of the day, the tunes had become objects of connoisseurship. The transformation in the conception of this music had begun in the 1950s, with the advent of the long-playing record, and it was nearly complete by the mid-1960s, when the LP was beginning to undergo a transformation of its own. It was on the first long-playing albums that popular songs that were no longer popular came together as a repertoire. The ongoing conception of this music as a canon is largely a secondary effect of a change in recording technology.

From the beginning of recording until the early 1950s, nearly all popular singers had sung new or recent songs almost exclusively, exactly as most pop singers do today. There seemed no point in recording material that the ticket- and record-buying public had already heard and had decided to purchase (or not) years earlier. With the advent of the long-playing album, which was introduced by Columbia Records as a mass-market product in 1948 and began to catch on with adult record buyers in the 1950s, singers and music producers found themselves with a need for material to fill twelve or so tracks on each disc, and there simply weren't enough new hits in supply to meet the LP's demands. Singers and producers turned to songs that had been written years earlier, paying special attention to musical theater songs, because they were plentiful and had been thoroughly vetted by the processes of show development and performance onstage.

Billy May, the swing-band arranger who worked often with Frank Sinatra, among others, recalled how Sinatra was early to suggest filling albums with songs he happened to like, regardless of their age. "Frank had his fill of singing crap at Columbia—chasing the hit parade," May remembered. "He went to Capitol [in 1953] and started making LPs, and he had no intention of filling those albums with shit. So he started singing old songs, because they were terrific songs and he loved them, and he could never have gotten away with it before the LP came along. The LP opened everything up. You didn't have to chase the goddamn hit parade anymore."

Sinatra, Ella Fitzgerald, Peggy Lee, Nat King Cole, Tony Bennett, and their peers all began filling albums with vintage theater songs that might have seemed too sophisticated, too character oriented, or too situational to have been recorded with hit making in mind. Thus, record buyers of the 1950s found LPs full of well crafted but already-old tunes from long-gone shows and films—things such as "Ill Wind," written by Harold Arlen and Ted Koehler for the *Cotton Club Parade* (1934); "Just One of Those Things," written by Cole Porter for the musical *Jubilee* (1935); "At Long Last Love" by Porter for *You Never Know* (1938); "Where or When," by Rodgers and Hart for *Babes in Arms* (1937); "It Never Entered My Mind," by the same collaborators for *Higher and Higher* (1940); and "Old Devil Moon," by Burton Lane and Yip Harburg for *Finian's Rainbow* (1947).

A recording format called the album got people thinking of the old music on recordings in new terms, as pieces in a portfolio of treasurable mementos, and a common repertoire of durable, adaptable songs—most of them originally written for the stage or the movies, others from Tin Pan Alley—began to take form. With men such as Sinatra now singing greater numbers of theater songs written originally for women, and with women such as Fitzgerald singing more show tunes composed for men, both the songs and their singers seemed to deepen and to expand in emotional range.

The LP, in providing a format for anthologizing songs, brought with it the necessity of an anthologizing rationale. Sinatra, as well as others, took up broadly conceived themes as frameworks for his albums at Capitol—love songs (*Close to You*), songs of rumination (*In the Wee Small Hours*), songs of despair (*Only the Lonely*), songs of brio (*Sinatra's Swingin' Session!!!*). Lee Wiley, a subtle, intimate singer with a jazz orientation, tried another approach and used the writers of the songs as an organizing principle. Wiley initially released a couple of book-like "albums" of 78 records, each dedicated to a song-writer or songwriting team—Cole Porter, Rodgers and Hart. She followed them with a sequence of LPs concentrating on the work of composers: first Vincent Youmans, then Irving Berlin. A few years later, Ella Fitzgerald, working closely with Norman Granz, the founder and head of Fitzgerald's label, Verve Records, refined this idea with a series of sophisticated, meticulously wrought albums and double-album sets, each devoted to one composer or songwriting team: Berlin, Kern, George Gershwin, Rodgers and Hart, Porter, Arlen, Duke Ellington, and Johnny Mercer. Granz titled them as songbooks—as in *Ella Fitzgerald Sings the Irving Berlin Songbook*—providing the emergent canon of American standards with the roster of canonical creators that every canon needs.

"A great singer should sing great songs," Norman Granz said. "Some would say, the greater the songs, the greater the singer. My contention was the greater the singer, the greater the songs. But that's immaterial. The concept of the songbooks—there were several ideas behind them—[was that] I wanted to present the music of the great songsmiths in a manner that demonstrated the gravity of their contribution and the uniqueness of the composers, and I wanted the public to consider Ella in a new way. By this, I mean [as] a master vocalist on the same plateau as these songs. People needed this to comprehend that she wasn't just the girl who used to sing with Louis Jordan."

It is no coincidence the debut albums in the Fitzgerald *Songbook* series, two LPs of Cole Porter material, were produced in 1956, the first year that rock and roll—the musical descendant of Louis Jordan's jump blues—overtook the pop charts, with Elvis Presley's "Heartbreak Hotel" the number one song of the year (and another Elvis record, "Don't Be Cruel," at number two). Granz had in mind to produce what he bluntly described as "anti–rock and roll," and he saw the album as the proper vehicle for it.

Fitzgerald herself had no aversion to rock, pop, R&B, or soul. In fact, she considered it her professional responsibility to keep up with popular trends. She not only recorded Beatles tunes such as "Can't Buy Me Love" but wrote and sang a riff tune about mop-top music, called "Ringo Beat." In the late 1960s, she belted a knockout version of Cream's "Sunshine of Your Love" in her stage show, and she was still experimenting with the latest sounds in the last concert she gave at Radio City Music Hall, in 1991, when, performing in a chair on stage at age seventy-four she ably recited a few couplets of rap. (I was there.) As she once told an interviewer, quoting Chick Webb, the bandleader who had hired Fitzgerald when she was eighteen, "He gave me the only advice I've ever needed. 'Honey,' he told me, 'in this business, you've always got to be the firstest with the mostest and the newest.'"

Granz, content to trade on Fitzgerald's open-mindedness and adaptability for the single market, released 45 rpm records of Ella singing "Can't Buy Me Love" and "Ringo Beat" with young listeners in mind and geared her LPs for their parents. For singles, he said, "you had to cater to the schoolkids." For albums, "you could play to adult sensitivity." As I've mentioned before, notably in the context of the transistor radio, this was standard thinking in Granz's time.

It was taken as a mark of the maturation of postwar, post–Tin Pan Alley music that its makers and their audience turned to the long-playing album format during the 1960s. Many things happened to happen at the same time. The young people who wrote, performed, recorded, and listened to music of the rock era grew older, and their interests and tastes changed. As everyone knows from every documentary movie collage about the 1960s, social unrest growing out of the civil rights movement and discontent over the Vietnam War stirred young adults to a certain seriousness of purpose and attitude—or, at the very least, the appearance thereof—and that grew widespread, if not faddish, on high-school and college campuses. The now-notorious baby boom was booming at full force. Postwar prosperity continued, with the boomers reaching adulthood in vast numbers, loaded with unprecedented purchasing power. The Japanese electronics industry expanded from the making of pocket radios to the mass production of high-quality stereo systems marketed to and priced within graduation-gift range of all those adult-age boomers. Recording technology advanced in synchronicity with the availability of affordable hi-fi playback equipment, so records could be produced with a degree of sonic complexity that justified close listening on stereo gear, and the FCC opened up the FM radio band, providing a free-to-listeners method of delivery of album content in high-quality sound.

By 1968, LPs were outselling single records for the first time, and the album format would be central to the way musicians, listeners, marketers, and most others would think about popular music until the invention of the MP3 and the rise of digital downloading in the twenty-first century. The LP, originally designed so that a full movement of a Berlioz symphony would fit on one side of a record, allowed for twenty to twenty-five minutes of music to play without the listener having to futz with the playing equipment. Because it was a nuisance to lift the tonearm and drop it again at precisely the right spot between bands on a spinning record, listening for twenty or so minutes straight became a near imperative. For the first time since songs became popular as mass-marketable products, through sheet music in the late nineteenth century, the form that popular music took changed substantively. Musicians and their audiences were now conceiving of and experiencing a work of popular music not as a three-minute thing but as a forty-minute thing—or a pair of twenty-minute things.

The way LPs were packaged made the album a physically appealing object. The cover was called a dust jacket, suggesting that it was both protective and an article of finery. At slightly more than twelve inches by twelve inches, the jacket was larger than the cover of a hardcover book and even larger than an eight-by-ten framed photograph. Looking over an album in the store to decide whether or not to buy it, you would hold it in two hands, and it would hold your attention. The size of the jacket allowed the creation of some ambitious, often beautiful, or, at the very least, complicated cover art: the graveyard dream collage of the Beatles, surrounded by cryptic symbols and standees of old celebrities on *Sgt. Pepper's Lonely Hearts Club Band*; the 3-D penis, dressed to the right, behind the pull-able zipper Andy Warhol designed for the Rolling Stones' *Sticky Fingers*; the song rundown in comix panels by Robert Crumb on Big Brother and the Holding Company's *Cheap Thrills* . . . Song lyrics could be printed on the inner sleeve that held the album itself, and if the package was a gatefold, more art and information or writing could be included. The printing of the words implied that the lyrics were worth printing, prodding songwriters to write for the eye as well as the ear. There was space for liner notes of half-decent length, and record companies took to commissioning writing on the subject of the record's artist by the likes of Bob Dylan (who wrote long prose poems for several albums by his friends in the early 1960s); Langston Hughes (for *Joan Baez 5*); Igor Stravinsky (for his own *Firebird*); and LeRoi Jones (Amiri Baraka) for John Coltrane's *Live at Birdland*. The multidimensional, tangibly gratifying entirety of the package reinforced the value of the music in the record grooves and, sometimes, provided enough of its own value to make up for not-so-great music.

Rock and pop artists grew to treat the album as a creative form rather than a way to re-merchandise a batch of singles. Singers and songwriters who came up through the folk craze, such as Bob Dylan, Judy Collins, and Simon and Garfunkel, were early among artists of the rock generation to do this, having occupied a sphere where some of the best-known albums—Harry Smith's *Anthology of American Folk Music*, Woody Guthrie's *Dust Bowl Ballads*, and Johnny Cash's *Songs of Our Soil*—were unified by theme. Each of Bob Dylan's albums had integrity as a whole and presented his latest mode of thinking as a package—social and political consciousness on *The Times They Are A-Changin'*, personal reflection on *Another Side of Bob Dylan* . . .

The LP, treated as something other than a kind of packaging, came to be a way for artists to repackage themselves, as Judy Collins did in 1966, when the album was beginning to come into its own as a form of art for the rock era. Collins, until then known solely as a guitar-strumming folkie, like Baez, worked with the twenty-two-year-old arranger Joshua Rifkin (a veteran of the jug bands who would go on to be a musicologist and classical conductor) to make an LP that altered her audience's conceptions of what she could do. Titled *In My Life*, for John Lennon's then-new and unexpectedly reflective autobiographical ballad, the Collins album took new songs by Dylan, Leonard Cohen, and Randy Newman, arranged as chamber pop, and juxtaposed them with pieces by Kurt Weill and Jacques Brel and a medley from *Marat/Sade*, the musical drama about madness and revolutionary politics. Tactically eclectic and unified by its *Village Voice*-ish artiness, *In My Life* constituted an argument for the maturity of songs by young writers of the rock generation.

There was an eruption of experimentation on albums in the second half of the 1960s as musicians and producers embraced the long form and pushed the potential of studio technology. While avant-garde composers such as Pierre Schaeffer, Karlheinz Stockhausen, and John Cage had been employing tape recorders, unconventional instruments, found objects, and synthesizers for more than a decade at this point, sonic experimentation had been fairly limited in music that reached the general population. Les Paul had employed overdubbing and double tracking on the jazzy pop singles he made with his wife and duet partner, the singer Mary Ford, though Paul's innovations were intentionally easy on the ear, barely apparent to listeners. Mitch Miller, the cynical populist who headed up production at Columbia Records, had spiced records with extramusical sound effects—a bull-whip cracking, honking geese—for novelty value in the 1950s; and Shadow Morton, the self-styled mysterioso of Brill Building pop, concocted cinematic aural pastiches by editing eerie sounds and spoken language into the pop tunes he recorded for the Shangri-Las in the early 1960s. But all that would feel like a prologue to 1966, and Morton would look impossibly prescient. Experimentation of all sorts—aesthetic, social, sexual, and political—had become chic, the ethos of the swingin' 1960s.

In 1966, two bands—the Kinks in London and the Beach Boys in Los Angeles—made LPs that demonstrated striking levels of intellectual ambition and musical adventurism. The Kinks' *Face to Face* was a loosely cohesive collection of character studies of people engaged in the small dramas of everyday life. In the version Ray Davies submitted to the record company, the songs were unified with snippets of sound effects between tracks, though the label had most of the effects deleted before release. The Beach Boys, working at about the same time (from mid-1965 to early 1966), made the record that would come to be regarded as the ur-text of the LP as an art form, *Pet Sounds*. A brainchild of the Beach Boys' man-child, Brian Wilson, and written by Wilson with the lyricist Tony Asher (with some compositional contributions by the Beach Boy Mike Love), *Pet Sounds* was sonically complex, unashamedly pretty, and lyrically veracious, telling simple stories of teenage life—dating, falling in love, and dreaming about growing up. Paul McCartney, stunned by the album's invention and musical sophistication, would describe hearing Brian Wilson's contrapuntal, harmonically advanced bass playing as a revelatory experience that altered his approach to the instrument, apparently unaware that it was not Wilson but the brilliant jazz-pop session musician Carol Kaye who was playing the bass on *Pet Sounds*. It was "the album of all time," said McCartney, and he set out to have the Beatles top it.

Their answer to *Pet Sounds*, we all know, was *Sgt. Pepper's Lonely Hearts Club Band*, the album that has been lavishly acclaimed ever since its release as a "concept album" revolutionary for its form. The Beatles themselves always resisted that claim for the album, and they were right to do so. For all its imagination and influence—*Rolling Stone* named it the number one greatest album of all time—*Sgt. Pepper* has never fully held together conceptually. According to McCartney, the original idea was for the album to tell the story of one man, the fictional Sgt. Pepper, from childhood to death. Abandoning that, the Beatles took up the notion of performing under an alias, the Lonely Hearts Club Band that they portray on the cover art, with the album's songs representing the imaginary group's repertoire. Yet the music on the album doesn't wholly fit that description, with George Harrison's hypnotic raga, "Within You Without You," played on Indian instruments and a chamber string section, and Lennon and McCartney's majestic "A Day in the Life," complete with a full symphony orchestra worked up to a volcanic finale.

I still remember the day I first heard *Sgt. Pepper*, listening from the hall outside my sister's room. Her friend Bonnie (upon whom I had a huge kid-crush, because she had a haircut like Diana Rigg) had come over with a portable record player and a copy of the record, and a third friend of theirs (whom I ogled less and cannot remember well now) joined them. I sneaked peeks though the crack in the door and could barely process what I was seeing. The girls had set up the record player on the floor, sat around it, and listened to the album from start to finish, barely speaking. I had never before witnessed such concentrated, deferential attentiveness to any art and had never seen teenagers so quiet, outside of church. This was a social ritual wholly unlike the giddy jerking and frugging to 45s that I had seen before.

"The technology was there now for us to sneak little bits in, you know, to discover if you listened closely enough," McCartney recalled in the first of two interviews I did with him, in 1989. "We had done the Cavern Club, and that was great. Now we didn't have to do that anymore. We gave up touring. The studio was our instrument. In the disguise of these alter egos [the Lonely Hearts Club Band], we could do whatever we wanted. We could be the Beach Boys or be Stockhausen or be Albert Ayler, if we wanted. We didn't have to be good little boys and do what the grown-ups told us anymore. We were all grown up ourselves."

In the late 1960s, the theme of maturation was on the minds of rock musicians and their audience as they aged into adulthood. As Lennon and McCartney did in their early conception of *Sgt. Pepper*, Paul Simon took on the subject of aging on the album he was making with Art Garfunkel at around the same time, *Bookends*. "I'm not interested in singles anymore," he told a journalist with *High Fidelity* magazine.

As Art Garfunkel quoted him, Simon said, "I'm going to start writing a whole . . . cycle of songs. I want the early ones to be about youth and the last song to be about old age, and I want the feel of each song to fit." At almost exactly the same time, the Pretty Things, a British group, made an album-length song cycle about a single person growing from childhood to old age, *S. F. Sorrow*.

Over the course of the late 1960s and into the early 1970s, albums by rock musicians grew grander and grander in aspiration and ambition, with cohesive albums growing into concept albums, such as the Who's *Who Sell Out*, a spiky parody of pirate radio, complete with mock commercials, and with concept albums growing into rock operas, such as Andrew Lloyd Webber and Tim Rice's *Jesus Christ Superstar*, which began life as a double-LP set in 1970, and *Tommy*, the Who's epic of pinball wizardry as a conduit to messianic superstardom. In the four years between the Kinks' *Face to Face* and *Jesus Christ Superstar*, the subject matter of albums went from ordinary people to God, or his Son. Rock and roll had not only grown up; it had grown into something that could be theatrically grand—indeed, grandiose. In the fall of 1971, an opulent production of *Jesus Christ Superstar* opened at the Mark Hellinger Theater, the venue with the largest stage on Broadway, where *My Fair Lady* had opened fifteen years earlier.

10

PUNK VERSUS DISCO

WHO NEEDS LOVE?

In the early hours of the morning on April 19, 1978, four people left CBGB and stopped in a deli a few blocks from the club, on Second Avenue and Fifth Street in the East Village. Two of them—Michael Sticca, a roadie for Blondie, and Marcia Leone, a stylist and photographer who at the time was the girlfriend of Billy Rath, the bassist for Johnny Thunders and the Heartbreakers—stood on the street, trying to hail a cab, while the other two—Johnny Blitz, the drummer for the Dead Boys, and his girlfriend Danielle—finished up in the deli. All four of them were drunk, as Sticca would later recall. By Sticca's account of the events, a car occupied by a group of Latino men and women swerved toward the curb, and Sticca yelled out, calling the driver an asshole. Leone hurried out of the way as several of the men in the car got out and surrounded Sticca. One of them had chains in his hand. Another had a baseball bat. Sticca pulled out a switchblade, swung it at one of the guys, and cut through his jacket to his chest. The Latino men turned back, and Sticca thought the confrontation was over, when Blitz came out of the deli screaming,

"I'll kill 'em!" Blitz ran after the men, and Sticca lost sight of them in the darkness. When Sticca found Blitz, he was lying on the street, butchered up, internal organs exposed, blood gushing onto the street. Sticca took him for dead.

Blitz recovered, over time, through extensive treatment at Bellevue Hospital that he had no means to pay for. There was talk that Blitz had nearly been left to die at the hospital, unattended by a doctor, presumed to be Jewish, because of the swastika around Blitz's neck, though the notion that a physician on emergency-room duty would abandon the Hippocratic oath over an ornament of punk jewelry is hard for me to believe.

The punk community in New York rallied to help Blitz, revealing publicly that it was indeed more of a community—a tightly united, almost hermetic society of spirits bonded by a set of narrowly defined tastes in music, style, and attitude—than the mob of antisocial individualists and anarchists that punks much preferred to be seen as. A group of Blitz's friends, admirers, and sympathizers led by Gyda Gash, a hardcore bassist, worked with the support of Hilly Kristal, the owner of CBGB, to organize a series of concerts at the club to help cover the cost of Blitz's medical care. There were four nights of shows with performances by many of the most important bands of the early punk era: the Ramones, the Dictators, the Dead Boys, the Fleshtones, Blondie, the Criminals, Sic Fucks, and about twenty more. The Ramones' house designer, Arturo Vega, had wide-neck black T-shirts made in honor of the occasion, with a list of the participating bands and Blitz's name printed in silver Gothic lettering.

I heard about the benefit from the English guitarist Robert Fripp, a recent escapee from the concept-rock land of gnomes and knights who was now living in Greenwich Village. I had recently interviewed Fripp for *The Real Paper*, the arts weekly in Boston. I was twenty-three, just out of NYU, living on Perry Street in the West Village, and starting to do my first professional music writing. I wrote quite a bit for *The Real Paper* for a few years and, in the course of this work, became friendly with both Fripp and his occasional collaborator at the time, Brian Eno, in the artificially cozy, mutually exploitative manner that over-eager journalists and media-savvy public figures can be, temporarily. Fripp let me tag along with him to the Blitz Benefit. He was planning to sit in with Blondie and, possibly, other acts.

Blondie was not strictly a punk band, a matter of some bearing in a realm as parochial as the CBGB scene, where a group had to be loud, rude, and crude to be accepted as legitimately punk. Blondie was more closely associated with New Wave, the poppish, electronically oriented style that arose around the same time as punk and ran parallel to it for a time with more commercial success, if less cultural impact in the end. Still, Blondie and its lead players—the mock-Weimar paper doll Deborah Harry and her lover, the songwriter and bandleader Chris Stein—were longtime fixtures at CBGB and accepted as cousins in the clan. Fripp, a veteran of the British art-rock group King Crimson, came from another sphere entirely but connected to punk by three degrees. He had played on the *Heroes* album with David Bowie, who had been working with Iggy Pop, who, as the leader of the Stooges in the 1960s, was one of the people who invented punk rock before it had a name.

Deborah Harry and Blondie were not yet well known nationally—their breakthrough on the pop charts would come the following year—but were already famous in the Village and were one of the main attractions at the Blitz Benefit, slotted late on the last of the four nights, May 7. With Fripp sitting in, standing to the side of Chris Stein, they played an abbreviated set of all or nearly all cover songs, as I recall. I remember that they did "Jet Boy," the punchy closing track on the New York Dolls' first album, a five-year-old historical artifact in 1978; and they played "Sister Midnight," one of the songs on the New Wave–ish album Bowie had recently produced for Iggy Pop, *The Idiot*. For their closing number, they did something utterly unexpected, a shock in a space where shock value was so normalized that true shocks had become rare. They played a dreamy, pulsing, slow-jam rendition of the Donna Summer disco hit from the previous year, "I Feel Love."

Looking back from the twenty-first century, when the mashing up of styles and genres is commonplace—a major genre of its own now—the idea of a bit of disco in a punk club may seem a quaint example of cultural dissonance. On the floor at CBGB that night, though, there was an almost physical feeling in the air that something very wrong had happened—something horrible in a way unlike the horrible stench of urine that was integral to the atmosphere of CBGB or the horrible house chili that was said to be seasoned with ejaculations by the Ramones. Disco, in its synthesized polyester-and-violins slickness, seemed, to the punks absorbed with crudity and raw noise, more distasteful than Ramone cum.

Fripp introduced me to Chris Stein and Deborah Harry, whom I had seen perform a couple of times, both at CBGB and at Max's Kansas City, but had never met. We talked for only a minute or so before a guy came up from behind Harry. I wasn't taking notes, but what he said was easy to remember. Standing at her shoulder, barking into her hair, he said, "You don't need *love*! You need *hate*!"

The "punk versus disco" conflict scheme is not simply a narrative device irresistible to writers like me, though it is that, too. Most of the punks hated disco music, as a qualification for being a punk, and disco dancers loathed punk rock for its proud ugliness and brutality. Disco and punk were the alternate-universe, good-Spock/goateed-Spock twins of 1970s music.

Both musics can be said to have started in the same year, 1974. Or perhaps I am overly inclined to mark that as a breakthrough time, because it was the year I moved to New York from New Jersey and found both disco and punk bubbling up around me. There are certainly important data points in 1974 for each sphere of music. That January, the single "Love's Theme"—an instrumental composed and conducted by Barry White with a studio ensemble billed as the Love Unlimited Orchestra—became a hit, the first string-orchestra record with no singer, no lyrics, to be number one on the pop charts since "Theme from *A Summer Place*," the smoothly swaying background music to every rec-room make-out session of the Kennedy era. (Later in the 1970s, "Theme from *A Summer Place*" would be rerecorded in a discofied version, as would scores of other pieces of music of every sort, from Cole Porter's "Night and Day" and Joni Mitchell's "Both Sides Now" to the first movement of Beethoven's Fifth Symphony.) It was early in 1974, as well, when four teenagers in Forest Hills, Queens, put together a band and took on stage names inspired by the pseudonym that Paul McCartney had briefly used when the Beatles were playing in Hamburg, Paul Ramon. Along with the Ramones, more than a dozen of the groups that established the punk movement in New York—the Patti Smith Group, Talking Heads, and Blondie, among them—would all be formed in 1974.

Like punk, disco existed as an alternative to the earthy, acoustic-guitar-based music of the singer-songwriters (James Taylor, Cat Stevens, and Don McLean) and the hippie bands (the Grateful Dead, the Allman Brothers Band, and the Doobie Brothers before their blue-eyed-soul phase) of the late 1960s and early 1970s. The same set of stimuli—the sight of suede boots and the sound of fingerpicking—triggered two opposite reactions: punk and disco. Punk responded by rejecting the laid-back sunniness and soft tunefulness of acoustic rock, in favor of grim nihilism and noisy rage. "I hate hippies and what they stand for. I hate long hair," Johnny Rotten of the Sex Pistols would say. Disco reacted by abandoning the internalism and casualness of the "head music" world, in the name of glamour, high style, and the pleasure of dolling up for the ballroom.

"That long-hair shit was never for me," said Frankie Valli, the lead vocalist with the 1960s harmony group the Four Seasons, who moved smoothly into disco in the mid-1970s. "When disco came and the kids threw out their filthy jeans and rotten sandals and started dressing up again and going to the Copa, that was a beautiful thing. Show business got back to what it's supposed to be."

As a dance music, disco belonged to one of the longest traditions—perhaps *the* longest tradition—in all of music. Generations before anyone was buying music on records, listening to it on the radio, or even playing it from sheet music in the parlor, people—especially young people—were dancing to it. From the days of the once-scandalously intimate minuet in colonial America, couples have been connecting through social dance and presenting their bodies, locking eyes, touching, and moving together in time to music. Dance has always been a mating ritual, and there is no dance without music—notwithstanding the formal experimentation of Yvonne Rainer, Merce Cunningham, and other avant-gardists of the second half of the twentieth century. Music critics like me often lose sight of the fact that a great deal of popular music has been created not for listening but for dancing. Its main purpose is not necessarily to stimulate the intellect nor even to stir the heart but to drive the body—not that these things are mutually exclusive.

The measures of value appropriate to dance music are not the same as the ones a critic would apply to music intended solely or primarily for the ears. The allure of the beat matters more than the sophistication of the melody, and the best melodies are the most *effectual* ones—the ones that contribute to the propulsion of the music by underpinning, prodding, or accenting the tempo. In music made for the dance floor, a simple, driving riff is often superior to a serpentine, legato melody. Shifts in tempo can be deadly; experiments in harmony, distracting. I'm not saying that music composed for movement cannot or should not be musically advanced. Stravinsky wrote *The Rite of Spring* for dancers. I'm talking about music made for public use rather than public appreciation, and there is a considerable difference between a ballet stage, where music is intended to suit trained dancers for the gratification of an observing public, and a dance club, where music is supposed to stimulate the public itself to improvised movement. Nor am I saying that its function as an inducement to movement makes dance music beneath careful consideration. To the contrary, I think the music of dance needs to be considered especially carefully, on its own terms.

For the people dancing, engaging with dance music is not simply a matter of taking in an art form as one would experience a chamber music concert or an Ornette Coleman record. It's a *practice*. As with religion, it's not solely a matter of subscribing to a set of traditions and beliefs; it's something you *do*—communally, in public.

Disco had much in common with some of the earliest fads in popular dance as a way of having fun that was also a laboratory for cultural experimentation and a mechanism for social change. Without getting too Ken Burns–ish about this, I'll point out the significance of the first dance craze of the twentieth century, the vogue for the fox-trot, in cross-fertilizing cultural values and democratizing social life (within the limits of racial segregation) for young people of the day. The fox-trot was introduced to the general public—I should say the white public—by Vernon and Irene Castle, the husband-and-wife vaudeville team, after Vernon Castle saw it danced by African American couples in a segregated club. Castle worked out the steps to music by W. C. Handy, the black composer who laid claim to having discovered the blues, and Castle called the step the bunny hug. At some point, it became associated with Harry Fox, a vaudeville performer whose stage prance resembled the dance, and it became popularly known as the "Fox trot," eventually depersonalized to fox-trot. Easy to learn, briskly paced, and intimate but not off-puttingly so, the fox-trot was critical to the rise of ballroom dancing as a national obsession in the first decades of the twentieth century. Single men and women went out at night to hotel ballrooms, met friends and perfect strangers—including people from other neighborhoods, other towns, and other social classes, though almost never from other racial groups—and held them in their arms. While the bands played ragtime, young Americans fox-trotted away from the strictures of Victorian propriety. (Stephen Sondheim, looking back at this era in the mordant pastiche musical *Follies*, built a saucy tune around the sexual subtext of ballroom dancing, called "Can That Boy Foxtrot!" Cut from the show, the song was rescued by the sultry nightclub singer Julie Wilson, who would stretch the *F* in the name of the dance to make sure the audience got the point.)

In the era of the fox-trot, record companies considered the danceability of a song so important that they would put the words "Fox Trot" next to the title, in large type. This practice would continue into the rock era, when the 45 rpm single of "Rock Around the Clock" was printed with the words, "Fox trot—vocal chorus by Bill Haley." At least forty tunes of the early twentieth century put the name of the dance in their titles, too: "Do the Funny Fox Trot, "Fox Trot Classique," "Black Satin Fox Trot," "The Raggy Fox Trot," and more. Like all popular dances, the fox-trot was a collectively delineated and flexible framework for individual improvisation, and it spawned immeasurable variations and copycat dances. The furry creature in the name of the dance caught the ballroom public's imagination, and Harry Fox was forgotten. By the end of the second decade of the century, there were half a dozen popular trots and related dances named for animals: the grizzly bear, the bunny hug, the camel walk, the kangaroo hop, the duck waddle, and the turkey trot. The last of which rivaled the fox-trot in popularity for a time and was explicitly condemned by civic and church leaders. In 1912, Father Edward F. Hannigan of Long Island City's St. Patrick's Church told a reporter, "If I was presiding as a judge and a couple were convicted before me of dancing the 'turkey trot,' I would sentence the woman to a year's imprisonment in a penitentiary and I would send the man to county jail for three months."

Within a decade of the animal-dance fad, the Charleston would carry on the social hybridization that the fox-trot established and take it further. The Jazz Age of flappers and Fitzgerald brought angular, limb-twisting movements derived from the African American juba dances of the slave period (with hints of the Spanish habanera in the music) to white America, and the steps were taken up as a symbol of the era's freedom of thought—or its decadence under Negro influence, depending on one's point of view. The popularity of the Charleston was propelled by the appeal of the song with the same title by James P. Johnson, the African American composer of songs and symphonic works, especially after the tune was interpolated into the Broadway revue whose name captured the ethos of the era, *Runnin' Wild*. Civic leaders warned of the corruption of youth, and pearls were clutched. As the *New York Herald Tribune* reported in 1925, "Unless it is suppressed or modified, it may be a great force toward the impairment of collegiate morals."

From the fox-trot and the Charleston to disco and beyond it to the contemporary era of club electronica, dance has been one of the great constants in American popular music. Yet it is a variable constant. (Yes, there is such a thing, in math as well as in music.) At times, dance has been the dominant force in pop music culture. This was certainly the case in the days of the fox-trot and the Charleston; it was the case in the swing era and also in the 1950s, when jump blues morphed into rock and roll, in the go-go 1960s, before rock became self-serious, and again in the disco years. There were, by contrast, periods when listening seemed to be the predominant mode of pop music consumption, most notably in the years immediately after each of the world wars, when the national mood grew sober. (During the times of both wars, counterintuitively, dance music thrived as a distraction and release, in the same way ballroom dancing flourished during the Depression.)

More often, however, the many varied audiences within the pop audience as a whole sought differing musics for differing purposes at the same time. While ballrooms in cities around the country filled with marathon dancers during the Depression, rural families in the South sat and listened to stark, sad Carter Family records on the radio. While children of the jet age with transistor radios listened themselves to sleep, as I did, slightly older kids were lining up to dance the twist at the Peppermint Lounge. In the heyday of the mopey singer-songwriters, James Brown and Sly and the Family Stone were getting teens of every color to get down with funk gems such as Brown's "Get Up (I Feel Like Being a) Sex Machine" and Sly's "Thank You (Falettinme Be Mice Elf Agin)." As I've said, disco arrived simultaneously with punk, and there was important funk music being made at the same time, by Parliament/Funkadelic, the Ohio Players, and the Isley Brothers, among others. Some people even danced, in a manner of speaking, at CBGB—hopping around stiffly in a way that would eventually be called the pogo. At any one concert by the Grateful Dead, a good portion of the audience would be listening, and another portion—up front, by the stage—would be dancing. The rest would presumably be doing both, listening while dancing somewhere in their minds.

Disco, like the fox-trot and the Charleston and the Lindy Hop and the twist, was a system of moves and attitudes with roots in multiple cultures. In the dancing of these dances, dancers brought a little whiteness, a little (or more) blackness, something of the Latino, perhaps a bit of high class, and, more often than not, something of the street into their bones in a literal way. Popular dance is cultural heterogeneity made physical and made personal. Yet disco was singular among dance crazes for the strength of its link not only to multiple ethnic groups and classes but also to gay society.

Popular music had always been informed by gay culture, of course. The very notion of "musicality"—an orientation toward music embedded in a person's being, in theory—was historically so closely associated with homosexuality that a gay man could ask another man if he was "musical" as a not-so-coded way to learn if he was companionably disposed. (When I was growing up, there was a tavern called the Musical Bar in my hometown, and I remember hearing in high school about a local teenager who entered it and "went gay." My father ordered me to cross to the other side of the street when I approached the bar on my walk to the barbershop.) Along with the ethnic parody acts in vaudeville, there were comparable "Nancy boy" shows of gay-male mimicry—a kind of homosexual minstrelsy performed in some cases by straight men. As I discussed in an earlier chapter, the blues was first popularized by steely women who performed a highly transgressive art, the early repertoire of which included a considerable number of songs of same-sex attraction (such as the "B.D. Woman's Blues," the initials of which were a lesbian slur). The show tunes of Cole Porter and Noël Coward were laced with naughty gay-boy innuendo and, more significantly, infused with the droll wit and blasé charm that can fairly be thought of as core qualities of gay sensibility. Little Richard, the self-proclaimed "Queen of Rock and Roll," added sexual fluidity to the transgressions of rock and roll, and a later generation of theatrical rockers—the Stooges, the Velvet Underground, the New York Dolls—updated Richard's gender twisting with metal guitars and gutter-poet lyrics to make the edgy/arty glam rock that prepared the way for both punk and disco.

"Disco was the soundtrack of the great gay coming-out party after Stonewall," recalled Edmund White, the memoirist and novelist whose books provide a deliciously vivid, literary chronicle of gay life in New York during the disco era. "No more hiding like frightened squirrels in sleazy little bars. Disco came into prominence at the same time as the gay renaissance, and there's no question that disco helped make it possible. Hundreds of men dancing together in these vast and lavish spaces. It was thrilling."

As the head of publicity for Fantasy Records told *Newsweek*, disco was "a symbolic call for gays to come out of the closet and dance with each other."

Moving to songs with words interpretable as messages of unity and celebration—"I Will Survive" and "I Am What I Am" by Gloria Gaynor, "You Make Me Feel (Mighty Real)" by Sylvester, and all the campy gay anthems by the Village People, like "Macho Man," "YMCA," and "In the Navy"—gay men found themselves grouped by the hundreds in a space where they could think of being homosexual as being part of a community, a collective body with the ability to work in synchronization. (Gay women also danced in clubs of their own, though the lesbian mobilization of the era was more political than musical.) Even the drugs in the discos, cocaine and amyl nitrate (sniffed from poppers, pop-open capsules), were potions of uplift, in contrast to the sedatives and hypnotics—pot, quaaludes, and heroin—more common in the punk clubs. (I'm speaking broadly here, because all drugs circulated in both spheres.)

For gay men, unlike the straight men and women who took up disco as the music caught on across the country, dancing was not necessarily a preamble to sex. There was sex everywhere in the clubs—in the balconies, in the back rooms, under the bars, and, often enough, on the dance floor. But dancing was something more than a sexual facilitator. "A gay man in the '70s could have all the sex he wanted," White said. "We didn't need to dance to get us in the mood." In the gay discos, the dancing itself was fully gratifying in its own way. The dancing was its own kind of sex.

Disco music, with its swirling strings and chant choruses about feeling good, had an insistent sexual positivity that punk fans saw as forced and overbearing. Over the course of the mid- to late 1970s, more than a dozen punk bands made anti-disco records: "Disco Sucks" by D.O.A., "Death to Disco" by the Vectors, "Kill the Bee Gees" by the Accident . . . When Blondie played "I Feel Love" at the Blitz Benefit, the carnal cheeriness of the song came across as a joke, and I presumed that was how Deborah Harry, Chris Stein, and Robert Fripp intended it. Disco fed on homosocial optimism and hope; punk, nihilistic cynicism and despair.

Both disco and punk were liberation movements, though music played a different role in each. In the case of disco, the music helped mobilize a society to prepare it to be liberated. For punk, a society came together to liberate the music itself; the music was not just the mechanism of liberation but its object. Rock and pop had grown so inflated, self-satisfied, and caught up in the pursuit of platinum-record glory and riches that they needed to be knocked down, kicked apart, and put into the hands of young people who could barely play their instruments.

Punk was and still is often misrepresented as a mission to restore the principles of amateurism and the values of chaos and danger to rock and roll. Yet the great service punk was engaged in was not simply one of restoration. It was more like repurposing. Rock and roll, at its most primal in the early and mid-1950s, had not really been so amateurish. The people who made it—Little Richard, Fats Domino, Chuck Berry, Elvis Presley, Jerry Lee Lewis, and their peers—were young, unseasoned (in most cases), self-taught (as a rule), and often undercompensated, but they were also highly skilled, and the conception of their music as chaotic and dangerous was a conceit inflated by both the music's fans and its critics, both of whom liked having rock and roll seen as a music for rebels.

Punk retroactively redefined rock and roll as something intrinsically brutal and rude, nothing less and nothing more. No matter that rock and roll had always been many things: gnarly and brash, at its radical best, elemental and sometimes proudly, wonderfully stupid, for sure. It had also been, in varying cases at various times, sexy, upbeat, fun, wishful, comic, and romantic. Musically, punk was narrowly defined, a formal art in a sphere where the standards were as rigid as those of, say, the early-music movement. At CBGB, three-chord, two-minute guitar-band songs became the new madrigals.

Blondie's performance of "I Feel Love" at the Blitz Benefit deepened the existing doubts about the group's punk loyalty. Deborah Harry and Chris Stein, unbowed, were looking toward a larger audience. Before the summer of that year, they arranged for a new producer, the pop-oriented Mike Chapman, to oversee the making of their third album. As Chapman explained to Lester Bangs shortly after the record's release that September, "I didn't make a punk album or a New Wave album with Blondie. I made a pop album." It included one of the first songs Harry and Stein had written together, a rhythmic ballad called "Once I Had a Love," now retooled, disco-style, with the new title "Heart of Glass." It put Blondie at number one on the pop charts.

As the band enjoyed popular success, *Stereo Review* reported in September 1979 that "some rock critics, the press in general, and possibly a lot of fans from Blondie's early days at the New York punk club CBGB claim that the group has sold out since breaking the single 'Glass.'" The record handily provided at least five of the qualities objectionable to authenticity fundamentalists since the days of the Lomaxes: (1) commercial intent, which can be fairly inferred by Harry and Stein's jump to Chapman; (2) commercial appeal, which is something different from intent and is apparent in the tune's bounciness and catchiness; (3) commercial success, which is a third thing and has only to do with the money the record made; (4) the use of technology such as electronic synthesizers, which "Heart of Glass" employed conspicuously, most notably in the Roland drum-machine track that anchors the song; (5) danceability. Selling out is a sin unrestricted to disco specifically.

A few days after the Blitz Benefit, I talked to Fripp about the decision to do "I Feel Love" at CBGB, and he told me it came from Harry and Stein, who, he said, were secret discophiles. Fripp loved "I Feel Love" himself. As Fripp explained, the producer Giorgio Moroder created the entire musical track electronically, without a single acoustic instrument. Fripp went on at some length about the expansive potential of electronic synthesizers and the weird beauty of new tonalities. This was a conversation in the spring of 1978, when the word "digital" referred to the new alarm clocks that used numbers instead of moving hands. I took what Fripp was saying as doe-eyed art-rock futurism and didn't think much about it for years.

≡ 11 ≡

VIDEO

MOONWALKERS

The moment of ecstasy and abandon that crystallizes the cheeky anarchy of *A Hard Day's Night* falls a little more than thirty minutes into the film, when the Beatles break away from their handlers and fans and Ringo shouts, "We're out!" Scooting down a fire escape and onto an open field, the boys race and jump and clown around in a virtuoso sequence of music-movie making, part faux cinema verité, part faux silent slapstick. There's no ambient sound—just the studio recording of "Can't Buy Me Love." A song written by Paul McCartney while the Beatles were staying in Paris, listening obsessively to *The Freewheelin' Bob Dylan* in their suite at the George V Hotel, "Can't Buy Me Love" is a cheery, mop-top version of a statement of antimaterialism. After a year of extravagant success on the pop charts with teen love songs such as "Love Me Do," "She Loves You," "I Want to Hold Your Hand," and "P.S. I Love You," the Beatles decided to say that love is something that cannot be bought or sold. Before long, McCartney would have second thoughts about this. Recalling a visit to Miami the Beatles took a month after recording

"Can't Buy Me Love," he told the biographer Barry Miles, "I remember meeting this rather nice girl and taking her out for dinner in this MG in the cool Florida night, palm trees swaying . . . It should have been 'Can Buy Me Love,' actually."

Two decades after the release of *A Hard Day's Night*, the "Can't Buy Me Love" scene would be packaged as a freestanding video for MTV, and the film's director, Richard Lester, would be honored at the first MTV Video Music Awards as the "father of the music video." Lester shrugged off the recognition and wrote to MTV demanding a paternity test.

It would have come out negative, naturally, because the music video form has innumerable progenitors and a lineage dating back to the earliest motion pictures. There were experimental short films centered on music in the silent era, when movies were not really soundless, after all, but usually projected to accompaniment performed by live musicians in the movie houses. Eva Tanguay mimed her songs and danced in early silent-era footage, dressed—or nearly undressed—in madcap headwear and well placed ostrich features. Georges Méliès, the French genius of cinematic effects, made wildly conceptual shorts such as *Le mélomane* (*The Music Lover*), which shows the conductor of a band of seven female musicians as his head pops off his body and reappears on-screen as the notes on a musical staff. A bit later, the American silent-comedy master Buster Keaton made another effects-driven short, *The Play House*, in which he portrayed all nine performers in a synchronized musical number, as well as all the musicians in the pit band on-screen. Keaton accomplished the feat by covering the camera lens with strips of light-blocking material; he removed one strip at a time, performed one role, then hand cranked the camera back to the beginning and performed the next role. He used one reel of film, exposed piece by piece, with no laboratory effects. Sixty years later, Paul McCartney would mimic the film with green-screen techniques, playing ten different musicians in a band (and his wife,

Linda, playing two more) in the music video for his synth-pop single "Coming Up."

With the advent of motion-picture sound, musical performances quickly became prevalent in feature films as the most impressive way to show off the new technology. The first talkie, *The Jazz Singer*, transplanted the biggest star of the musical stage, Al Jolson, to a medium that was still learning its own strengths, and he sang and danced—in blackface, yet—with all the outsized gusto appropriate to a live performance in one of the thousand-seat theaters where he customarily performed. Musical revues abounded in the early talkie period, although the song numbers tended to be stage-bound, little more than filmed musical theater, until the choreographer Busby Berkeley began experimenting with the visual vocabulary of cinema, employing regimens of half-nude chorines to produce living, moving geometric forms.

Sequences were built around individual songs, making musical numbers mini-movies within movies. From the mid 1930s onward, the musical numbers in most films could stand on their own; indeed, many were conceptual flights detached from and often superior to the films they were in: Fred Astaire and Ginger Rogers, performing their sublimely romantic duets in otherwise disposable musicals; Astaire, dancing on the walls and the ceiling in *Royal Wedding*; Gene Kelly, Frank Sinatra, and Jules Munshin, exultant in "New York, New York" in *On the Town*; Gene Autry, salvaging his juvenile westerns with a plaintive song; Donald O'Connor's balletic clowning to "Make 'Em Laugh" in *Singin' in the Rain*; Jerome Robbins's rooftop battle of cultures and sexes in "America" in *West Side Story*; and on and on and on . . .

By the time the film version of *West Side Story* was released, in 1961, its conception of teenage music—Lindy Hop swing and mambo—was already outdated. *Blackboard Jungle*, with its opening sequence set to rock and roll, was six years old. A string of quickie drive-in movies were made to exploit the momentary fad that many people, including Elvis, thought rock to be: *Rock, Rock, Rock!* (1956, starring a thirteen-year-old Tuesday Weld), *Don't Knock the Rock* (1956), *Rock Baby, Rock It* (1957), *The Big Beat* (1958), *Go, Johnny, Go!* (1959, featuring a teenage Sandy Stewart, before she took up jazz), *Juke Box Rhythm* (1959), and, the best among them, *The Girl Can't Help It* (1956, with Jayne Mansfield, directed by Frank Tashlin in the crazed style of his Looney Tunes cartoons). Nearly every one of these pictures repurposed the generational conflict over music and social values that was the plot of *The Jazz Singer*. Thrown together with mismatching scenes of rock and pop acts such as Chuck Berry and the Moonglows edited in, the films had an incoherent scrappiness that was demeaning to rock at the same time it reinforced the music's image as something marginal and disreputable—beneath adults and, therefore, dear to its young fans.

Because the art form of popular music in the rock era was the record, not the composition, the work seemed less adaptable to the big screen than pre-rock music, which had been written to be interpreted by the largest possible number of singers in a variety of settings. *Blackboard Jungle* had, extraordinarily for the time, used a pop single on the movie soundtrack in place of a conventional background score. The images accompanied the record. Richard Lester, with *A Hard Day's Night*, applied the same approach throughout the film, setting the Beatles' recordings to imagery. This was the case even in the ostensible live performances in the movie, including the four-song concert at the end. The boys mime to their records, with the crowd's screaming edited in. (In three of the concert songs, "If I Fell," "I Should Have Known Better," and "She Loves You," we hear John Lennon strumming an acoustic guitar as we watch him playing an electric.)

Before making feature films, Richard Lester had directed novelty shorts and TV commercials, and his experience with both helped make *A Hard Day's Night* an enjoyably kinetic, mildly radical work of branding. It foreshadowed MTV by melding commercial and creative purposes to the sound of pop. After *A Hard Day's Night*, the Beatles started making short films set to their singles for promotional use on television, to cut down their need to travel and perform live, and the idea caught on with other acts. The Rolling Stones, the Who, the Kinks, and Bob Dylan all started making video clips of their songs. The idea wasn't entirely new; in the 1940s, dozens of pop singers, swing orchestras, jump blues bands, and country acts made short music films called Soundies, which could be watched for ten cents a play on coin-operated machines about the size of a refrigerator in bars and bus terminals. Soundies were exclusively performance films, though, and rock artists veered further and further away from straightforward documentation to make more ambitious, if often more pretentious, little movies. By the end of the 1970s, there would be almost enough rock clips to fill an entire TV channel.

Late in 1979, I started working as an editor for a new magazine called *Video Review*, about the emerging home video scene. We reviewed movies and other releases on videocassette and cable and covered technology with drooling nerdiness. It was a day job but not a bad one, and it led me in the summer of 1980 to Monterey, California, to interview Michael Nesmith, the former guitarist and songwriter for the Monkees, who had started a video production company with backing from his mother. She was the inventor of Liquid Paper, the brush-on, fast-drying goo that was an essential office supply until the invention of the home computer. I was excited about meeting Nesmith, having once been kicked out of a Monkees cover band.

Nesmith, working with the director William Dear, had begun producing whimsical video shorts set to his solo recordings. One, called "Rio," had him flying by way of green screen on his own power, with three women riding on his back; another, a parody of his ballad "Joanne," had Nesmith turn into Rodan, the cheesy Japanese movie monster. In sober, businesslike tones, Nesmith explained to me that he was building a catalog of video clips for use on a cable series he was producing, which would be dedicated exclusively to music videos. The show would be called *PopClips*, and it would start on the Nickelodeon network later that year. The idea was a kind of "music television," he said, and I wrote down the phrase thinking, *That's a pretty good idea*. Like everyone who grew up after Elvis had appeared on *The Ed Sullivan Show*, I was raised on TV and pop records. The notion of combining the two seemed a smart application of the narrowcasting that cable had made possible, and it seemed only fitting that the idea would come from one of the stars of a made-for-TV band.

PopClips made such an impression in the young cable industry that John Lack, the CEO of the Warner Amex Satellite Entertainment Company, tried to buy it, but Nesmith demurred, wanting to retain his company's independence. Lack went to the president of Warner Amex, Jack Schneider, and proposed a twenty-four-hour channel devoted to music videos, using *PopClips* as evidence of the appeal of music television. With Schneider's approval, Lack initiated MTV.

To create their new hybrid of music and television, the founders of MTV needed to break two industries of entrenched habits of practice. The WASEC people thought of MTV as a kind of "radio with pictures," as Schneider called it, and thus expected the record companies to supply them with clips at no cost, much as they gave free singles to DJs. The record people saw MTV as a television channel and wanted it to license music the way the broadcast networks did. The cable operators, meanwhile, were reluctant to devote airtime to rock music content, which they thought of as having a small television audience.

MTV's first office was a room in the Sheraton Hotel in midtown Manhattan. Bob Pittman, a cocksure former radio programmer, dealt with the record companies, while Fred Seibert, a onetime jazz record producer, worked on the visual style and corporate personality of the channel. The soon-to-be-famous "moon man" station ID made a virtue of MTV's financial limitations: Seibert chose the imagery because it was in the public domain. At the same time, the reference to one of the landmarks of human achievement made clear the channel's image of itself. "We actually thought what we were doing was important," Seibert would later recall. "We thought, *We're going to change the face of television!*"

This sense of self-appointed importance would be one of MTV's defining qualities, an appropriately rock-star-like faith that people *needed* the channel. It was evident from the first few moments of MTV's launch on August 1, 1981: a countdown, a rocket launch, the moon-landing footage, and the first clip, "Video Killed the Radio Star," a video produced a few years earlier by the Buggles, an English art-pop band that made a specialty of ironic futurism. The early broadcasts did not go well, with wrong music cues, technical problems with the stereo sound, and a limited selection of videos. Fortunately for the network, most cable markets were not yet carrying it. The staff of MTV had to watch the launch of its own channel in the ballroom of a bar in Fort Lee, New Jersey, because Manhattan Cable had no deal with WESAC.

An inadvertent positioning tool, its limited exposure worked to MTV's advantage. In 1981, cable TV was still a novelty in most American households. For teens, watching cable was, by necessity, a social activity centered on the houses of whoever had cable service, and MTV was the newest, most exotic thing available. Its scarcity, combined with the relative obscurity of many of the acts it featured, enhanced MTV's mystique. Just as earlier music buffs traded rare blues records for both the thrill of discovery and the status that interest in them conferred, the children of Reagan's America sought out and talked up the latest videos on MTV.

Before long, record companies started noticing that some lesser-known performers such as Devo, the Stray Cats, Billy Idol, and Duran Duran were seeing a dramatic sales uptick in those secondary markets where MTV was transmitted. Few of these acts were getting much promotion by their labels or significant radio play. But they were video-friendly, and their clips were being played on MTV. The labels and their artists began to recognize MTV's usefulness. "If it weren't for MTV, we'd still be spud boys in Ohio," said Gerald Casale, who directed many of Devo's videos, along with writing and singing some of their material.

From its start, MTV defined itself as a rock-format station, reflecting the AOR (album-oriented rock) background of its top executives. MTV promoted New Wave acts, young hair-metal bands, and established rock stars. The channel shied away from R&B and virtually ignored hip-hop. The tone of the channel was resolutely white, notwithstanding the occasional inclusion of upbeat commercial music from black artists such as "Rockit" by Herbie Hancock, "Pass the Dutchie" by Musical Youth, and "She Works Hard for the Money" by Donna Summer. Even Michael Jackson, who was a major pop star before he began making videos, had trouble breaking through on MTV. When Jackson's record company submitted the video for "Billie Jean," the second single from Jackson's *Thriller* album, there was a delay in MTV's accepting it for broadcast. Enraged, the head of Columbia Records, which owned Jackson's label, Epic, threatened to pull every video controlled by Columbia from the network's roster. MTV relented and started playing what would become one of the most popular videos ever to air on the channel. Jackson followed up with "Beat It," a more rock-oriented track with an Eddie Van Halen solo that suited the network's AOR orientation.

At the center of both videos was Jackson's extraordinary dancing, a limberly mechanical-looking hybrid of break-dance moves and classic showbiz steps developed by Cholly Atkins, the house choreographer at Motown. Music video, as a medium with pictures, and moving ones at that, was especially hospitable to performers who could move, and Michael Jackson was the most thrilling dancer in pop since Jackie Wilson and James Brown. Jackson brought pop music dance to a new level of virtuosity and established the ability to dance as a prerequisite for pop stardom for decades to come.

Jackson's instantly iconic set piece, the moonwalk, grew out of a step called backsliding that the *Soul Train* dance team Eclipse performed (notably in a televised performance of Jackson's "Workin' Day and Night," from his breakthrough solo album, *Off the Wall*). In Jackson's masterly adaptation, the moonwalk was so impressive that Fred Astaire called Jackson and asked him to teach it to him. Jackson, jerking his body as if in fast motion, suddenly freezing, and moving backward, seemed the very embodiment of the video experience, as if his body were directed not by his mind but by an internal remote control.

With his follow-up to "Beat It," "Thriller," Michael Jackson established the video release as a pop culture event. A fourteen-minute film directed by John Landis (then best known for the frat comedies *Animal House* and *The Blues Brothers*), the video for "Thriller" introduced all the elements that would subsequently identify prestige video releases: a celebrity-potted premiere, a forty-five-minute "making of" documentary, and saturation play on MTV. It also proved definitively that music videos could sell records. The *Thriller* album was already a huge hit, having spent a year on the charts, but had definitely peaked. After the "Thriller" video, sales of the album doubled. Thirty years later, *Thriller* would remain the bestselling album of all time, and the "zombie dance" from the video would be reenacted around the world on Halloween. In 2007, fifteen hundred Filipino prisoners reenacted the "Thriller" video as part of their rehabilitation therapy, and in 2009 more than thirteen thousand people danced the "Thriller" routine in Mexico City in honor of Michael Jackson's birthday. Both occasions became digital-era events on YouTube, MTV's successor as the main platform for the distribution of music videos in the early twenty-first century.

Much as the phenomenon of recording affected the art of live performance, with pop acts striving to replicate the sound of their records onstage, the rise of videos had an impact in the concert arena. Rock and pop shows started to look like videos. Performers began to be costumed, choreographed, and lit for the benefit of video cameras, whose feeds would be edited in real time for projection on giant screens in the concert halls. This setup is so commonplace today that it barely seems notable. But I was stunned the first time I saw it, at a Madonna concert in Radio City Music Hall in June 1985.

Madonna had emerged by then as something of a counterpart to Michael Jackson, a star of the video age who employed the medium with mastery to cast and periodically recast her celebrity image. Within two years of the release of her first, self-titled album, she had a string of hits on MTV: "Borderline," "Like a Virgin," "Material Girl," and "Crazy for You," all very good songs and even better videos. To support her second album, *Like a Virgin*, Madonna did a twenty-seven-city tour of major halls such as the Universal Amphitheatre in Los Angeles and Radio City in New York. Before this, she had performed only in much smaller venues such as the Mudd Club and Danceteria, and I had never seen her onstage. I went to the Radio City show as an admirer but was taken aback for the first ten or fifteen minutes of the concert, until I realized that I needed to adjust my expectations. Her voice sounded thin and weak, and she sang slightly sharp for much of the show and significantly off-key a few times. After a while, I didn't notice any of this anymore; I was too caught up in the spectacle of Madonna dancing nonstop with a small troupe of boys, in three or four costume changes, including a slutty-bride Halloween-costume gown.

For the finale, she performed "Like a Virgin" in that gown, with part of Michael Jackson's "Billie Jean" interpolated. The point seemed to be to suggest that the kid in the latter song was not the singer's son, because she was a virgin until recently, or something like that. For the encore, she did "Material Girl," her trademark statement of sexual and economic agency that neatly trashed the Beatles' proposition about money not buying love.

There were four video screens set up behind the stage, and I ended up looking at them all night, instead of watching the stage, even though I had an excellent seat somewhere around the twelfth row. The name of the hall was Radio City, but the aesthetic was pure video.

Popular music had always involved both sight and sound. Unless we're listening in the dark or with our eyes closed—or doing both, as I did with my transistor radio in bed—we're taking in images as part of the music experience. We're watching performers, onstage or on-screen, or we're glancing around the room, reading, or gazing at a lover. Although the Beatles never made a video for "Tell Me What You See," I see the same thing in my mind's eye every time I hear it: the eyes of Mary Jane Pence. What videos did was replace the imagery of personal experience with prepared images organized by the grammar of the screen: close-ups, long shots, pans, slow motion, crosscutting, montage, and special effects—all that. Videos, a kind of recorded imagery parallel to recorded sound, did for the visual component of the music experience what records did for the aural: they replaced a set of stimuli to the imagination with a fixed and permanent, unchangeable piece of work.

At the same time, they got us all used to hearing recordings as the accompaniment to things we see. Listening to music on the street, with headphones or earbuds—on a Walkman, in the 1980s, and after that with digital devices—would be a familiar experience, like living in a music video.

12

HIP-HOP

BEATS WANT TO BE FREE

The persistence of the human urge to make music has rarely been demonstrated as vividly as it was in the wreckage of the South Bronx during the late 1970s and early 1980s, when a group of young people without musical instruments, money, or access to the power centers of the music business used their record collections and their wits to create a new form of music that would come to be known as hip-hop. I was not part of this scene, personally. I was still hanging around CBGB and just beginning to immerse myself in jazz at a bar in the Village called Bradley's when hip-hop was taking form. But I heard from some NYU schoolmates a couple of years younger than I that radical things were going on in black music. A woman I went out with had a friend living in Weinstein Hall, one of the university dormitories, and the friend played us a cassette tape produced by a guy on her floor, Rick Rubin, who was running a record label out of his dorm room. I felt like an interloper, listening to music not meant for my ears, and it bothered me that this Rubin person, a white kid, was packaging it. What I heard—"I Need a Beat" by LL Cool J,

I know, and something by T La Rock and Jazzy Jay—felt to me like the blackest black music I had ever been exposed to, and I felt guilty for loving it and wanting more.

Hip-hop, like most arts, had no single point of origin, no one inventor. Among the music's earliest innovators was a Kingston, Jamaica, native named Clive Campbell, who, as a boy, had encountered the island tradition of "dancehall" parties hosted by disc jockeys with mobile sound systems set up in vacant spaces. Campbell learned from the sound system shows, where the success of a DJ was based on the uniqueness of his records, the loudness of his gear, and the cleverness of the comments and rhymes he improvised over instrumental sections of the music. The DJs in Kingston assumed stage names in the spirit of the sovereigns who had once ruled Jamaica from imperial Britain—King Tubby, Duke Reid, Sir Coxsone Dodd—and they conducted their business like monarchs of rivalrous fiefdoms. One DJ would steal a competitor's records. One would sabotage another's equipment. Not yet rap or hip-hop as we would come to know it, Kingston sound system music was the center of a society where creative people with good business sense took on outsized personalities to practice an art that combined curation, improvisation, and technological expertise.

Campbell's family moved to the South Bronx when he was twelve, in 1967, and settled in a yellow-brick high-rise building for working-class families a couple of blocks north of the Cross Bronx Expressway. By the age of eighteen, Campbell was going by the name of DJ Kool Herc and hosting sound system parties in the community room of his building, in school yards, and in empty lots around the neighborhood. Chief among Kool Herc's innovations was the use of a turntable technique he called the merry-go-round, which would soon become better known as the break-beat style. Herc focused on the point in a record when the singer and most of the band step aside—take a break—and all you hear is the beat, just drums or drums and bass. In 1960s and 1970s funk music, James Brown had exploited the dramatic potential of the break, stretching out the sections of bare rhythm while he egged the musicians on with gibes and prods, meticulously timed. "Don't turn it loose, 'cause it's a mother!" "I wanna give the drummer some of this funky soul we got here!" (In the first two decades of recorded rap music, the drumming by Clyde Stubblefield on James Brown's record of "Funky Drummer" would be sampled on more than a thousand recordings, including tracks by Boogie Down Productions, LL Cool J, Big Daddy Kane, Public Enemy, and the Fat Boys.) Herc worked out a way to manipulate multiple turntables to mix back and forth between similar breaks on separate records, extending the effect from a few teasing seconds to an ecstatic five minutes or more. Dancers took to using the break as the aural equivalent of a spotlight, the signal to show off their stuff, and a new class of dancers—break-dancers, break boys, or b-boys—competed for status (and prizes in drugs and sexual favors) in this new cultural space.

DJs in the making studied Herc's technique and built upon it. One of them was Joseph Saddler, a Bronx teenager of Caribbean ancestry who was studying electronics at vocational school when he started DJing his own parties under the name Grandmaster Flash. More fluid a mixer than Herc, Flash devised a way to match the beats between two records so the transition was imperceptible. He also added percussive elements to Herc's style, including the punch, a short phrase from one record played atop the break of another, and the rub, which involved turning a track up before he had finished cuing it, revealing the scratching sound the needle makes as it vibrates in the record's grooves. One of Flash's younger protégés in the Bronx, a DJ called Grand Wizard Theodore, loved rubs and treated them as a new musical instrument, scratching records with deftness and precision to produce a range of percussive accents and trills. Around the same time, another Bronx resident and member of the Black Spades gang, Kevin Donovan, started DJing and promoting parties as a constructive alternative to the gangs. Inspired by what he learned during a trip to Africa that he had earned in a high-school essay contest, Donovan renamed himself Afrika Bambaataa, and he dubbed his informal group of followers the Universal Zulu Nation. Nearly fifty years after the closing of the Cotton Club, New York street culture was once again conjoining with motifs from Africa and a tinge of romance with gangsterism.

As Kool Herc, Grandmaster Flash, Afrika Bambaataa, and other DJs developed progressively complex methods of mixing music, they started delegating the rapping, assigning others to microphone duty as masters of ceremonies. Although part of the MC's job was to glorify the DJ, the MCs inevitably became attractions themselves, either individually or in groups such as the Cold Crush Brothers or the Furious Five. From ad hoc parties in the South Bronx, rap spread to dance clubs in Harlem, lower Manhattan, and Fort Greene and other black neighborhoods in Brooklyn, as well as in Philadelphia, Washington, and other cities in roughly the same period. MCs rapped streams of slick talk as the records spun—urging the crowds on, boasting, and riffing on the music they were playing. There were many precedents for the rhythmic, improvised interplay of speaking voice and recorded music that the MCs were practicing: the banter of AM-radio disc jockeys, the spoken-word records of Gil Scott-Heron or the Last Poets, the kinetic dialogue between James Brown and his musicians, and the patter of the Kingston sound system DJs. But rap evolved quickly into an art of its own kind. Increasingly, MCs were showing that their rapping could be something more than an inducement to entertainment; it could be a form of entertainment itself.

The technical innovations that Herc, Flash, and others came up with were made possible in part through a fortuitous confluence of developments in the production of electronics hardware. Audio mixing and cross-fading technologies, used in professional radio and recording studios for many years, became available to DJs hosting house parties in the early 1970s. When Japanese and Korean companies started producing cheaper, smaller mixers geared to the semiprofessional market, kids in the Bronx projects could get their hands on them. Meanwhile, direct-drive turntables such as the Technics SL-1200 series made it easier to maintain the music's tempo as the DJ scratched, and there were now portable high-quality speaker systems and low-cost programmable drum machines.

Rap music, unlike every form of popular music preceding it, was made from existing recordings by artists working with record collections. Their tastes were formed primarily by listening to records, and their authority as artists was rooted largely in their command of their collections. They absorbed and produced culture in a way specific to the electronic age, in which everything that has ever been recorded is seen as a creative resource. Rap artists drew freely from music of a great many traditions: the electro rhythms of the German art-rock ensemble Kraftwerk, which Bambaataa interpolated into his hit single "Planet Rock" in 1982, the hard rock samples in countless records from Def Jam (the label Rick Rubin founded in Weinstein Hall and built with the African American impresario Russell Simmons), or the classic rock and Top 40 songs that rappers referenced in both their music and their lyrics. One of my favorite examples is Boogie Down Productions' "The Bridge Is Over" from 1987, in which KRS-One dismisses his rivals Marley Marl and MC Shan to the tune of Billy Joel's "It's Still Rock and Roll to Me," a cranky song that I never much liked on its own but relished in repurposed form.

Like rock and roll with "Rock Around the Clock," rap broke through to the mainstream public—meaning, to young record buyers of all colors—as a novelty. The music's first commercial hit, the Sugarhill Gang's "Rapper's Delight," was released by the independent label Sugarhill Records late in 1979 and made the *Billboard* chart early in 1980. Kids all over the country tried to memorize the singsong rap, competing to see who could recite the whole thing. (My wife committed it to memory while she was in high school and can still do it, top to bottom.)

Built around the bass line of the single "Good Times" by Chic, "Rapper's Delight" was a studio concoction that emulated the DJ-based music that had developed in the clubs. The members of the Sugarhill Gang weren't established rappers. They didn't come from Sugar Hill, the once-tony area in Harlem celebrated in the lyrics to the composer Billy Strayhorn's theme for the Duke Ellington Orchestra, "Take the 'A' Train." The Sugarhill Gang came from Englewood, a middle-class suburb on the Jersey side of the George Washington Bridge. The three rappers—Big Bank Hank, Wonder Mike, and Master Gee—were brought together by Sylvia Robinson, a veteran R&B singer and producer (at one time, half of Mickey and Sylvia, the duo that had a hit in 1957 with "Love Is Strange," co-written by Robinson, her partner Mickey Baker, and Bo Diddley, writing under his wife's maiden name, Ethel Smith). Robinson had heard and liked and tried unsuccessfully to sign the early rapper Lovebug Starski—a delicious name that embodies rap's free pillaging from pop culture, a mash-up from a Disney movie about a car and a TV cop show. When Starski declined to record with her, Robinson cast around for someone who would and found three enthusiastic amateurs. She gave the group its name and formed Sugarhill Records to capitalize on what she recognized astutely as the next big thing.

Some musicians in other spheres warmed up quickly to the music. Two years after Blondie played "I Feel Love" at CBGB, the band recorded an original disco number, "Rapture," which ended with Deborah Harry pulling off a credible rap coda. Around the same time, in 1981, the Clash tried rapping on the single "The Magnificent Seven" and inviting Grandmaster Flash and the Furious Five to open for the band in New York. The groove and rap on "The Magnificent Seven" came off well enough for the record to get heavy airplay on New York's black music station WBLS.

Critics took a little longer. Three years after "Rapper's Delight," Sugarhill released "The Message," a single credited to Grandmaster

Flash and the Furious Five, though it was not Flash but one of the members of the Five, Melle Mel, rapping on the track. Ominous in tone and grim in subject matter, "The Message" was among the first rap records to be taken up by critics as an example of the music as a serious form. "The Message" conjured a bleak picture of black life in the early 1980s, a landscape of rape and broken glass and piss on the stairs. It was just the kind of thing that critics could use to defend rap as more than a novelty.

Like other works of the avant-garde, hip-hop defied entrenched standards and expectations, challenging both critics and listeners to apply new measures of value to a new kind of art. When I first heard hip-hop, on the mixtape Rick Rubin gave to my girlfriend's friend, I found it thrilling but destabilizing. I was unequipped for it. I listened for the things I thought of as necessities to good music: melody, harmony, good tonal production, and well crafted words. I mistook the rhythmic chanting of LL Cool J as lacking a tune. It would take time for me to recognize the melodic content in the exactingly intricate cadences and microtonal variations in rap. It would take longer still for me to shake my predisposition to applying the standards I was used to and stop expecting chromatic harmony where it simply did not belong. Only after I stopped listening for "perfect" rhymes did I hear the perfection in great rappers' virtuosic slapping down and fucking around with the English language. Hip-hop set and met aesthetic values of its own choosing—groove and flow, layering, rupture. Aesthetically, I realized, hip-hop was interested not in assimilation but in sovereignty.

Initially a party music, blunt and earthy but entertainingly so, rap grew darker and more explicitly violent and sexual as the music evolved into hip-hop as it would come to be known. In hip-hop lyrics, African American artists used the graphic imagery of social realism to construct a hyperbolic dreamscape where black artists—typically men, but not always—dominated everything. The lyrics' glorification of violence, sexual prowess, and material gratification made it too easy a target for critics who took the work at face value as raw expression rather than dramatic material.

Take, for example, the Notorious B.I.G.'s 1994 track "Gimme the Loot," a dialogue between two black men as they set off on a crime spree and kill several other black men, rob pregnant women, and finally shoot it out with the police. Precise in its details and tactically extreme, the piece works in the realm of the cathartic imagination. It is gripping and disturbing, meant to be both.

Violent imagery had had an important place in black music since the first days of the blues. Created by and for poor African Americans in the South, the blues gave voice to the discontent and anxieties of a subjugated, suffering people. It was an outlet for rage—as well as joy, sometimes, to palliate that rage—coded in language about domestic matters, to throw off any eavesdropping whites. In the blues, the reasons (or rationales) for the violence were ostensibly amatory or otherwise personal, though really societal by implication: a broken heart, wounded pride, maltreatment by the boss (standing in for white society).

Robert Johnson, the country-blues musician whose legend tells how he sold his soul to the devil in exchange for his enigmatic guitar style, laid the bedrock for violent hip-hop lyrics when he sang freely about gunfire in songs such as "32-20 Blues," a rewrite of a tune by one of his contemporaries, Skip James, which Johnson recorded in 1936:

> She got a .38 special but I believe it's most too light
> I got a 32-20, got to make the caps all right . . .
> I'm gonna shoot my pistol, gonna shoot my Gatling gun
> You made me love you, now your man have come.

Wrath and weaponry of various kinds infused virtually every style of blues. Bessie Smith barked, in "Black Mountain Blues," "I'm bound for Black Mountain, me and my razor and my gun . . . / I'm gonna shoot him if he stands still and cut him if he run." Lonnie Johnson, a virtuoso of delicate, chamber-style guitar blues, crooned, in "Got the Blues for Murder Only," "I'm going to old Mexico, where there's long, long reaching guns / When they want real excitement, they kill each other one by one." Lead Belly, the pardoned convict who composed lyrical folk-blues, entertained nightclub audiences with his tribute to a bartender who shot a policeman, "Duncan and Brady": "Brady, Brady carried a .45, said it would shoot half a mile / Duncan had a .44, that what laid Mr. Brady so low."

Gunpowder helped keep the blues ignited as it spread over the twentieth century to give us innumerable musical styles from jazz to rock, and nearly every style has an element of the outlaw ethos at its core. Country music has always celebrated renegades, bandits, and gunslingers—Jimmie Rodgers warbled about being "free from the chain gang now," and Johnny Cash came to epitomize outlaw cool, despite having served only a day in jail. Even swing had an aura of roguishness, with one early big band called the Rhythm Racketeers.

The Notorious B.I.G. would have felt at home in Robert Johnson's world. His songs, like those of many other rappers, overflow with references to barrel gauges and bullet types. "Gimme the Loot" alone mentions .45s, Tec-9s, and .357 slugs. Rap lyrics, in their dramatic use of the imagery of violence and gunplay, were, if anything, old-school.

While MCs edged DJs out of prominence once rap started being recorded, it was DJs and their successors, the producers, who developed one of hip-hop's most influential innovations: sampling as a form of creative expression. Rap music anticipated the transformation from analog culture to digital culture and prepared the world for that change. Rap showed, in an entertaining way, that recorded sound—and by extension any recorded information—is unfixed. It can be edited, changed, reconfigured, and turned into something new. The early hip-hop DJs began to demonstrate this, in a limited manner, with turntables and mixers. Technology took a few years to catch up with the way they thought.

The premise underlying sampling—that part of one artist's music can be creatively interpolated into another artist's music—had been accepted practice in music long before recording codified sound as the work itself. As I discussed in the context of folk music and the blues, informal music of many kinds has taken form over time through the accretion of additions, subtractions, and variations by many contributors. Woody Guthrie used the melody of a song he had heard on a Carter Family record, "When the World's on Fire," for "This Land Is Your Land," and there's no knowing where A. P. Carter found the tune he used.

In classical music, there are countless instances of composers incorporating musical quotations from other composers' works in their pieces. Mozart quoted Bach in his Piano Concerto no. 12. Ravel quoted Stravinsky in his first Piano Concerto, and Stravinsky quoted Ravel, among many others. "I could go through Stravinsky's *Rite of Spring* with you and point out what comes from Mussorgsky and Ravel—note-for-note passages from Ravel—outright, out-fucking-rageous steals!" Leonard Bernstein told the writer Jonathan Cott. "I could go through Beethoven at his most revolutionary, bar by bar, and show you the derivations from Handel and Haydn and Mozart." Charles Ives went further still and made quotations part of his aesthetic, evoking the American egalitarianism he prized in music over-packed with musical allusions: in his Symphony no. 2, Ives quotes Beethoven's Symphony no. 5, "American the Beautiful," "Turkey in the Straw," and at least half a dozen other pieces.

In jazz, moreover, virtually every major improviser has nodded to other musicians, either in respectful homage or as ironic commentary. Charlie Parker, in his recording of "Salt Peanuts" for Verve Records, quoted Stravinsky's *Rite of Spring*. Sonny Rollins, trading solos with Parker on Miles Davis's "Serpent's Tooth," teasingly referenced "Anything You Can Do I Can Do Better." All of this was a kind of sampling without sampling gear. The difference in the case of digital sampling was its explicit challenge to the privilege of a recording to represent creative expression in immutable form.

Technologically, rudimentary sampling had been possible since the invention of magnetic tape in the 1940s. Avant-garde experiments with sound collage and musique concrète during the late 1940s and the 1950s started seeping into the pop music consciousness during the 1960s, most visibly through the Beatles, who used tape loops ("Tomorrow Never Knows," "Revolution 9") and tape-based samplers such as the Mellotron ("Strawberry Fields Forever"). With the emergence of digital recording and the production of portable equipment such as the Fairlight CMI and Akai S900 samplers, sampling became accessible and affordable and seemingly unstoppable.

Through the techniques of break beat and scratching, the early hip-hop DJs invented the sonic vocabulary that rap producers would apply to sampling. For some producers, at first, sampling provided a handy way to mimic what the DJs were doing in the clubs. More adventurous producers such as Hank Shocklee and the Bomb Squad began to create tracks of complexly edited and layered sounds, montages of bits from recordings and fresh material, melded into a dizzying, multiformed new kind of whole.

Shocklee was a major innovator who layered samples on top of samples, after samples, next to samples, between samples, to create a three-dimensional version of Phil Spector's "wall of sound." Shocklee's sonic constructions had four, five, and six walls, some standing and some crumbled in heaps. He'd put an Isley Brothers vamp and a David Bowie backing vocal over a groove from the J.B.'s, then run a blaring car alarm or a free-jazz saxophone improvisation through the whole thing.

Samples became more prominent in rap: in 1990, the rap songs on *Billboard*'s Top 100 R&B singles chart used seventy-one samples from no fewer than fifty-seven earlier recordings, and as rap became more prominent in the marketplace, the artists whose work was being re-used started to take notice. In 1991, the rapper Biz Markie sampled part of "Alone Again (Naturally)" by the English-Irish singer-songwriter Gilbert O'Sullivan without permission. O'Sullivan sued for copyright infringement, and the Court for the Southern District of New York ruled in O'Sullivan's favor. The decision quickly changed the record industry's attitude toward sampling. Every sample now had to be cleared by the copyright holder, who would inevitably demand a fee. The ruling ensured that copyright holders retained control of their creative property while turning a laboratory of free experimentation into a marketplace.

The high cost of licensing established music for sampling inspired hip-hop producers to hunt more widely for material. Producers such as Pete Rock dug out tracks such as the Beginning of the End's "When She Made Me Promise" from 1971 for use on CL Smooth and Rock's 1992 single "They Reminisce over You (T.R.O.Y.)," exposing listeners to material they might not otherwise have heard while boosting the producers' reputations as vinyl archaeologists. At the same time, sampling a famous song became a way of signaling a producer's financial wherewithal, a kind of sonic bling. When Sean Combs used the Police's "Every Breath You Take" for his Notorious B.I.G. tribute "I'll Be Missing You" in 1997, or when Kanye West sampled Ray Charles's "I Got a Woman" for his "Gold Digger" in 2005, they were not only taking advantage of a great riff; they were demonstrating the size of their disposable income.

Sampling was among the first phenomena to stir the debate over ownership of creative material, music, and images before art and information came to be categorized together as "content." In the mid-1980s, around the same time that hip-hop was becoming broadly popular, technophiles envisioning a world connected by data started spreading the slogan "Information wants to be free." It was an unconscious echo of the philosophy of hip-hop's architects. The DJs in the projects, siphoning electricity from power lines to make new music from parts of existing recordings, could well have been rapping, "Beats want to be free."

Technophiles would provide the tools that allowed the hip-hop artists to re-create the licensing-fee-free space of their music's origins: the digitization of sound, the development of cheap sampling software, and the theoretically infinite capacity for distribution that the Internet offers. These tools have given rise to the subcultures of rap mixtapes, mash-ups, and remixes, wherein the music of everyone from James Brown to Belinda Carlisle is used to make new music, without the exchange of payment. This does not represent a rejection of the capitalist impulse in hip-hop; it is just an accommodation. Mixtapes and mash-ups, legal or not, are seen as forms of promotion, ways to spread word of one's work and create buzz. At the same time, they serve to reinforce artists' connections to and positions in the hip-hop community by embracing the work of fellow artists and influences. If the potential reach of this underground is vast, the fundamental need it fulfills is the same one that motivated teenagers in the South Bronx more than three decades ago. Hip-hop started with the communal appreciation of the beat, the moment the break emerged from the DJ's speakers and the crowd lost control.

≡13≡

DIGITIZATION

THE IMMATERIAL WORLD

The mere physicality of records and CDs carries so much novelty today that it obscures the fact that people who bought plastic discs in the days before digital delivery did not, as a rule, buy them in order to own plastic discs. They got them to hear music. There were niceties in the physicality of records and CDs, for sure—the package art, the information on the record sleeves or CD booklets, the tactile pleasure in holding the objects, and the material pride in gazing at one's collection on a shelf. Yet those were all value-added qualities. The main reason to buy a record was to be able to hear a piece of music on your own terms, without having to wait for either a radio station to play what you wanted to hear or the artist to give a concert near you. Records and CDs were technologies of delivery, and the immediate, on-demand access to music they provided was their primary benefit.

In the earliest days of recording, record companies promoted the breadth of their offerings as a major selling point of the young medium. "New Victor Artists in Popular Field—List of Names Is Long

One," read the headline in an ad from the 1920s, showing an array of thirty-four photographs of varied musical acts, from the young contralto Marian Anderson to the ragtime duo of Noble Sissle and Eubie Blake, the hillbilly fiddler Eck Robertson, and the fox-trot dance band the Yale Collegians (featuring Rudy Vallee). "There is nothing stranger than human taste," read the body copy of the ad. "Take two compositions, or two organizations, of equal merit, and their partisans will divide themselves clearly. The big thing about the Victor repertoire is the satisfaction it brings to all musical needs and tastes."

Every subsequent technology for delivering music has brought with it new terms of delivery. When radios became small enough to be installed in cars, listening became mobile—and, in a way, more private, with car radios supplying background music not only for driving but also for parking. The lack of listener control over radio content, the commercials between songs, and the often spotty reception in some locations were liabilities offset by the experience of having music in the background, almost as if you were living in a movie. The transistor radio, as I've discussed, made listening more personal and private, a development advanced considerably by the invention of the Walkman and other portable cassette equipment. Because cassettes were recordable, the Walkman brought content control and personalization to private, mobile listening.

I got my first Walkman as a handout at the media event Sony staged to announce the product in 1979. I had just finished college and was working as an editor for a trade magazine, *Consumer Electronics Monthly*, while doing freelance writing for *The Village Voice*. Initially, the device was being marketed under the trademark Soundabout. Walkman, a term of politically incorrect Janglish, was Sony's trade name for the product in Japan. As the indelibly awkward term migrated east through people traveling between the countries, Sony abandoned the Soundabout name in America. (In the U.K., Sony called it the Stowaway.) Because the original model had no voice-recording ability and no speaker for playback, I thought of it at first as a bad version of a tape recorder, but as soon as I tried it on the street, playing music with headphones, I realized it was a much improved version of a transistor radio.

Like most of my friends and untold other music fans, I spent the 1980s with phones on my ears and a Walkman clipped to my belt, listening to mixtapes I had made by recording songs from records or FM-radio broadcasts or, eventually, from other cassettes, using a dual-cassette recorder. Mining every source of recordings at my disposal, sometimes borrowing hard-to-find jazz and original-cast albums from the Lincoln Center Library for the Performing Arts, I organized songs by theme and sequenced them on cassettes and neatly filled out the little J cards with the song titles and credits. One of the mixtapes I made was a "Plagiarism Mix" of songs that owed too-obvious debts to earlier compositions (the well known cases of George Harrison's "My Sweet Lord" and the Chiffons' "He's So Fine," and the Beach Boys' "Surfin' U.S.A." and Chuck Berry's "Sweet Little Sixteen"; as well as a couple of examples I had stumbled on myself: Woody Guthrie's "This Land Is Your Land" and the Carter Family's "When the World's on Fire," and John Lennon's "Happy Xmas (War Is Over)" and Peter, Paul, and Mary's arrangement of "Stewball"). Another mix was "Grouse On!," a collection of songs by rock stars complaining about how awful it is to be a rock star (the Who's "Success Story," the Byrds' "So You Want to Be a Rock 'n' Roll Star," David Bowie's "Fame," and such). As a gift for a woman I was trying to persuade to warm up to me, I made a whole tape of different versions of "My Funny Valentine." I don't know if she played it. We didn't talk much after that. I probably should have left off the Stan Kenton.

The home craft of making mixtapes was a geeky harbinger of the digital curatorship that would become central to the experience of music in the twenty-first century, when listeners would put together playlists from songs culled from the seemingly bottomless mine of materials online. The recordability of cassettes enacted, in a limited but prescient way, a transformation in the relationship between recorded music and its audience, members of which were now engaging creatively with the music, selecting tunes and organizing them in mixes. There was an element of authorship in the making of mixes—collections of things are copyrightable as creative works, after all. Just as in the sheet music era, when families used to play and sing the songs they purchased in their parlors, amateurs were treating professionally produced music as a resource for the making of something they could think of as their own.

The process of making cassette mixtapes was laborious, and their gift value was connected to the labor involved. The effort represented care. That said, it is too easy to romanticize the mechanics of cassette tape making. I would have much preferred to have had a faster, easier way to access music and curate it for sharing with my friends.

People were working on that, trying to figure out how to exploit the information-processing ability of computers for the sake of music. The first IBM Personal Computer had been introduced in 1981, followed by the Apple Macintosh in 1984. (Though I was no longer working for *Consumer Electronics Monthly*, I got invited to the press conference introducing the IBM PC. On the CBS News report on the event that night, I could be seen tapping something on a sample keyboard and looking dumbstruck.) There was a vague assumption among people interested in both computers and music that the new machines might eventually be of use for some purpose other than keeping a database of your record collection.

Among the first of those known to have conceptualized a scheme resembling the way music would be delivered in the twenty-first century was a young Briton named Kane Kramer, a high-level tinkerer who in the early 1980s made some progress developing a handheld digital audio player with the ability to retrieve songs over phone lines from a hypothetical data bank. In 1979, when he was twenty-three, Kramer made concept designs of the device, collaborating with a friend, James Campbell, who was twenty-one, and proposed it to investors. According to Kramer, one of the first backers was Paul

McCartney. In 1981, Kramer filed for a patent for the technology, and it was granted in 1987. Kramer had essentially invented the iPod, as Apple's attorneys would later acknowledge. Unfortunately, he did so before the Internet was established as a global system of instant communication. Kramer's idea, however inspired, would not make practical sense until the rise of the World Wide Web in the early 1990s and the invention of the MP3 as a standard of data compression in the same period.

The Web established a framework for the distribution of digital material of all kinds, and home computers provided the means to access it. The only problem was a sizable one, and the matter of size was, in fact, the problem: it was impractically time-consuming to send the enormous files required for music storage over the Internet. Music, like every type of sound, could be translated into the ones and zeros of digital data by sampling the sound waves at micro-tiny intervals and assigning a number to each point in the sampling process. But the procedure generated so many ones and zeros that it would take more than an hour to send the data for a three-minute song across the Web by phone lines in the early 1990s.

The solution was a technique developed primarily by Karlheinz Brandenburg, a bubbly and fiercely intelligent German engineer who, in the late 1980s, was studying how the ear and the mind work in union to perceive sound. For his Ph.D. dissertation, Brandenburg looked at the phenomenon known in the field of psychoacoustics as auditory masking, meaning the way some sounds drown out or distract us from other sounds being made at the same time. You're watching TV, and your phone rings, and you miss a few words of dialogue in the show. The sound of the dialogue you missed still existed, but because you didn't perceive it, it could just as well have been edited out of the broadcast, and you would never have noticed. Brandenburg, building on his dissertation as part of a German group of engineers called the Fraunhofer Society, worked out a way to take advantage of that quirk in human perception, eliminating sounds from recordings that most people wouldn't hear anyway, thus reducing the size of digital music files. The team presented the technique for use by an organization called the Motion Picture Experts Group, because its charge was to shrink the size of digital files well enough for full movies to be sent over the Internet, and the system of audio compression it developed, the MPEG Audio Layer III, became better known as the MP3.

Typically described as compression, the process is really one of strategic excision. It relies on determinations Brandenburg and his colleagues made about what kinds of sounds and how much of them could be removed (either wholly or partially, by reproducing some sounds less fully than others) without most people sensing that something was lost. If the average listener sat down and did a careful comparison of the same recording of the same song as it sounded on (*a*) a CD and (*b*) an MP3, the difference would probably be apparent. Heard independently, though, an MP3 sounds all right. More to the point, in the view of many people in the music audience, the convenience an MP3 provides by making it as easy to exchange a song electronically as it is to send a text message more than compensates for the compromised sound quality. From Edison cylinders through the whole history of recorded music, sound quality has always been a matter of compromise. The main point of any delivery technology, for listeners, has been the access it offers, and nothing has ever made more music more accessible to more people than the MP3.

It was first popularized, notoriously, through the trading of songs by college students through the early file-sharing network Napster. The system was founded in the summer of 1999 by Shawn Fanning, an eighteen-year-old computer science student who had just dropped out of Northeastern; his thirty-five-year-old uncle, John Fanning, the organization's moneyman and token grown-up; and Sean Parker, a nineteen-year-old whom Shawn Fanning had befriended on the Internet, bonding over chats about theoretical physics. The title of the service, Napster, was Shawn Fanning's nickname in high school, given for the nappy way his curly hair tended to look. It had nothing to do with napping, though the image of being caught dozing would end up serving neatly as a symbol of how Napster found the music industry.

There had been earlier networks for distributing digital files of music and other materials by way of the Internet—Usenet, Hotline, and others long forgotten now. Napster's difference was its use of the data-skimping MP3 as a file format. By February 2001, the network had more than twenty-six million users around the world, many of them students using their first computers. More significantly, they were among the first students ever to be using computers. They were not merely learning what digital technology could do but inventing digital culture, and one of the main things they learned—and invented—was the notion that music should be free.

The music business, being a business, was accustomed to having people pay for its products. Confronted with spiraling CD sales, a consortium of record labels brought suit against Napster for facilitating copyright infringement and won in a ruling by the Ninth Circuit Court of Appeals in February 2001. Napster folded, though the name would later resurface as the trademark for a paid-downloading service. Peer-to-peer file sharing would continue in the legally dubious gray patches of the Web, and the act of taking music from the Internet without payment would come to be talked about as piracy—nothing so crude as *stealing*, but something more romantic with the aura of costumed swashbucklers in the Caribbean.

Digitization did not really bring immateriality to popular music for the first time. Music has been disseminated in immaterial form since the invention of radio. As wondrous as it would be for people everywhere to be connected wirelessly through computers on Wi-Fi, it was the revolutionary extent of that connectedness, not the fact of its wirelessness, that was news for music. Radio had been referred to as "the wireless" in Edison's time. The wide and instant connectedness possible through digital communication made the exchange of music (and everything else that could be digitized) so easy that the value of the music came to be measured by the frequency of its exchange.

Since Marx, the idea of exchange value had had to do with how the perceived worth of a thing changes through a sale; with digital music, the value was contained in the exchange itself. Nothing needed to be sold at all.

The ephemeral nature of all digital content, along with the virtually limitless quantity of it on the Web, conspired to diminish the value of digitized music in the public consciousness. What does one have, exactly, when one has a digital file? Music, reduced to data, becomes an abstraction harder to grasp than sound waves. At a loud dance club, you can feel the sound from the speakers pulse through your body from fifty feet away. Even the invisible air has a palpable physicality that makes it real to us. Digital data has . . . what? Nothing we can sense or touch as it flits around the virtual universe from database to device to device and we use it or share it or store it or ignore it. Digital data, in the way most of us tend to conceive of it, is a kind of nothingness, and we attach the appropriate value to it: none.

With the introduction by Apple of the iTunes Music Store for purchasing music, two years after the collapse of Napster, Apple institutionalized a pricing structure that fixed a monetary value on digital music: $.99 for a single song (at first, later $1.29), $9.99 for an album, more for releases of extended lengths and other special cases. In its first week in business, the iTunes Music Store reported selling more than one million songs, and musicians, producers, and music label people exhaled. "Nobody was going to pay for digital music, seriously, until somebody was selling it seriously," said Roger Ames, chairman and CEO of Warner Music, one of the five major labels contracted with the iTunes Music Store at the time.

By decreeing that digital music would now cost something, Apple asserted that it was worth something, and the act of using the iTunes Music Store was enough like traditional shopping to provide users with the satisfactions of acquisition and ownership. Searching through the site's offerings by genre or artist name, perhaps clicking to hear a short sample of a song, constituted a much more efficient method of browsing for music than thumbing through the discs in a record bin, even if its very efficiency precluded the serendipity of discovery that vinyl shoppers sentimentalize. You paid for a digital track and then saw it appear in your iTunes folder. You could listen to it as often as you'd like, use it in playlists, duplicate it, or e-mail it to someone else as an attachment. The file was your property—much like a record, however ephemeral.

Not all people care about such things, of course. For all the material benefits of ownership, a great many if not most music lovers are still more interested in having access to music than in having music in their possession. The popularity of music streaming services in the second decade of the twenty-first century makes this clear. YouTube, introduced two years after the iTunes Music Store as a platform for sharing homemade video clips, indoctrinated the world in the benefits of streaming before the word had come into common use. Why pay for works of entertainment, whether they're videos or song clips— or even go through the effort of downloading them for free and collecting them—if you can enjoy what you want whenever you feel like it, in real time on YouTube?

Within a few years of its launch, YouTube had become a repository for millions of songs of nearly every sort—obscurities and current hits, bootlegs, live recordings, demos, and everything else that YouTube users got their hands on and felt like sharing—uploaded in listenable if less than hi-fi sound quality. A considerable amount of this material appears on YouTube illegally, because it is against the law to upload copyrighted songs to a public forum without the permission of the copyright holder. Unfortunately for the music's creators, as well as for the integrity of intellectual property rights in general, the monolithic power of YouTube is such that it does whatever it wants. By 2007, YouTube was using as much digital bandwidth as the entire Internet had used in the year 2000.

Subscription services for streaming music, such as Spotify, Apple Music, and SoundCloud, have sought a ground somewhere between selling songs and albums on a one-by-one basis, as iTunes does, and making everything available for free, as YouTube does. I have subscribed to Spotify since the week it was introduced in the United States in July 2011, and I signed up for Apple Music on the day it began, in June 2015. I still pay for a lot of music, buying at least one or two albums every week, typically as downloads but sometimes on vinyl or CD. I even buy 45 rpm singles and 78s on occasion, because I have both a 45 jukebox and a windup Victrola in my house. But I use Spotify on and off all day, almost every day, and I feel horribly guilty for doing so, knowing that songwriters are being inadequately remunerated by Spotify for my use of their work. (I write songs myself, most often as a lyricist collaborating with composers; as a member of ASCAP, I receive a modest payment of royalties on a quarterly basis for radio play and performances of my songs in concerts.) Using Spotify on my phone, listening with earbuds, I crank the sound up loud enough to drown out my conscience and console myself with the delusion that my commitment to purchasing CDs and vinyl, in small numbers, somehow compensates for my gluttonous consumption of streaming music for next to nothing.

At a symposium on copyright and the arts at the Columbia University Law School in 2014, the president of the Songwriters Association of Canada, Eddie Schwartz, provided some unsettling data on streaming. By his calculations, the writer of a song that sold a million records (in the form of CDs, vinyl albums, and cassettes) in the year 2000 would have earned approximately forty-five thousand dollars—"middle-class economic status," in his words. By comparison, a songwriter who had a composition streamed a million times in 2015 would make about thirty-five dollars—enough, Schwartz said, for "a pretty good pizza— maybe an extra-large with a couple of toppings."

The failings of its revenue structure for creative artists are not the only liabilities of streaming in my experience. The act of listening by streaming changes the music for me. In a literal sense, first, the music itself is altered. The severely compressed character of streaming audio—light and thin and metallic—is not well suited to some of the music I love best, such as the early acoustic recordings of Joni Mitchell. (Streaming actually befits Mitchell's late-period synth-infused albums, which Elvis Costello once described as "the aural equivalent of being trapped in a Chinese restaurant.") When I'm using Spotify, I find myself playing more contemporary pop than I would otherwise listen to. On the morning I wrote this, for instance, I noticed a new single by Carly Rae Jepsen, "Your Type," hyped on the New Release section on Spotify. I gave it a listen, and its icy, synthetic Europop production seemed perfectly appropriate for streaming.

It would be easy but inaccurate to say that the degradation of sound quality in recordings of popular music since the rise of the MP3 and the proliferation of handheld devices and earbuds, exacerbated by the compression employed by the most successful streaming services, has degraded the quality of popular music. Rather, it has made pop music sound *different* today—not necessarily lesser, but surely not the same as music produced for listening through speakers on hi-fi stereo sound systems. If it's designed properly, music geared for being downloaded or exchanged as MP3s or streamed for listening with buds plugged into your phone uses the narrower dynamic range, the limited frequency response, and the essential, inescapable *electronicness* of digital delivery as well as music of the stereo-gear era used hi-fi sound. Among the reasons for the prominence of Scandinavian producers, the musical descendants of ABBA, in contemporary pop is the companionability of their aesthetic and contemporary delivery technology. The chirpy, blissfully artificial music made by producers such as Max Martin, the whiz behind Taylor Swift's 2014 album, *1989*, is music created for digital delivery. The fact that Swift declined Apple Music's overtures at first, holding out for a better offer— sipping her drink, sitting sideways at the bar—shows only that she and streaming were truly made for each other.

If streaming is responsible for a certain degradation, it is one of public tastes and expectations. The problem is an unexpected consequence of having an almost inconceivably vast amount of music available at any time, and it has some precedent in YouTube. When everything seems to be available, the value of each thing shrinks; I should emphasize "seems," because vastness is not completeness, and great quantities of great music are not yet available for streaming. The process of purchasing something—weighing the options, applying critical standards (however vague they may be in one's mind), gambling or trusting one's tastes, and making the small sacrifice of spending a bit of money—instills a commitment to the purchase. I remember buying the album *Hejira* in 1976, to use the example of Joni Mitchell again, and finding it tuneless and confusing. But, damn it, I spent a whole seven dollars on the thing. So I stuck with it, hoping to find a way to appreciate it and get my money's worth. Within a few days, I did, and my taste expanded in the process.

Today, I skip around Spotify while I'm on the subway or walking down the street, and when I find myself hearing something I don't much like, I click out of it and listen to something else, because countless alternatives are always a click away. Tastes broaden and sometimes improve through both exposure to art of many kinds, something streaming facilitates, and commitment to individual works, particularly the ones most challenging, which streaming fights against. Spotify and Apple Music, through their easy and instantaneous access to more options than we can indulge, inhibits perseverance and impedes challenge. They're super-easy and fast and put a universe of music in your hands, and all that comes at a price dearer than free.

As we download and stream and share music files, we're well attuned to the importance of digital technology in the popular music experience today. At the same time, we may not recognize how profoundly digitization is affecting the music we hear, because we're not supposed to hear all its effects. Among the most pervasive uses of digital tech in both recording studios and concert halls is one intended not to be noticed: the electronic manipulation of the oldest musical instrument, the human voice, by means of Auto-Tune.

The ur-text of Auto-Tune—the narrative that established the use of technology for pitch correction as a key to popular success and a nexus of ethical debate—actually predates the digital age by half a century. That text is *Singin' in the Rain*, the movie musical produced for MGM by Arthur Freed, the Tin Pan Alley tunesmith turned production unit chief, in 1952. Set on the cusp of the silent and sound eras, the film pokes gentle, toe-tapping fun at Hollywood's first panic at the prospect of technological change—a crisis embodied in the character of Lina Lamont, a shrewish, cellophane-haired silent-movie queen who can barely speak in English sentences, let alone sing on key, as she needs to do to meet the demands of the new all-talking, all-singing pictures. Technology, having started the problem, provides a nettlesome solution as Donald O'Connor hatches a scheme to have a perky unknown with a pretty voice, Kathy Selden (played by a nineteen-year-old Debbie Reynolds), dub Lamont's voice offscreen. Lamont mouths the words to "You Are My Lucky Star," and the movie audience within the movie hears Debbie Reynolds trilling sweetly in perfect intonation—until the unraveling of things in the happy ending, when O'Connor and his pals literally pull the curtain on the scam. The good girl, who can really sing, triumphs over the bad one, who had betrayed the public with electronic trickery.

Since the late 1990s, digital sound processing has made pitch correction possible without the necessity of hiding Debbie Reynolds. The technology commonly referred to as Auto-Tune (the brand name for the first and best known of several software programs for the manipulation of pitch, tone, and other aspects of sound) does Reynolds's work with improved efficiency and flexibility, if less perkiness. Meanwhile, most of the discourse on the use of technology to fix the sound for off-tune singing has the same thematic content as an old movie musical. The natural voice stands for virtue; technology, vice. Vocal technique—specifically, the skill sufficient to produce notes in accord with the twelve-tone tempered scale—is perceived as legitimizing. Digital processing, when employed to accomplish something that used to be the exclusive domain of living beings, is taken as a cheat. More than sixty years after MGM's Technicolor vindication of vocal and moral purity in the form of Kathy Selden, undoctored singing would still be thought of as right as the rain that splashed around Gene Kelly's tap shoes. Yet, just like manufactured showers, that conception is more complicated than it appears.

Invented as an afterthought, the by-product of research in a related field, Auto-Tune was developed by Harold Hildebrand, a onetime engineer for Exxon, as an outgrowth of his research in the analysis of seismic data for the purpose of finding oil. The quasi-accidental nature of Auto-Tune's origin makes for a cute story, one that puts the invention broadly in the company of the transistor, Teflon, the microwave oven, and the Frisbee, while offsetting any suspicion of Machiavellian intent on the part of Hildebrand, who left Exxon to start the company that introduced and still markets Auto-Tune. (Founded as Jupiter Systems in 1990, the firm would later be renamed Antares Audio Technologies.) Hildebrand, an amateur flutist who got his undergraduate education on a music scholarship and later earned a Ph.D. in electrical engineering, goes by the nickname Andy and likes to be called Dr. Andy, in the manner of a self-help author or pediatric dentist. In interviews, he gives Auto-Tune a sagely public face, talking with noncritical affection for both music and technology, shrugging off ethical questions with folksy humor. "Well, I don't know if it's bad or good," Hildebrand said in an interview with *The Seattle Times*. "I'm not a judge of that. It's very popular, so in that sense it's good. I don't place value judgments on things like that. Someone asked me at one point in time if I thought that Auto-Tune was evil. I said, 'Well, my wife wears make-up. Is that evil?' And yeah, in some circles that is evil. But in most circles, it's not."

To the extent that use is a measure of popularity, Hildebrand is correct about Auto-Tune. (Attitudes are a different kind of measure, because users of things can have mixed feelings about the things they use.) Auto-Tune is a fixture in popular music in the twenty-first century, employed far more widely than most people probably realize. There are no hard statistics to quantify the use of digital pitch correction; Antares has declined to release its sales figures, and so has its main competitor, the German company Celemony, which calls its software Melodyne. In recording studios, pitch correction tends to be employed discreetly, if not surreptitiously, to preserve the reputation of singers. Each day, meanwhile, less and less pop recording takes place in the foam-padded studios of the old-paradigm record industry, and more and more is done in private, at home, with laptop software. Pitch-correction plug-ins are all but standard accessories for home recording as the old lines between professionalism and amateurism, vocation and avocation, dissolve. The physics are simple: the lower the singers' levels of skill, experience, and/or talent, the greater the utility of Auto-Tune. The fact that one can or cannot sing no longer has much bearing on whether one will or will not.

When most of us think of Auto-Tune, the sound we likely conjure in our minds is not the sound Auto-Tune provides on the pitch-corrected hits that have filled the pop charts since the first decade of the twenty-first century. We probably think of the novelty uses of pitch correction that first brought Auto-Tune attention and made it the subject of some controversy. As I write this, it is more than fifteen years now since Cher and her producers pushed Auto-Tune past its safety settings on the single "Believe," producing that quavering, metallic chipmunk sound—"the Cher effect"—that established Auto-Tune as a gimmick. Over the years since, dozens of acts prominent in pop and hip-hop have followed Cher and pushed Auto-Tune further for conspicuous effect or stunt purpose: Lil Wayne, with his juvenile fantasy of cheap sex, "Lollipop"; the Black Eyed Peas, with their unctuously catchy "Boom Boom Pow"; Kanye West, almost approaching irony with the plastic crooning on "Heartless"; Daft Punk, the electronic dance music duo, with their spacey "One More Time"; T-Pain on "Buy U a Drank" and twenty or thirty other tracks that wallow in Auto-Tune as an aural equivalent to the extravagant excesses in his lyrics; Rihanna, exulting in multiple modes of disorientation on "Disturbia"; and Ke$ha, whose voice gains most of its character from the electronic aura imposed by Auto-Tune—a digital essence that neatly inverts Walter Benjamin's formulation to give electronic creations an aura nonexistent in life.

None of the music I just mentioned has much to do with the way Auto-Tune has come to dominate contemporary pop, however. Since the rise and decline of Auto-Tune as a mere gimmick, digital pitch correction has pervaded recorded music, but in a way more significant and even creepier than "Buy U a Drank": in stealth. If we don't think of Auto-Tune when we hear the pop songs wafting around the shampoo aisle as we shop, that's just because we don't recognize it. We don't hear what we're hearing. As Dr. Andy has explained in an online interview, he intended his invention to be imperceptible, and it is to most ears, most of the time. "Auto-Tune can be used very gently to nudge a note more accurately into tune," Hildebrand says. "In these applications, it is impossible for skilled producers, musicians, or algorithms to determine that Auto-Tune has been used."

What does it mean to say that someone "can sing"?

My wife, the singer Karen Oberlin, is a third-generation musician. Her parents met at Tanglewood when they were both playing in a youth orchestra under Zubin Mehta. Karen's paternal grandparents were vaudeville performers who sang and played light classics and comedy songs on the Chautauqua circuit. Karen and I have an adolescent son, and since he was in preschool, his teachers have been telling us the kid has musical talent. But what are they saying, exactly?

As I just suggested by relaying that family history, it's natural to think of musical ability as naturally ingrained, a gift—something endowed, if not by genetic inheritance, then by God. There's evidence of the inheritability of artistic talent in gene research, and there's a case for the divine in every concert review that describes a piece of music as transcendent or miraculous. Most of us likely have some faith that creative skills (in music or any of the arts) can be learned, to some degree, or developed through training and experience. Without such belief, where would the M.F.A. industry be? Still, the Nietzschean conception of talent as a natural endowment—and more than that, a supernatural one—persists, dressed up now in DNA lingo. This line of thinking underlies the widespread contempt for Auto-Tune as an extra-natural method of accomplishing what should supposedly come naturally, and it helps preserve our enduringly romantic conception of artists as special creatures, anointed or made differently from the rest of us. We resent Auto-Tune not so much because it's nonhuman—we put our faith (and, increasingly, our affection) in electronic devices every day—as because the power it applies, in providing a way to sing in perfect intonation, seems superhuman and, in practice, indiscriminate. Auto-Tune defies the myth of the creative gift.

To say someone can sing suggests a physical endowment, as well as a metaphysical one, though technology has influenced the physical process of singing in the past. When my wife's grandmother performed "Under the Greenwood Tree" onstage in Pittsburgh, part of the proof that she could sing was her ability to project her voice from the footlights to the balcony, as Olive Fremstad or Al Jolson could. As I discussed in an earlier chapter, that ability to project became an irrelevance, if not a liability, after the invention of the microphone and electronic amplification, along with the development of radio and records. The microphone, in a sense, was the Auto-Tune of its day, doing for amplitude what Hildebrand's invention has done for pitch.

Yet the analogy between the mic and pitch correction is imprecise—or perhaps still incomplete. With the microphone, singers did not simply sing quietly and sound loud; they sang differently from Fremstad, Jolson, and the song belters of the proscenium era. In the electronic age, singers learned to work more intimately, conversationally, sensually, and subtly, establishing a new set of aesthetic standards for pop vocalists. Auto-Tune has not much changed the way singers sing, though it may well end up doing so in ways I cannot foresee. Digital pitch correction is a technology more active than the microphone; rather than capturing a singer's voice, passively, it alters it, raising or lowering the tone to match the settings on the controls. It is, indeed, all about control—specifically, about conforming strictly to a traditional standard of correctness, the Western tempered scale.

There, to me, lies the tyranny of Auto-Tune. To say that someone can sing can mean simply that the person can sing on key, and it is elementally important to hit the right notes. The trouble with Auto-Tune is that it applies too rigid a definition of rightness. It has the ability to adjust every tone with unyielding precision, squarely in the mathematical center of the note. But no one sings that way—not even the world's most esteemed opera singers. In every form of vocal music, the scale is a framework for expressive interpretation, not a system of regimentation. What it means to say that someone can sing, above all, is that the person can communicate the content of the words and music, and emotional expression, in vocal music, involves the deft, intelligent manipulation of pitch. A skilled singer knows how to shade a moment in a song by, say, hovering near the bottom of a note—within the note, in tune, but just below the center of the tone. A great blues singer may use three chords but find countless possibilities for tonal variation in a single note. The music, the art, is contained in those variations. Billie Holiday, processed through Auto-Tune, would have all the soul of Siri.

It's easy to see the problem with the "auto" in Auto-Tune. Automation is by definition not human; still, automation is merely a method of production, and even automated music can be interesting intellectually. Music is sound, and I can think of no sound quite as oppressive as the systematic execution of technical perfection. Auto-Tune, by making every song perfectly correct, makes every song wrong.

More than being correct, music has to sound right, and to this date few works in any art exemplify the distinction between reality and perception better than *Singin' in the Rain*. After all, when Kathy Selden is dubbing for the voice of Lina Lamont and we hear the sound of Debbie Reynolds crooning "You Are My Lucky Star," we aren't really hearing Debbie Reynolds. We are actually hearing a ghost singer named Betty Noyes, who dubbed Reynolds's voice, without credit.

Some years ago, I learned about this at a press event for one of the video releases of the film, and Reynolds was on hand for pictures and a few questions. When the subject of Noyes's once-secret dubbing came up, Reynolds smiled her Kathy Selden smile and said, "Oh—my singing was too good to use."

The spark for the idea to do a Donna Summer song at CBGB seems to have come from West Berlin in the summer of 1977, half a year before the Blitz Benefit, when David Bowie and Brian Eno were recording Bowie's *Heroes* album, with Robert Fripp playing guitar. Eno, once a funk music hater who wore a button that said "Join the Fight Against Funk," had recently reformed and had started raving about Parliament/Funkadelic and its sensational bassist, Bootsy Collins. As Bowie would remember, he was working in the recording studio when "Eno came running in and said, 'I have heard the sound of the future.'" Eno put the Donna Summer record of "I Feel Love" on the studio turntable. "Eno had gone bonkers over it, absolutely bonkers," Bowie recalled. "He said, 'This is it, look no further. This single is going to change the sound of club music for the next fifteen years.'"

Eno was wrong, we now know. The hypnotic, all-electronic synthesized pulsing of "I Feel Love" changed the sound of club music for more than thirty years, and its influence spread far beyond the relatively insular club culture of the 1970s and 1980s. By the end of the first decade of the twenty-first century, electronic dance music had become the new rock and roll. By the term, I refer to a whole class of musics comprising dozens of styles and sub-styles and sub-sub-styles of work, from the decades-old genres of house and techno music to their younger offshoots, dubstep and dub techno, to a stunning variety of splinter styles, including Rotterdam techno and cosmic disco. As a class, this music falls under the general heading of electronica, not only because it is made by electronic means, often entirely by computer, but also because it's intended to evoke the electronic realm; it's made with electronics to sound like electronics.

As rock and roll once did, electronica dominates the soundtrack of social life for young adults, though it's far from the only music for hooking up today. Brooklyn still has blocks full of bars with bands playing live music, including old-fashioned rock—and jazz and old-timey music and salsa—on instruments other than MacBooks. Electronica, in varied forms, permeates the big dance clubs, as it has for years, and plays also now in the arenas and on the festival grounds where, just a couple of seasons ago, one would see lots of bearded guys with accordions. Meanwhile, strains of electronica not geared for dancing have been flourishing as downloads for people, one by one, to take in with earbuds or headphones, and there is a meaningful distinction here between the essentially passive act of *taking in*, which is appropriate to this vein of electronica, and *listening* in the traditional, more active sense of hearing with close attention. Electronica, the sound of our time, has much in common with the earliest known music, the accompaniment to ancient ritual: neither was made just for listening.

"If you're 15 to 25 years old now, this is your rock and roll," Michael Rapino, head of the event promotion company Live Nation, told a reporter for *The New York Times*. As a promoter, Rapino was basically matching a category of customers to a classification of product, though he was getting at something more interesting. To relate electronica to rock and roll is to apply a historical pattern to the new music. One generation's rock and roll is, more than anything, a music that veterans of the preceding generation do not like, approve of, or grasp. My parents' rock and roll was swing. Their parents' rock and roll was Dixieland, whose fans the swing kids derided as "moldy figs." I like to describe myself as a product of the punk era, though that's mainly posturing. When I was in my early twenties, I really loved disco but was too insecure among the crowd I knew at CBGB to admit it. Disco was my secret rock and roll. Electronica certainly qualifies as a counterpart to the many past styles of popular music whose successes seemed largely predicated on their ability to confound and alienate old-timers. In that sense, electronica is almost quaintly traditional.

While rock is essentially a vocal music, electronica is concerned with absolute sound; it uses the human voice—often heavily processed and manipulated, when it's used at all—as one of innumerable sources of tonal effects employed in service to the groove and the mood. While rock takes the song as its standard form, electronica seems, but is not really, formless. It's elliptical; it's built on repetition, through which variations can occur so subtly that unconditioned ears might not hear them. Rock has earthiness; electronica, atmosphere. Rock is descended from Louis Jordan and Little Richard and before them the blues. Electronica's grandparents are Stockhausen and Cage, their antecedents the abstractionists of the early modern era.

Notionally, as a proposition that new methods of production can help liberate music from the ostensible tyranny of melody and harmony imposed by traditional instrumentation, electronica has roots in the polemical musings of Ferruccio Busoni, the Italian composer and teacher who wrote the prescient "Sketch of a New Esthetic of Music" in 1907. Calling for vaguely conceived challenges to ingrained musical conventions, above all those of the Western tempered scale, Busoni proposed that technology could have value in music making before much technology had been devised for the purpose. "Music was born free, and to win freedom is its destiny," Busoni wrote in language as intemperate as the scales he dreamed of. "We have formulated rules, stated principles, laid down laws; we apply laws made for maturity to a child that knows nothing of responsibility! [Music's] state is one of development, perhaps the very first stage of a development beyond present conception, and we talk of 'classics' and 'hallowed traditions'! I almost think that in the new great music, machines will also be necessary and will be assigned a share in it."

The rhetoric of aesthetic liberation, entwined with a utopian-futurist idealization of machinery conspicuously at odds with Adorno, followed electronic music as it traveled over the course of the twentieth century from the imaginings of theorists to the labs of the Princeton and Columbia Music Departments to the dance clubs of Chicago and Detroit. In the words of George Lewis, a current-day composer who has produced a body of serious-minded works of music with his laptop, "The history of electronic music—in fact, the history of the avant-garde, to a certain degree—is a history of artists getting their hands on something new—it could be a computer, it could be almost anything—and saying, 'Well, this is interesting. I wonder if I can change the *rules* with this.'"

Contemporary electronica has obvious precedents in both house music (the hard-throbbing, minimalist dance music first developed at the Warehouse, a gay club in Chicago, during the late 1970s and early 1980s) and techno (the more sonically complex, multilayered dance music that emerged in Detroit sometime around the mid-1980s). Each of these styles offered, in its essence, an embedded critique of the mainstream music of its day and the culture that supported it. House music, in its primal relentless and carnal muscularity, was the near antithesis of the dozy Southern California folk-pop all over the radio, and it provided overnight fuel for the gay awakening of the post-Stonewall period. Techno, developed in the birthplace of Motown Records for an emerging generation of African Americans and Latinos, took its name from an Alvin Toffler book and rejected the romantic smoothness of R&B for a command of digital effects that demonstrated a kind of prowess more technical, more cerebral, than physical.

"The Detroit underground has been experimenting with technology, stretching it rather than simply using it," said Juan Atkins, who produced one of the first important techno tracks, "No UFOs," under the name of Model 500. "Basically, we're tired of hearing about being in love or falling out, tired of the R&B system, so a new progressive sound has emerged."

Over the decades since, as house music and techno evolved into (typically) denser, (often) slower, and (sometimes) moodier styles, electronica's historical identity as a music for dancers—and gay, black, and Latino ones, at that—seems not to have helped its reputation in the pop music establishment. *Rolling Stone* and *Spin* largely ignored electronic dance music for decades, and the Grammys gave it little more than token attention as a specialty category until 2012, when Skrillex, a half-decent but not great electronica composer and performer who has a rock-star aura, received five Grammy nominations. (He won three, for Best Dance Recording, Best Dance/Electronica Album, and Best Remixed Recording, Non-classical, but lost Best New Artist to Bon Iver, the emo-ish indie band that had been recording for four or five years by then.)

Among the marvels of electronica is the sheer number of subgenres that the genre accommodates: ambient house, illbient, Baltimore club, funky breaks, liquid funk, folktronica, breakcore, cybergrind—literally hundreds, as well as I can count them. Many are defined so narrowly, down to the acceptable number of beats per minute and the beat on which a snare sound may occur, that a deviation does not constitute a variation, but calls for a new subgenre name. Dubstep, for instance, employs a syncopated rhythm of 138 to 142 bpm, with a snare sound acceptable on the third beat of the bar. Wind down to 130 bpm, and you have post-dubstep. The regimentation within this system of classification may be matched only by the rules of harmony in the Western tempered scale from which Busoni looked to machines for liberation.

Electronic dance music has grown more and more listenable— indeed, more cerebral, not that that has made it better by the standards of the dance floor. A whole school of electronic music for use with earbuds has been flourishing under the names of chill-out, ambient, or trance. Much of this work is related to dub techno, which grew out of dubstep, which emerged after house music and techno traveled from the urban Midwest of the United States to Britain and got mixed up with Eurodisco and the stylized German intellectualism of Kraftwerk. Andy Stott, a dub techno producer out of Manchester, started making especially strong music in the school of electronica for listening—meticulous but unfussy, serious but unpretentious collages of processed voices, sounds, and effects.

One can appreciate the high achievement of his work without fully accepting the narrative cliché of pop music migration, in which important styles of music are born among disenfranchised Americans and end up in Britain, inflated and prettified as art music. After all, the techno that Juan Atkins helped invent in Detroit was profoundly artful—original and immeasurably influential, as well as danceable. Techno didn't need a Briton to turn it into art.

Some people I respect can't accept EDM. A friend and colleague of mine, a former editor at *Spin*, finds the repetitions tedious and the lack of words unsatisfying. But he's applying inappropriate standards. The history of other kinds of music, jazz in particular, suggests that electronic dance music, being dance music, is susceptible to long-standing biases against work whose first mission is to engage the body rather than the mind.

In 1996, I went to the ninety-fourth birthday party for the alto saxophonist Benny Waters, for a magazine piece I was writing. Waters got to reminiscing about his early days in the New York jazz scene, in the 1920s, when he played with King Oliver, and he said, "There was a lot of criticism of what we were doing. 'It's all just a beat. There's no melody.'" The parallel to electronic dance music—and to hip-hop, as well—is glaring in this fable: the music was thought of as limited, if not dangerous, because it seemed best at inducing movement rather than thought. As Waters went on to explain, critics of the jazz he made with Oliver soon caught on to the fact that the music had a "real lot more than meets the eye"—or the feet: it offered gratifications for both the body and the mind. But this moral applies to only some electronic dance music—to the techno of Juan Atkins and Richie Hawtin, for sure, and even more so to the broody music made through dubbing (dub techno) by artists such as Deadbeat and Andy Stott. And the lesson is a limited one, in that it denies the legitimacy of the physical and the value of the power to stir a person to dance. It's not for nothing that we say, when music affects us deeply, in our bones, that the music *moves* us. A great deal of high-quality electronic dance music—the work of Machinedrum or Derrick Carter and Mark Farina, for instance—derives its quality from its utility, from its usefulness as an inducement to movement. If we stopped to think about the music, we would be stopping, and the music would have failed—not simply as a form of expression, but as a stimulus to personal expression through dance.

CODA

By the middle of the second decade of the twenty-first century, my youngest son, Nate, was almost exactly the age I had been when I had walked to the Gateway diner to meet the only songwriter in the north Jersey factory town where I was raised. Nate has grown up in the Morningside Heights area of Manhattan, in housing provided by Columbia University, where I teach. It's a factory town, too. He has been exposed to music of many kinds, his mother being a punk rocker turned jazz singer, his father a music critic, his older brother and sister both millennial musical polyglots, and many of the parents of his friends involved in music and the arts. Several years ago, when Nate first saw *Santa Claus Is Comin' to Town*, the animated Christmas special from 1970, he noticed that the train conductor in the show has the same voice as Fred Astaire. Starting at the age of twelve and a half, he became, appropriately, obsessed with the commercial pop hits produced for young people of his generation. Somewhere in his head, I am sure, he has a sense that the Fred Astaire recordings for Verve Records that his mother and I play in the house were once something that had somehow been considered popular. But he really doesn't care about that, because the matter seems to have no bearing on the music he loves. The songs Nate compiles in his Apple Music playlists and plays so loudly in his earbuds that I can hear them without having to stream them myself—"Don't Tell 'Em" by Jeremih (featuring YG), "Somebody" by Natalie La Rose (featuring Jeremih), "Money and the Power" by Kid Ink—are precious to him because they belong to him and his friends. The music is theirs and all theirs, by intent and design.

Listening to the music Nate loves through earbuds of my own, I've heard quite a bit that sounds duly jarring to my ears. As it always does, popular music is acting today as a for-profit laboratory of both social and aesthetic experimentation, a place where young people can take up and try out notions that challenge the values of their parents. Just as the fox-trot helped break down barriers of Victorian propriety, putting strangers in each other's arms, and just as rock and roll advanced an exultant image of integration during the rise of the civil rights movement, contemporary pop has been playing a part in the much-talked-about transformation of social and sexual habits of young—and ever-younger—people. The pop hits of the early twenty-first century are the soundtrack of the hookup culture, in which sex has a much different place in social life—or in the way social life is broadly conceived—than it had in the past. Instead of dating in hopes of growing close and, before too long, having sex, strangers meet and have sex and, over time, maybe grow closer and maybe not, rarely going on old-style dates until they're committed in exclusive relationships. That's the sexual paradigm of the pop music world of Nate's generation. It's explicit in songs like "Tik Tok," by Ke$ha, which opens with the singer waking up in a stranger's place and brushing her teeth with Jack Daniel's; "Drunk in Love," by Beyoncé, which has her waking up in a kitchen and asking, "How the hell did this shit happen?"; and "Sex in the Lounge," by Nicki Minaj, which is about what it says.

Of course, a great deal of popular music has always been fixed on sex, if only by association with romance or in code language about dancing. A lot of the love that songs have sold has been sex by other names. Some tunes, such as "What's Love Got to Do with It?" by Tina Turner and "Ain't Talkin' 'bout Love" by Van Halen, were unabashedly more concerned with eros than amore, and plenty of hits of the past were bluntly about nothing other than pure fucking: "Let's Get It On," by Marvin Gaye, "That's the Way (I Like It)," by K.C. and the Sunshine Band, and, long before them, as I discussed earlier, the bawdy-mama numbers of the vaudeville blues queens. There are a couple of differences today, though: one, the high quotient of songs glorying in sex without romance, relative to the number of more traditional love songs; another, the widespread portrayal of sex partners as interchangeable parts in a scheme of endless, unfixed possibilities. Any night out could lead to any number of hookups, perhaps all at once. It was a savvy act of branding for Onika "Nicki" Maraj to change her last name to a word for group sex. Ménages à trois are referred to in more than a dozen songs I've heard since the turn of the century, including a number one hit by Katy Perry, "Last Friday Night (T.G.I.F.)," released on a 2010 album titled *Teenage Dream*.

Popular music is part of the cultural feedback loop through which ideas emerge from all corners of society to be sorted, mixed, enhanced, enlarged, and reintroduced as new ideas. In this way, songs helped lay a path for the women's movement in the 1960s. Gloria Steinem, referring to "You Don't Own Me," a Top 10 hit in 1963, said, "Lesley Gore was there before me. She primed a whole generation of teenage girls to become feminist women." Much the same, the glamorization of rebels, outsiders, and nonconformists in pop music (and movies and other entertainments) helped set the framework for the gay rights movement. "Elvis was so cool and sexy and deliciously unconventional, he made it easier to be gay," said Edmund White. "And he wore eye makeup." Relatedly, songs (and, again, other works of popular culture) surely played a role in preparing Americans for same-sex marriage by advancing the proposition that marriage is about love rather than the propagation of the species.

With all this in mind, it seems plausible to me that not only the prominence of sex in contemporary pop but also the fluidity of sexual partnership in the music could influence young listeners in ways hard to conceive of now. Some futurists, speculating about the next frontier in civil rights, have talked about the prospect of growing acceptance of polyamory, the having of relationships among three or more people. The idea is difficult for me to accept, because it's something I associate mainly with bigamy and porn. My son Nate and his friends, having grown up with a star named Minaj and after hearing "Last Friday Night (T.G.I.F.)" hundreds of times, could come to have a different point of view someday. I'm not predicting or lobbying for any such thing. I know the future is unknowable, but I've learned that popular music, being an art designed to help young people feel different from people older than they, has a long tradition of inciting its audience to defy traditions.

Musically, as well as socially, pop endures as a laboratory of experimentation, though, like many labs outside the realm of metaphor, it has been computerized and automated in recent years. The music that's most popular today—the dance-oriented teen pop that plays in tight rotation on what programmers call CHR (contemporary hit radio) and that *Billboard* ranks on its Hot 100 chart—is produced and distributed by methods that, in many ways, are more regimented and mechanized than the means by which any music of the past had been made. Songs are created by the track-and-hook method: producers generate instrumental tracks by sample mining and synthesis, using software and keyboard plug-ins; teams of "topliners" add melodic hooks and lyric phrases onto the tracks; and the results are cut and pasted, Auto-Tuned and processed, then digitally tested with software that compares the sonic patterns of new songs with those of past hits to measure their chart potential. The world of this music is both familiar and unique, connected in elemental ways to the factory-model production methods of Tin Pan Alley and, at the same time, utterly inconceivable in any era before the digital age.

The music of CHR is created by systematic methods that can make songs sound awfully similar. Then again, every form of music has systems of training and production, as well as modes of practice and aesthetic standards, that could be seen as overly regimented and stultifying. In classical music, conservatories endorse practice regimens and guidelines for tonal production and score interpretation that can seem nearly as regimented as the track-and-hook system. Besides, songs in every genre of music tend to sound alike—especially to listeners not steeped in the work, while devotees of the genre revel in the parsing of minute distinctions between songs. To a musical theater buff, the blues of the Mississippi Delta might sound inexplicably repetitive. Hip-hop fans may not pick up the subtle variations between songs that bluegrass aficionados hear in their music, and vice versa. To a listener deeply engaged in current-day pop, such as my son Nate, the bebop records I play in the house can sound annoyingly alike.

A few years ago, an old friend of mine named Thomas Bucci, a painter who is an enthusiast of Americana "roots" music, came to visit me, and I was listening to Frank Sinatra's melancholy album *Only the Lonely*, from Sinatra's prime in 1958, when he arrived. We yakked for a while as "Willow Weep for Me," "Angel Eyes," "Ebb Tide," and "Spring Is Here" played in the background. After a while, my friend said, "How can you tell those songs apart? They're all the same."

The worst sin of music making by machine, to my thinking, is the fact that mechanization can be dehumanizing. Sampling and synthesizers have made it possible to create and record complex, sonically rich, and varied works of music without anyone involved playing a traditional musical instrument. Pro Tools and other digital software packages *are* the instruments by which pop is constructed today. Yet it's human beings who use the software, making creative decisions— alone, sometimes, but often in teams of people collaborating, trading ideas, competing, squabbling, feeding off one another, and inspiring each other. And it's the human voice—even if it's augmented by Auto-Tune—at the center of the songs. The story of music making by the track-and-hook method is one of human beings involved in the profoundly human activities of invention, collaboration, rivalry, triumph, and disappointment. For all their efforts, often working obsessively day and night, most of the people making pop today spend most of the time working on music that is never released or falls short of becoming a hit. The ostensible hit makers are engaged, often, in the most human of acts: failure.

Contemporary pop is often described as an industrial product. A more accurate and useful way to approach today's music would be to think of it as *post*industrial, a phenomenon of the information age. After all, music is made now by excavating the vast digital repository of recordings of the past, or by emulating or referencing them through synthesis, and then manipulating the sounds and mashing them up—through the human fallibility and inspiration that have always informed popular music and probably always will. It is access and processing, the methods that digitalization facilitates, not gearing and stamping for uniformity and mass production, that distinguish the pop of the twenty-first century. Like machine-age plants everywhere, the old song factories of the record industry have closed, and the work of the day is being done electronically.

I like quite a bit of the music on my son's playlists, including some of the music most jarring to me at first, more than I probably should. Without question, a fair share of the songs on the *Billboard* Hot 100 are unexceptional—derivative and redundant. Too many songs sound like too many other songs on the same chart, and some tunes are, by all critical measures I value, just awful. But these things have always been true of popular music and many other forms of art, popular or not. A high proportion of fine-art works in the New York galleries in any season tend to bring other works to mind, and relatively few endure as masterpieces. The miracle of popular music, for me, is that so many songs provide the satisfactions and the surprises that they do, considering the sheer quantity of work produced every week, every year. In the first few years of the second decade of the twenty-first century, I've found myself loving and admiring quite a few songs: "Royals," the spare, tuneful cry of protest to the bling culture, written and recorded by Lorde, the New Zealand singer-songwriter, when she was sixteen; "Alright" and "The Blacker the Berry," two singles by Kendrick Lamar from his majestic jazz-pop-hip-hop hybrid, *To Pimp a Butterfly*; "Bad Blood," an almost abusively infectious style mash-up by Taylor Swift, featuring Lamar; and "FourFiveSeconds," the unpredictably harmonious collaboration by Rihanna, Kanye West, and Paul McCartney. I could go on.

I try not to show too much enthusiasm for this music to my son, for fear of siphoning the work of its proprietary value to him. I have not forgotten being his age, sitting with Red Mascara in that booth at the Gateway. When Mascara finished showing me the music to "I'm from New Jersey," he caught me glancing at the remote jukebox station, and he asked me if there was a song I wanted to play. I was thinking, *Well, sure*—"Ruby Tuesday"—but I said, "No." I didn't want him to listen to the Stones and tell me, *What a pretty song*, or *How interesting that they've employed the Renaissance woodwind instrument the recorder*, or *Did you know that the bowing technique they're using on the bass is called arco?* I didn't want him liking *my* music any more than I liked *his* song. "Ruby Tuesday," with "Let's Spend the Night Together" on the B side, was number one on the pop charts at the time. Like a million kids around the world, I thought of the song as mine and mine alone.

NOTES

INTRODUCTION

3 *"doomcore"*: The music writer Simon Reynolds wrote that "doomcore" music is "hardcore, but it's midtempo and melodic, characterized by cavernous reverb, slimy synth textures, and macabre cadences." See Simon Reynolds, "Future Crusader," *Village Voice*, June 15, 1999.

3 *"neurofunk"*: According to Reynolds, "neurofunk" features "clinical production, foreboding ambient drones, blips 'n' blurts of electronic noise, and chugging, curiously inhibited two-step beats that don't even sound like breakbeats anymore." See Simon Reynolds, *Generation Ecstasy: Into the World of Techno and Rave Culture* (New York: Routledge, 1999), 355.

4 *"I Got Rhythm"*: The chord progression known as Rhythm Changes is derived from the harmonic structure of George Gershwin's "I Got Rhythm." See Ronald McCurdy and Willie Hill, *Approaching the Standards* (Miami, Fla.: Belwin-Mills, 2000), 22.

5 *promoted as the A side*: See Bruce Spizer, *The Beatles' Story on Capitol Records: A Narrative and Pictorial History of Beatlemania, Part One: Beatlemania and the Singles* (New Orleans: 498 Productions, 2000), 83. To see

the variations of cover art, visit www.45cat.com/record/5498 and Getty Images at www.gettyimages.com/detail/news-photo/view-of-the-cover-of-the-45rpm-single-yesterday-b-w-act-news-photo/106532056.

5 Guinness Book: Mark C. Young, ed., *The Guinness Book of World Records 1997* (New York: Bantam Books, 1997), 284.

5 *seven million times*: See "Yesterday Top Song in U.S.," *Evening Standard*, Dec. 17, 1999; "No, Not That Song Again," *Globe and Mail*, Dec. 23, 1999.

5 *three thousand versions*: Barry Miles, "Still Fab After 40 Years: They Began as a Teen Craze but Turned into a Cultural Force That Changed the World," *Times* (London), Sept. 12, 2009.

5 *McCartney has attempted*: Geoff Boucher, "Paul's New Arrangement Is Flip Side of Lennon-McCartney," *Los Angeles Times*, Dec. 15, 2002.

6 *"I go to restaurants"*: Quoted in David Sheff, *All We Are Saying: The Last Major Interview with John Lennon and Yoko Ono* (New York: St. Martin's Griffin, 2000), 56.

6 *"It's the thing to do"*: From the transcript of an interview between Bob Dylan and Robert Shelton in the repository of the Experience Music Project, Seattle.

6 *Laura Binetti and Steven Blessing*: The couple was married on December 27, 2014. A wedding guest posted a photograph during the wedding on Twitter with the caption "Yesterday by the Beatles for the 'father' daughter dance—absolutely beautiful."

6 *Meredith Ewart*: Angus Loten, "Gathered to Recall Terror's Toll: Church Overflows at Service for Montreal Woman Killed in Sept. 11 Attacks," *Montreal Gazette*, Oct. 28, 2001.

7 *who is a jazz singer*: Visit Karen Oberlin's website at www.karenoberlin.com.

7 *"If the critic cannot reveal"*: Alfred Kazin, "To Be a Critic," in *Contemporaries: From the 19th Century to the Present*, rev. ed. (New York: Horizon Press, 1982), 9.

9 *chatter about that endures:* See the caption to an online photograph of the Gateway: "The legend was that the Rolling Stones ate here in the 1970s and raved about its authentic 'Jersey diner culture.'" www.pbase.com/meg96/image/129080597.

9 *"I'm from New Jersey"*: Red Mascara passed away on June 20, 2015, after this text was written but before it was published. See Kate Zernike, "Red Mascara, 92, Dies; His 'I'm from New Jersey' Almost Became

State Song," *New York Times*, June 26, 2015. For more on Mascara, see Ben McGrath, "You Say Tomato," *New Yorker*, March 21, 2005.

10 *radio stations refused to play it*: See "Stones OK for 5th Gold Disk," *Billboard*, Feb. 11, 1967.

10 *Mascara labored*: A bill to honor "I'm from New Jersey" passed the New Jersey state assembly three times and the senate three times but always failed to be signed by the governor. In 2014, New Jersey's legislature sought to honor "I'm from New Jersey" by naming it one of five official state songs. See Matt Friedman, "NJ Has No State Song. Some Lawmakers Want It to Have Five," NJ.com, Sept. 28, 2014; www.welcometoasburypark.com/acr121.shtml.

12 *Top 10 hit*: See "Billboard Hot 100," *Billboard*, Sept. 23, 1967.

I. THE SHEET MUSIC ERA: THE ZENITH OF THE POPULAR MUSIC CRAZE

13 *The 45 was cheap*: In 1950, a 45 rpm record typically cost $.79 to purchase, compared with $2.85 for a ten-inch 33⅓ rpm LP. See John Broven, *Record Makers and Breakers: Voices of the Independent Rock 'n' Roll Pioneers* (Urbana: University of Illinois Press, 2010), 78.

14 *come and gone like fashion*: Lyrics from the Pretenders' song "Don't Get Me Wrong," written by Christine Hynde, from the album *Get Close*, Sire Records, 1986.

14 *"The boys got their musical education"*: George Martin, interview with author.

15 *"day of great hits"*: See "Day of Big Song Hits Gone, Sheet Music Trade Dying," *Boston Daily Globe*, Oct. 24, 1920.

15 *When commercial song sheets*: For more on the evolution of the sheet music industry, see Derek B. Scott, *Sounds of the Metropolis: The 19th Century Popular Music Revolution in London, New York, Paris, and Vienna* (New York: Oxford University Press, 2011), 24–27; David Suisman, *Selling Sounds: The Commercial Revolution in American Music* (Cambridge, Mass.: Harvard University Press, 2009).

15 *"Polar Bear Polka"*: The 1856 song was composed by Albert W. Berg. For the cover image, visit www.library.upenn.edu/collections/rbm/keffer/b36an32.html.

15 *"The Carrier Dove"*: The sheet music for "The Carrier Dove," a ballad by Daniel Johnson, was published in 1841. For the cover image, visit http://pastispresent.org/wp-content/uploads/IMG_0015.jpg.

16 *ten thousand dollars for the right*: See John Shaw, *This Land That I Love: Irving Berlin, Woody Guthrie, and the Story of Two American Anthems* (New York: PublicAffairs, 2013), 17.

17 *parlor grand piano*: A new Sohmer parlor grand piano cost five hundred dollars in 1892. See *Illustrated American*, Jan. 16, 1892.

17 *five million copies*: Russell Sanjek, *American Popular Music and Its Business: The First Four Hundred Years*, vol. 2, *From 1790 to 1909* (New York: Oxford University Press, 1988), 322.

17 *thirty to forty cents*: See Vernon Lue, "Doings of Song Writers and Publishers," *San Francisco Chronicle*, May 30, 1897; Reebee Garofalo, "From Music Publishing to MP3: Music and Industry in the Twentieth Century," *American Music* (Fall 1999): 321.

17 *eight to ten dollars*: To adjust prices across time, visit the Federal Reserve Bank of Minneapolis's Consumer Price Index Calculator at www.minneapolisfed.org/community/teaching-aids/cpi-calculator -information.

17 *around seventy-six million*: For the census figures, visit www.census .gov/population/estimates/nation/popclockest.txt.

17 *proportionally the equivalent*: The U.S. population was 281 million in 2000. Visit www.census.gov/main/www/cen2000.html.

17 *"Maria Maria"*: "Best Selling Records of 2000," *Billboard*, Feb. 10, 2001.

17 *about a hundred songs*: See William Ruhlmann, *Breaking Records: 100 Years of Hits* (New York: Routledge, 2004), 16.

17 *around ninety million*: For the census figures, visit www.census.gov /population/estimates/nation/popclockest.txt.

18 *always attracted sizable audiences*: At the Metropolitan Opera, Puccini's *La bohème* was performed 1,245 times between 1883 and 2013, making it the most performed opera in the institution's history. See William Forde Thompson, ed., *Music in the Social and Behavioral Sciences: An Encyclopedia* (Thousand Oaks, Calif.: SAGE, 2014), 184. Rossini's *Il barbiere di Siviglia* was performed at least 600 times between 1883 and 2013 at the Met, consistently playing throughout those 130 years. See https:// archives.metoperafamily.org.

18 *at first on Union Square*: Philip Furia and Laurie Patterson, *The Songs of Hollywood* (New York: Oxford University Press, 2010), 10.

18 *twenty publishing businesses*: Howard Pollack, *George Gershwin: His Life and Work* (Berkeley: University of California Press, 2006), 62.

18 *"Nowadays, the consumption"*: See "How Popular Song Factories Manufacture a Hit," *New York Times*, Sept. 18, 1910.

19 *Between 1890 and 1904*: See Daniel Akst, *Temptation: Finding Self-Control in an Age of Excess* (New York: Penguin, 2011), 60.

19 *three hundred American piano makers*: In 1910, the United States was the largest piano manufacturer in the world, with more than 350,000 pianos produced yearly. See *"The New York Times" Guide to the Arts of the 20th Century, 1900–1929* (Chicago: Fitzroy Dearborn, 2002), 2705.

20 *"He could not separate"*: Jan Swafford, *Charles Ives: A Life with Music* (New York: W. W. Norton, 1998), 88.

20 *"The composition of popular songs"*: See "How Popular Song Factories Manufacture a Hit."

21 *"Song writers, publishers"*: "The Popular Songs So Guilelessly Sung by Our Daughters Are Vicious, Warns Mme. Fremstad," *New-York Tribune*, Jan. 14, 1915.

21 *like many others*: For more articles containing criticism of popular music, see "'Ragtime' Under Fire: It Is Not, However, Lacking in Able Defenders," *New-York Tribune*, Oct. 29, 1911; "Banish the Suggestive Song," *Advance*, May 15, 1913; "Are Americans Really Music Lovers?," *New-York Tribune*, June 18, 1916.

22 *Richard Strauss's Salome*: The opera's premiere date was January 22, 1907. To read about the production, visit the Metropolitan Opera archives at http://archives.metoperafamily.org/archives/scripts/cgiip.exe /WService=BibSpeed/fullcit.w?xCID=38600&limit=500&xBranch =ALL&xsdate=&xedate=&theterm=&x=0&xhomepath=&xhome=.

22 *up to ten dollars*: Larry Hamberlin, *Tin Pan Opera: Operatic Novelty Songs in the Ragtime Era* (New York: Oxford University Press, 2011), 99.

24 *more than three hundred "Chinee" songs*: The song titles included "The Heathen Chinee" (1870), "Poor Chinee!" (1876), "Ah Sin, Chinee Song" (1877), "Wing Tee Wee: The Sweet Chinee" (1890), and "The Wedding of the Chinee and the Coon" (1897). See Krystyn R. Moon, *Yellowface: Creating the Chinese in American Popular Music and Performance, 1850s–1920s* (New Brunswick, N.J.: Rutgers University Press, 2005), 170–72.

24 *more than six hundred "coon" songs*: The song titles included "New Coon in Town" (1883), "The Whistling Coon" (1888), and "Little Alabama Coon" (1893). See Karen L. Cox, *Dreaming of Dixie: How the South Was Created in American Popular Culture* (Chapel Hill: University of North Carolina Press, 2011), 15; John Ogasapian and N. Lee Orr, *Music of the Gilded Age* (Westport, Conn.: Greenwood Press, 2007), 137.

24 *including "All Coons Look Alike to Me"*: See Robert Jefferson Norrell, *Up from History: The Life of Booker T. Washington* (Cambridge, Mass.: Harvard University Press, 2009), 120.

24 *"If the Man in the Moon Were a Coon"*: See Stephen G. N. Tuck, *We Ain't What We Ought to Be: The Black Freedom Struggle from Emancipation to Obama* (Cambridge, Mass.: Harvard University Press, 2010), 84.

24 *he had come to regret*: See Cox, *Dreaming of Dixie*, 15.

25 *Broca's area*: See Yosef Grodzinsky and Katrin Amunts, eds., *Broca's Region* (New York: Oxford University Press, 2006).

26 *Silvertone acoustic*: Visit the Silvertone World website for a description of the models: www.silvertoneworld.net/acoustic.html.

2. THE RISE OF RECORDS: WHISPERING

30 *as a song "plugger"*: Sigmund Spaeth, *A History of Popular Music in America* (New York: Random House, 1948), 428–29.

30 *"The Japanese Sandman"*: For more on Paul Whiteman and His Orchestra, who recorded the song, visit www.gracyk.com/whiteman.shtml.

31 *As early as 1874*: Bell began work on the acoustic telegraph in 1874. His first telegraph-related patent was US161739, which was granted on April 6, 1875.

32 *1,093 patents*: See Randall E. Stross, *The Wizard of Menlo Park: How Thomas Alva Edison Invented the Modern World* (New York: Three Rivers Press, 2007), 283. For an online record of Edison's patents, visit http://edison.rutgers.edu/patents.htm.

32 *cylinder recording-and-playback system*: To view Edison's 1877 patent, visit http://edison.rutgers.edu/patents/00200521.PDF.

32 *toilet paper rolls*: See "From Cylinders to Disks: Sound Recording Becomes a Mass Medium," in Richard Campbell, Christopher R. Mar-

tin, and Bettina Fabos, *Media and Culture: An Introduction to Mass Communication*, 8th ed. (Boston: Bedford/St. Martin's, 2013), 74.

32 *Lonnie Johnson*: Johnson, a noted vaudeville guitarist, recorded in the early 1920s. See Dean Alger, *The Original Guitar Hero and the Power of Music: The Legendary Lonnie Johnson, Music, and Civil Rights* (Denton: University of North Texas Press, 2014), 63.

33 *William Jennings Bryan*: To hear Bryan's recorded speech, visit the Library of Congress National Jukebox website: www.loc.gov/jukebox /recordings/detail/id/1463.

33 *Ellen Terry*: For more on Terry, who recorded speeches from such Shakespeare plays as *The Merchant of Venice* and *Much Ado About Nothing* for Victor, see the *1922 Catalogue of Victor Records: With Biographic Material, Opera Plots, New Portraits, and Special Red Seal Section*.

33 *J. M. Gates*: For more on Gates, see Lerone A. Martin, *Preaching on Wax: The Phonograph and the Shaping of Modern African American Religion* (New York: New York University Press, 2014).

33 *Murry K. Hill*: For more on Hill's career, visit the Library of Congress National Jukebox website: www.loc.gov/jukebox/artists/detail/id/3181/.

35 *magazine ad from 1915*: To view the ad, visit the Library of Congress's National Jukebox website: www.loc.gov/jukebox/images/advertisements /ColorVicAd_TMW_1915.jpg.

35 *A low-end Victrola cost about fifteen dollars*: For more on the history and pricing of phonographs, visit www.antiquephono.org/encounter ing-antique-phonographs/.

35 *wardrobe trunk*: For the wardrobe trunk ad from Saks & Company, see *New-York Tribune*, Dec. 20, 1915.

36 *fabric gloves*: For the gloves ad from Filene's, see *Christian Science Monitor*, March 30, 1915.

36 *Some stores*: Recollection of author's mother, Angelina Hajdu.

36 *"gaudiness and show"*: To view the Library of Congress's image of the Landay's advertisement, visit www.loc.gov/jukebox/features/victor -advertising.

36 *at least five million*: *The New York Times* reported that RCA Victor estimated that Caruso sold fifty million records through 1964. See Donal Henahan, "Met Remembers Caruso, Whose Voice Few Can Forget," *New York Times*, Feb. 20, 1973.

38 *Walter Benjamin*: Benjamin's much-cited 1936 essay examined the social, political, and aesthetic impact of mechanical reproduction on the
arts. Benjamin argued that the reproduction of an artwork diminishes
the aura of the original. See Walter Benjamin, "The Work of Art in the
Age of Its Technological Reproducibility" (Second Version), in *The Work
of Art in the Age of Its Technological Reproducibility and Other Writings on
the Media*, ed. Michael W. Jennings, Brigid Doherty, and Thomas Y.
Levin (Cambridge, Mass.: Belknap Press of Harvard University Press,
2008), 19–55.

39 *"Both are Caruso"*: Advertisement from 1915 reprinted in Benjamin
Aldridge, *The Victor Talking Machine Company* (New York: RCA Sales,
1964), 54.

39 *"Vesti la giubba"*: See Philipp Blom, *The Vertigo Years: Europe, 1900–1914*
(New York: Basic Books, 2008), 316.

39 *half a million record players*: Through 1910, 606,596 phonographs had
been sold by Victor. See Thom Holmes, ed., *The Routledge Guide to
Music Technology* (New York: Routledge, 2006), 323.

41 *Paul Whiteman was one*: Victor sold two million copies of Whiteman's
"Three O'Clock in the Morning." See David A. Jasen, *Tin Pan Alley:
An Encyclopedia of the Golden Age of American Song* (New York: Rout-
ledge, 2003), 197.

41 *commissioned George Gershwin*: See Don Rayno, *Paul Whiteman: Pioneer
in American Music, 1930–1967* (Lanham, Md.: Scarecrow Press, 2013), 2.

43 *Yakima Canutt*: See Gary Giddins, *Visions of Jazz: The First Century*
(New York: Oxford University Press, 1998), 285.

44 *"They felt like prisoners"*: George Martin, interview with author.

3. THE COTTON CLUB: JUNGLE NIGHTS IN HARLEM

47 *neo-Georgian-style building*: Architecture style suggested by the Columbia University architecture professor Andrew Dolkart.

47 *Lenox Avenue and West 142nd Street*: The building was built in 1918. The
ballroom, before becoming Club DeLuxe, was initially the Douglas
Casino, a large dance hall. For more on the club, see Carlos E. Cortes,
ed., *Multicultural America: A Multimedia Encyclopedia* (Thousand Oaks,

Calif.: SAGE, 2013), 591; A. H. Lawrence, *Duke Ellington and His World* (New York: Routledge, 2001), 105.

47 *White Steam Touring Car*: White Steam Touring Cars were made by Cleveland's White Sewing Machine Company, which produced vehicles from 1900 until 1980. See *The White Bulletin: Presenting the Characteristics and Achievements of the Incomparable White Steam Touring Car*, Oct. 1903. For the image of Jack Johnson's White Steam Touring Car advertisement, visit www.josportsinc.com/item_images/12063 64505.jpg.

48 *"White people began"*: Langston Hughes, *The Big Sea: An Autobiography* (New York: Hill and Wang, 1993), 224.

49 *"a white man's fantasy"*: Cab Calloway, interview with author.

49 *"They tried to make us out like cavemen"*: Ibid.

49–50 *"The boys behind the music"*: Ibid.

50 *McHugh would say*: See Alyn Shipton, *I Feel a Song Coming On: The Life of Jimmy McHugh* (Urbana: University of Illinois Press, 2009), 93.

50 *"I Can't Give You Anything but Love"*: Though the song is copyrighted in the names of Jimmy McHugh and Dorothy Fields, some claim that Fats Waller might have sold the melody to McHugh in 1926 and that the lyrics were in fact by Waller's frequent collaborator, Andy Razaf. See Paul S. Machlin, *Thomas Wright "Fats" Waller: Performances in Transcription, 1927–1943* (Middleton, Wis.: A-R, 2001), 69.

50 *"the Negro-est white man"*: See Edward Jablonski, *Harold Arlen: Happy with the Blues* (Garden City, N.Y.: Doubleday, 1961), 68.

51 *Arlen would recall*: Ibid., 36.

51 *"Of all the better song writers"*: Alec Wilder, *American Popular Song: The Great Innovators, 1900–1950* (New York: Oxford University Press, 1972), 255.

52 *"That song was the perfect expression"*: Ethel Waters, *His Eye Is on the Sparrow: An Autobiography*, with Charles Samuels (New York: Da Capo, 1992), 221.

53 *"At the Cotton Club"*: Duke Ellington, *Music Is My Mistress* (Garden City, N.Y.: Doubleday, 1973), 419.

54 *William Morrison Patterson*: See "Why 'Jazz' Sends Us Back to the Jungle," in Edward J. Wheeler, ed., *Current Opinion* 65 (July–Dec. 1918): 165.

54 *"Music has charms"*: "How 'JAZZ' MUSIC Originated in the JUN-GLE," *San Francisco Chronicle*, Oct. 20, 1918.

54 *"Barbarism has entered popular music"*: Aldous Huxley, *Complete Essays*, vol. 1, *1920–1925* (Chicago: Ivan R. Dee, 2000), 347.

55 *"Nathan Huggins"*: Huggins (1927–1989) was a historian who served as W. E. B. Du Bois Professor of History and Afro-American Studies at Harvard. His books included *Harlem Renaissance* (New York: Oxford University Press, 1971) and *Slave and Citizen: The Life of Frederick Douglass* (New York: Little, Brown, 1980).

55 *some three hundred thousand listeners*: WFBH began broadcasting from Manhattan in 1924 with a 500-watt signal. At the same time, New York–based WEAF was broadcasting at 5,000 watts and claimed a daily audience of one million people. During the 1928 Federal Radio Commission hearings, the radio engineer John V. L. Hogan explained that 5,000-watt stations broadcast good-quality sound within a hundred-mile radius while 500-watt stations broadcast good-quality sound within a thirty-mile radius. Proportionately, the potential audience of WFBH could have been around three hundred thousand. See Bill Jaker, Frank Sulek, and Peter Kanze, *The Airwaves of New York: Illustrated Histories of 156 AM Stations in the Metropolitan Area, 1921–1996* (Jefferson, N.C.: McFarland, 1998), 60, 70; John V. L. Hogan, *Radio Facts and Principles: Limiting the Total Number of Broadcasting Stations Which May Operate Simultaneously in the United States* (Washington, D.C.: U.S. Government Printing Office, 1928), 9.

56 *begun in the United States only in 1920*: Alfred Chandler Jr. and James Cortada, eds., *A Nation Transformed by Information: How Information Has Shaped the United States from Colonial Times to the Present* (New York: Oxford University Press, 2000), 147.

56 *"The Cotton Club enjoys the distinction"*: See "Hurtig and Seamon Offer the Cotton Club Revue," *New York Amsterdam News*, March 25, 1925.

56 *the Hotel Majestic*: See "Hotel Majestic Upheld Fighting WFBH's Suit," *New York Herald/New-York Tribune*, May 28, 1925.

56 *"So far as we were concerned"*: Ellington, *Music Is My Mistress*, 77.

59 *"the future of rock and roll"*: Jon Landau, "Growing Young with Rock and Roll," *Real Paper*, May 22, 1974.

4. THE CHARTS: MAKE-BELIEVE ISLAND

64 *exclusively female groups*: For a thorough history of the female bands, see Sherrie Tucker, *Swing Shift: "All-Girl" Bands of the 1940s* (Durham, N.C.: Duke University Press, 2000).

64 *"Only God can make a tree"*: George T. Simon, *The Big Bands* (New York: Macmillan, 1967), 261.

64 *in at least one census*: U.S. Census 1920, Census Place: Chicago Ward 3, Cook (Chicago), Illinois, roll T625_312, p. 6B, Enumeration District 135, image 882. To learn more about Hutton, see Bob Stanley, "Ina Ray Hutton: The Forgotten Female Star of 1930s Jazz," *Guardian*, July 7, 2011.

65 *record made in April 1940*: For more on the record, see "Rating the Records," *Baltimore Afro-American*, Sept. 21, 1940; http://searchworks .stanford.edu/view/8393890.

66 *Lena Horne came out of . . . semiretirement*: Her new album was titled *We'll Be Together Again*, Blue Note Records, 1994. David Hajdu, liner notes.

66 *"a better woman"*: Lena Horne, interview with author.

66 *The microphone*: John Woram, "50 Years of Studio Mikes," *Billboard*, Dec. 18, 1976.

66 *The first vocalists to exploit*: See David Hajdu, "Imperfect Pitch," *New Republic*, June 22, 2012.

67 *three-part series of profiles*: See E. J. Kahn, "The Voice with the Golden Accessories," *New Yorker*, Oct. 26, 1946; E. J. Kahn, "The Fave, the Fans, and the Fiends," *New Yorker*, Nov. 2, 1946; and E. J. Kahn, "Just a Kid from Hoboken," *New Yorker*, Nov. 9, 1946.

68 *Looney Tunes short*: The 1944 film was *Swooner Crooner*, directed by Frank Tashlin. It was nominated for the 1945 Academy Award for Best Short Subject (Cartoons).

68 *in a wheelchair*: The wheelchair-bound Sinatra was featured in the 1946 cartoon *Book Revue*, directed by Bob Clampett.

68 *a song about him*: The song, "Dear Mister Sinatra," was performed by Eileen Barton, who co-starred on Sinatra's CBS radio program in the 1940s. The song has music by Jerry Livingston, words by Al Hoffman. See "Sinatra's Song Partners Sing About Him," *Life*, Dec. 11, 1944.

68 *"The Billboard Music Popularity Chart"*: This was the first national chart to rank the popularity of songs by specific artists. For more, see Silvio Pietroluongo, "Hot 100 Spotlight," *Billboard*, July 22, 2000.

71 *Frank Sinatra, briefly in 1943*: See Nancy Sinatra, *Frank Sinatra, My Father* (New York: Pocket Books, 1985), 53.

72 *Danny Goldberg*: For more on his career, see Danny Goldberg, *Bumping into Geniuses: My Life Inside the Rock and Roll Business* (New York: Gotham Books, 2008).

73 *"A song is on the chart"*: Danny Goldberg, conversation with author.

73 *"Russ Morgan is the latest"*: "Swing Sessions with Bill Gottlieb," *Washington Post*, Aug. 11, 1940.

74 *"It was all you heard"*: Quoted in Donald Clarke, *All or Nothing At All: A Life of Sinatra* (New York: Fromm International, 1997), 50.

74 *"the biggest thing since"*: Bill Gottlieb, "Swing Sessions with Bill Gottlieb," *Washington Post*, Nov. 3, 1940.

74 *"If he listens"*: See Jean-Paul Sartre, *Critique of Dialectical Reason*, vol. 1, *Theory of Practical Ensembles* (London: NLB, 1976), 650.

75 *typical price of a 78 rpm single*: See David Baskerville, *Music Business Handbook and Career Guide*, 8th ed. (Thousand Oaks, Calif.: SAGE, 2006), 302.

76 *number seven*: See "Billboard Hot 100," *Billboard*, July 2, 1966.

76 *first song to sell*: Gary Trust, "Adele Says 'Hello' to No. 1 Hot 100 Debut; First Song to Sell 1 Million Downloads in a Week," *Billboard*, Nov. 2, 2015.

5. GOING WEST: HOLLYWOOD BARN DANCE

79 *the Highwaymen*: See Robert Hilburn, *Johnny Cash: The Life* (New York: Little, Brown, 2013), 503–506.

79 *Nassau Coliseum*: See John Anderson, "Highwaymen Travel Country Memory Lane," *Newsday*, March 16, 1990.

81 *"The Jolly Cowboy"*: See John Avery Lomax and Alan Lomax, *Cowboy Songs and Other Frontier Ballads* (New York: Macmillan, 1922), 284.

82 *"a work of real importance"*: See Frederick Winthrop Faxon, ed., *Bulletin of Bibliography and Dramatic Index*, vol. 9, *January 1916–October 1917* (Boston: Boston Book Company, 1917), 71.

82 *"Out in the wild"*: Lomax and Lomax, *Cowboy Songs and Other Frontier Ballads*, xix.

83 *"The songs represent"*: Ibid.

84 *shooting 69 animals*: See Howard Ensign Evans, *The Natural History of the Long Expedition to the Rocky Mountains* (New York: Oxford University Press, 1997), 111; Clement Augustus Lounsberry, *North Dakota History and People: Outlines of American History* (Chicago: S. J. Clarke, 1917), 1:34.

84 Buck Taylor, King of the Cowboys: See David Hamilton Murdoch, *The American West: The Invention of a Myth* (Reno: University of Nevada Press, 2001), 60.

86 *A. P. Carter would also bring in material*: See Mark Zwonitzer and Charles Hirshberg, *Will You Miss Me When I'm Gone? The Carter Family and Their Legacy in American Music* (New York: Simon & Schuster, 2004), 119.

87 *did not know if corn*: See Charles K. Harris, *After the Ball: Forty Years of Melody* (New York: Frank-Maurice, 1926), 318.

87 *more than 350 songs*: See Ron McFarland, *The Long Life of Evangeline: A History of the Longfellow Poem in Print, in Adaptation, and in Popular Culture* (Jefferson, N.C.: McFarland, 2010), 161.

87 *so were other tunes*: Nineteenth-century songs performed by the Carter Family included the 1879 "I'll Be All Smiles Tonight," the 1888 "Lula Walls," the 1849 "Wildwood Flower," the 1865 "Shall We Gather at the River," and the 1893 "When the Roll Is Called Up Yonder." See Wayne Erbsen, *Rural Roots of Bluegrass* (Pacific, Mo.: Mel Bay, 2003), 90; Richard Matteson Jr., *Bluegrass Picker's Tune Book* (Pacific, Mo.: Mel Bay, 2010), 160, 203, 232, 239.

87 *based on a poem*: Zwonitzer and Hirshberg, *Will You Miss Me When I'm Gone?*, 186.

88 *released by Victor*: A version of "Single Girl, Married Girl" was released on Montgomery Ward records, which were reissued Victor and Bluebird records advertised and sold through Montgomery Ward stores. See http://honkingduck.com/discography/artist/carter_family; Tony Russell and Bob Pinson, *Country Music Records: A Discography, 1921–1942* (New York: Oxford University Press, 2004), 21.

89 *"sold and kept selling"*: Zwonitzer and Hirshberg, *Will You Miss Me When I'm Gone?*, 105.

89 *"old, weird America"*: Greil Marcus, *The Old, Weird America: The World of Bob Dylan's Basement Tapes* (New York: Picador, 2011), 87.

93 *More than 160 such programs*: For more on the barn dance radio phenomenon, see Richard A. Peterson, *Creating Country Music: Fabricating Authenticity* (Chicago: University of Chicago Press, 1997).

94 *twice the strength*: In 1935, the most powerful station in the United States—and the world—was Cincinnati's WLW, which broadcast at 500,000 watts. See Volney D. Hurd, "U.S. Experts Plan Powerful String of Radio Stations," *Christian Science Monitor*, Oct. 15, 1935; Alden P. Armagnac, "Weird Electrical Freaks Traced to Runaway Radio Waves," *Popular Science*, June 1935.

94 *played over the fillings*: See Gene Fowler and Bill Crawford, *Border Radio: Quacks, Yodelers, Pitchmen, Psychics, and Other Amazing Broadcasters of the American Airwaves*, rev. ed. (Austin: University of Texas Press, 2002), 44.

95 *"The worst thing that ever happened"*: Quoted in Douglas B. Green, *Singing in the Saddle: The History of the Singing Cowboy* (Nashville: Vanderbilt University Press, 2002), 69.

96 *"That Silver Haired Daddy of Mine"*: See Rick Koster, *Texas Music* (New York: St. Martin's Press, 2000), 5.

98 *only two thousand dollars per film*: See Jeremy Agnew, *The Old West in Fact and Film: History Versus Hollywood* (Jefferson, N.C.: McFarland, 2012), 58.

98 *more than eighty westerns*: See Gary A. Yoggy, ed., *Back in the Saddle: Essays on Western Film and Television Actors* (Jefferson, N.C.: McFarland, 1998), 83.

99 *"Monarch of Merchandising"*: Elliott V. Bogert, *1953 Program for Profit: Roy Rogers, King of Cowboys, Monarch of Merchandising* (Hollywood, Calif.: Roy Rogers Enterprises, 1952).

100 *more than 150 movies*: Over their entire careers, Autry and Rogers made around 90 movies each. See Richard W. Slatta, *The Cowboy Encyclopedia* (New York: W. W. Norton, 1994), 130.

100 *No fewer than one hundred million*: Gene Autry alone sold one hundred million copies of his records between 1929 and the early 1960s. See Holly George Warren, *Public Cowboy No. 1: The Life and Times of Gene Autry* (New York: Oxford University Press, 2007), 2.

6. ROCK AND ROLL: THEY WENT CA-RAAAAAZY FOR IT!

101 *observer effect*: In science, the term "observer effect" refers to changes that observing something will make on the phenomenon being observed. In many cases, the changes are the result of instruments that alter the state of what they measure in some manner. The observer effect is often confused with Werner Heisenberg's uncertainty principle. Introduced in 1927, the uncertainty principle finds that in the field of quantum mechanics the more precisely the position of some particle is determined, the less precisely its momentum can be known, and vice versa. See Aya Furata, "One Thing Is Certain: Heisenberg's Uncertainty Principle Is Not Dead," *Scientific American*, March 8, 2012.

102 *"Mother of the Blues"*: See the article used to announce Ma Rainey's 1924 concert at Pittsburgh's Lincoln Theater: "Mother of the Blues," *Pittsburgh Courier*, Oct. 25, 1924.

102 *respected actress*: Ethel Waters was the second African American to be nominated for an Academy Award. She earned her nomination as Best Supporting Actress for Elia Kazan's 1949 film, *Pinky*. See Stephen Bourne, *Ethel Waters: Stormy Weather* (Lanham, Md.: Scarecrow Press, 2007), 72.

102 *"the very sound of the blues"*: Albert Murray, interview with author.

102 *"Empress of the Blues"*: See Floyd G. Snelson, "Theatrical Comment," *Pittsburgh Courier*, Nov. 1, 1924.

102 *she gave separate concerts*: Bessie Smith played whites-only concerts in Memphis in 1923. See "Hit on Radio," *Chicago Defender*, Oct. 6, 1923. For more on her popularity with mixed audiences, see Robert C. Cottrell, *Icons of American Popular Culture: From P. T. Barnum to Jennifer Lopez* (New York: Routledge, 2010), 98.

103 *more than two million copies*: See Steve Sullivan, *Encyclopedia of Great Popular Song Recordings* (Lanham, Md.: Scarecrow Press, 2013), 1:15.

103 *Cookery at lunchtime*: Though the author met Teddy Wilson briefly at the Cookery, he never saw him perform there.

105 *"Ah, swing, well"*: Quoted in W. C. Handy's 1941 book, *Father of the Blues: An Autobiography* (New York: Da Capo, 1991), 292. The actual date of the Bing Crosby broadcast that Handy quotes from is unclear.

105 *"Invisibility, let me explain"*: Ralph Ellison, *Invisible Man* (New York: Vintage, 1995), 8.

106 *Henderson sold dozens*: See Marshall Winslow Stearns, *The Story of Jazz* (New York: Oxford University Press, 1956), 209.

106 Let's Dance: See John R. Tumpak, *When Swing Was the Thing: Personality Profiles of the Big Band Era* (Milwaukee: Marquette University Press, 2008), 17.

106 *two million people of all colors*: See Michael Kimmelman and Francis Davis, "'King of Swing' Benny Goodman Is Dead at 77; 'You Could Spell Jazz B-e-n-n-y G-o-o-d-m-a-n,'" *Philadelphia Inquirer*, June 14, 1986.

106 *Goodman, to his credit*: Goodman would refer to Fletcher Henderson as a "genius." See Ross Firestone, *Swing, Swing, Swing: The Life and Times of Benny Goodman* (New York: W. W. Norton, 1993), 117; Scott Yanow, *Jazz: A Regional Exploration* (Westport, Conn.: Greenwood Press, 2005), 58. For more on Henderson's career, see Jeffrey Magee, *The Uncrowned King of Swing: Fletcher Henderson and Big Band Jazz* (New York: Oxford University Press, 2005).

107 *"Of its pioneers"*: Gama Gilbert, "Swing: What Is It?," *New York Times*, Sept. 5, 1937.

107 *"There is a distinct difference"*: Lige McKelvy, "After-Beat: Musicians' Row Against Race Mixing on the Bandstand; Earl Geiger Lands Society Job," *Orchestra World*, March 1937.

107 *federal excise tax*: The tax, known as the cabaret tax, went into effect on April 1, 1944. See "Taverns Plan to Absorb Tax on All Drinks," *New York Herald Tribune*, April 1, 1944; James E. Powers, "Village Life Dimmed by Taxes: 30% Levy Strikes Heaviest Blow at Cabarets Here in Greenwich Village," *New York Times*, April 24, 1944.

108 *"rock and roll"*: The *Billboard* writer Maurie Orodenker first used "rock-and-roll" to describe spiritual singing in 1942. He would again use the term "rock and roll" in his "Caldonia" review. See M. H. Orodenker, "On the Record," *Billboard*, May 30, 1942; M. H. Orodenker, "Record Reviews," *Billboard*, April 21, 1945.

109 *"The first time I heard"*: From an interview with Berry in the 1987 documentary *Chuck Berry Hail! Hail! Rock 'n' Roll*, directed by Taylor Hackford.

109 *"To my recollection"*: Quoted in Arnold Shaw, *Honkers and Shouters: The Golden Years of Rhythm and Blues* (New York: Macmillan, 1978), 64.

110 *also a slang term*: Murray, interview with author.

110 *number four*: See William E. Cleghorn, "Hank Williams Rides on

Down Trail of National Popularity on Air Records," in *The Hank Williams Reader*, ed. Patrick Huber, Steve Goodson, and David Anderson (New York: Oxford University Press, 2014), 20. The *Billboard* "Country and Western" chart was, until 1949, called the "Hillbilly" chart.

110 *"changed everything"*: Quoted in Paul Hemphill, *Lovesick Blues: The Life of Hank Williams* (New York: Viking, 2005), 69.

111 *when he murdered his wife*: For more on the murder case, see Nick Tosches, *Country: The Twisted Roots of Rock 'n' Roll* (New York: Da Capo, 1996), 160.

112 *for another year*: Elvis recorded his first song on acetate in 1953. See "Elvis Presley's 80th Birthday: The King's First Song, Recorded in 1953, Up for Auction," Associated Press, Jan. 8, 2015.

112 *Nick Manoloff instruction book*: See Chuck Berry, *Chuck Berry: The Autobiography* (New York: Harmony, 1987), 42.

112 *Jerry Lee Lewis was seventeen*: See Linda Martin and Kerry Segrave, *Anti-rock: The Opposition to Rock 'n' Roll* (New York: Da Capo, 1993), 75.

112 *choir in Lubbock*: See Ellis Amburn, *Buddy Holly: A Biography* (New York: St. Martin's Press, 1995), 21, 29.

112 *"new hard-driving 'swing boogie' style"*: See Peter Guralnick, *Sam Phillips: The Man Who Invented Rock and Roll* (New York: Little, Brown, 2015), 116.

113 *Alan Freed*: See James L. Baughman, *The Republic of Mass Culture: Journalism, Filmmaking, and Broadcasting in America Since 1941*, 3rd ed. (Baltimore: Johns Hopkins University Press, 2006), 68.

113 *"King of Rock and Roll"*: See "Payola Axes 'King' Freed," *Life*, Dec. 7, 1959.

113 *attempted to copyright the phrase*: John A. Jackson, *Big Beat Heat: Alan Freed and the Early Years of Rock and Roll* (New York: Schirmer Books, 1991), 85.

113 *Berry drew heavily*: See Berry, *Chuck Berry*, 143.

113 *"Ida Red"*: "Ida Red" incorporated lyrics from a nineteenth-century ballad titled "Sunday Night" by Frederic W. Root.

114 *Richard Brooks*: For the entire story, see Peter Ford's website entry "Rock Around the Clock and Me": www.peterford.com/ratc.html.

114 *reports of juvenile arrests*: See "An Outrage: Youth and Crime," *New York Herald Tribune*, May 5, 1955.

114 *30 percent* decline: See Eve Edstrom, "Juvenile Complaints Down 30%," *Washington Post and Times Herald*, Dec. 22, 1954.

116 *Alan Freed was making headlines*: See, for instance, Marty Richardson, "Today's Youngsters: Teen-Agers or Moon-Doggers?," *Cleveland Call and Post*, April 26, 1952.

116 *"Moondog Coronation Ball"*: See Jackson, *Big Beat Heat*, 1–8.

116 *twenty thousand young people*: See Valena Williams, "Call and Post Women's Editor Caught in Wild Melee as Moon Doggers 'Break It Up,'" *Cleveland Call and Post*, March 29, 1952.

116 *after the first song*: Don Michael Randel, ed., *The Harvard Dictionary of Music*, 4th ed. (Cambridge, Mass.: Harvard University Press, 2003), 196.

116 *The Supreme Court ruled*: See James T. Patterson, *Brown v. Board of Education: A Civil Rights Milestone and Its Troubled Legacy* (New York: Oxford University Press, 2001).

117 *Frank Sinatra and Nat King Cole*: In a 1956 article, Cole said, "The teenagers have taken over the popular recording business. They're on the threshold of adulthood. They're showing off, and there's a note of defiance in them occasionally." He continued, "In a few years, they'll look back hungrily at a growing-up period almost void of melody because the song publishers are mistaking youthful enthusiasm for musical taste." See Phyllis Battelle, "Rock n' Roll Beat Irks People the Nation Over," *New Journal and Guide*, July 23, 1956.

117 *"Rock and roll is the most brutal"*: See Frank Sinatra, "The Diplomacy of Music," *Western World*, Nov. 1957.

118 *"Rock 'n' roll bears"*: Leonard Feather, *The Encyclopedia Yearbook of Jazz* (New York: Horizon Press, 1956), 24.

118 *"Rock 'n' roll shows that morally"*: Quoted in "Baptist Pastor Sees Evil in Rock 'n' Roll," *Los Angeles Times*, Sept. 2, 1956.

118 *diminishment of a music*: The African American writer George E. Pitts observed that white musicians were taking over the rock-and-roll field, which was once dominated by black performers. Pitts wrote, "What's wrong with this? Nothing, except whites are now capitalizing on what they once termed 'distasteful and lurid' and blamed for juvenile delinquency. They are moving in and taking the big money." See George E. Pitts, "Are Whites Taking Over Rock 'n' Roll Field?," *Pittsburgh Courier*, Feb. 22, 1958.

118 *"torturous rhythm"*: Phyllis Battelle, "Rock 'n' Roll Has Muddled Origin," *Courier-Gazette*, June 18, 1956.

119 *Within three months*: The single of "That's Alright (Mama)" was released

on July 19, 1954, and the performance on *Louisiana Hayride* occurred on October 16, 1954. See Scotty Moore, *That's Alright, Elvis* (New York: Schirmer Books, 1997), 70; Glen Jeansonne, David Luhrssen, and Dan Sokolovic, *Elvis Presley, Reluctant Rebel: His Life and Our Times* (Santa Barbara, Calif.: Praeger, 2011), 76.

119 *"I'd like to know just how"*: Quoted in the October 16, 1954, *Louisiana Hayride* episode. To listen to the audio, visit www.youtube.com/watch?t=159&v=bLaPnpjw-pc.

119 *"King of Rock and Roll"*: See Molly Ivins, "Elvis Presley Entombed," *New York Times*, Aug. 19, 1977.

120 *"King of Swing"*: See John S. Wilson, "Benny Goodman, King of Swing, Is Dead," *New York Times*, June 14, 1986.

120 *"Ragtime King"*: See Janet Byrne, "Sour Notes in the Life of Irving Berlin," *Wall Street Journal*, Aug. 3, 1990.

120 *appears on the writing credits*: Vallee's songwriting credits included "I'm Just a Vagabond Lover," co-written with Leon Zimmerman, and "Talk to Me," co-written with Eddie Snyder and Stanley Kahan.

120 *"They tell me I'm another Rudy Vallee"*: Quoted in Roy Hemming and David Hajdu, *Discovering Great Singers of Classic Pop* (New York: Newmarket Press, 1991), 32.

121 Blackboard Jungle *was released*: See Bosley Crowther's March 1955 review: "'Blackboard Jungle': Delinquency Shown in Powerful Film," *New York Times*, March 21, 1955.

7. THE TRANSISTOR: MINE COMPLETELY

123 *monaural sound*: For more on monaural sound, see Quentin Wells, *Guide to Digital Home Technology Integration* (Clifton Park, N.Y.: Delmar, 2009), 172. Radio stations in the United States began to broadcast in stereo in 1952, and stereo vinyl records appeared on the market in 1958. See "W-G-N and WGNB to Unveil New 'Visual' Sound," *Chicago Tribune*, May 19, 1952; David Morton, *Sound Recording: The Life Story of a Technology* (Baltimore: Johns Hopkins University Press, 2006), 147.

123 *Phil Spector*: Spector's hit singles included the Ronettes' "Be My Baby" (1963), the Crystals' "Da Doo Ron Ron" (1963), the Chiffons' "One Fine Day" (1963), the Dixie Cups' "Chapel of Love" (1964), and the

Shangri-Las' "Leader of the Pack" (1964). See Tom Larson, *History of Rock and Roll* (Dubuque, Iowa: Kendall/Hunt, 2004), 58–59.

124 *Silvertone series 1205*: For more about this model, visit www.abetterpage .com/transistors/trans/US/1az3SilvertoneShtpkts.html.

124 *atom symbol*: To view the Sears and Roebuck atom logo, visit http:// guitarhunter.blogspot.com/2009/03/vintage-1970s-sears-harmony -acoustic.html.

126 *commonplace in cars*: See Lewis Coe, *Wireless Radio: A Brief History* (Jefferson, N.C.: McFarland, 1996), 88.

126 *invented in the United States*: For more about the invention and the impact of the transistor, see Michael Riordan and Lillian Hoddeson, *Crystal Fire: The Invention of the Transistor and the Birth of the Information Age* (New York: W. W. Norton, 1998).

126 *U.S. patent*: The patent, filed on June 17, 1948, is US2524035.

126 *Nobel Prize*: See Francis Leroy, *A Century of Nobel Prize Recipients: Chemistry, Physics, and Medicine* (New York: Marcel Dekker, 2003), 163.

126–27 *battery-powered radio*: For more on the development and the sale of the pocket radio, see Michael B. Schiffer, *The Portable Radio in American Life* (Tucson: University of Arizona Press, 1991), 176.

127 *Steve Jobs was conceived*: Steve Jobs was born on February 24, 1955. See Walter Isaacson, *Steve Jobs* (New York: Simon & Schuster, 2013), 3.

127 *Regency brand*: Schiffer, *Portable Radio in American Life*, 176–79.

127 *a man's suit cost around $40.00*: For fashion prices, visit www.thepeoplehist ory.com/50smensfashions.html.

127 *typically $63.00*: Cara S. Trager, "Business and Family Grew with Levittown," *Newsday*, Jan. 24, 1997.

127 *one hundred thousand Regency radios*: Schiffer, *Portable Radio in American Life*, 178.

127 *based its sales estimates*: Megan Fernandez, "The Pod Father," *Indianapolis Monthly*, March 2007.

127 *sold millions of transistor radios*: See Christopher H. Sterling, ed., *The Concise Encyclopedia of American Radio* (New York: Routledge, 2010), 778.

128 *average cost of a transistor radio*: See *Sears, Roebuck Catalogs*, Fall/ Winter 1960.

128 *as low as fifteen dollars*: Mary Braswell, "Looking Back a Half-Century to 1965," *Albany Herald*, Jan. 3, 2015.

128 *oversized breast pockets*: See Patricia Ebrey and Anne Walthall, *East Asia: A Cultural, Social, and Political History*, vol. 2, *From 1600* (Boston: Wadsworth Cengage, 2013), 469.

128 *registered their radios as toys*: See Ced Kurtz, "1950s Transistor Radios Pointed to More Tech Changes," *Pittsburgh Post-Gazette*, July 12, 2009.

128 *first jazz album to sell*: *Time Out* would eventually go double platinum in 2011. See Nicholas Cook and Anthony Pople, eds., *The Cambridge History of Twentieth Century Music* (New York: Cambridge University Press, 2004), 403.

128 *around $5.98 in 1960*: See "Mono 33 Single No Negation of Fall Price Cut," *Billboard*, June 27, 1960; Sam Goody advertisement, *New York Times*, Sept. 6, 1959.

129 *"serious listeners"*: For use of the term, see "Shopping for a Record Player?," *Changing Times: The Kiplinger Magazine*, Feb. 1958; "JansZen Loudspeakers," *Hi-Fi Review* 3 (1959).

129 *Brill Building*: For more on the history of the Brill Building, see Ken Emerson, *Always Magic in the Air: The Bomp and Brilliance of the Brill Building Era* (New York: Penguin, 2006).

130 *seventeen and twenty years old*: See David Hinckley, "Gerry Goffin Dead at 75," *New York Daily News*, June 19, 2014.

130 *a hit from 1960 called "Tonight's the Night"*: See Gillian G. Gaar, *She's a Rebel: The History of Women in Rock and Roll* (New York: Da Capo, 2002), 33; Carole King, *A Natural Woman: A Memoir* (New York: Grand Central, 2012), 94–95.

131 *"Like any kid, I think"*: Transcription of an interview between Marc Maron and David Byrne on episode 603 of the *WTF with Marc Maron* podcast, May 18, 2015.

132 *"Technological advances"*: Elmer Bernstein, "Listening to Music Is an Art," *Los Angeles Times*, Nov. 5, 1961.

132 *Compared with hi-fi stereo*: See Christopher H. Sterling, ed., *Encyclopedia of Radio* (New York: Fitzroy Dearborn, 2004), 1974.

132 *AM waves, modulated*: See Christopher H. Sterling and Michael C. Keith, *Sounds of Change: A History of FM Broadcasting in America* (Chapel Hill: University of North Carolina Press, 2008), 229; Allan Watson, *Cultural Production in and Beyond the Recording Studio* (New York: Routledge, 2015), 141.

132 *two-and-a-half-inch speaker*: See Toshiba Midget Transistor Radio advertisement, *Life*, March 30, 1959.

133 *"When we were growing up"*: Joe Harrington, "We Were Squares, But—," *Daily Boston Globe*, Aug. 24, 1958.

8. SINGERS AND SONGWRITERS: POTTY ABOUT DYLAN

135 *with twelve Top 10 hits*: See "Fool's Paradise" in "Retailers Pick," *Billboard*, Nov. 26, 1949; "Sitting by the Window" in "Most Played Juke Box R&B," *Billboard*, April 15, 1950; "I Wanna Be Loved" and "My Foolish Heart" in "Best-Selling Pop Singles," *Billboard*, July 1, 1950; "The Show Must Go On" in "The Disk Jockeys Pick," *Billboard*, Sept. 16, 1950; "Bring Back the Thrill" in "The Operators Pick," *Billboard*, March 3, 1951; "If" in "Records Most Played by Disk Jockeys," *Billboard*, March 10, 1951; "I'm Yours to Command" and "What Will I Tell My Heart?" in "The Retailers Pick," *Billboard*, April 21, 1951; "I Apologize" in "Best-Selling Pop Singles," *Billboard*, April 28, 1951; "Love Me" in "The Retailers Pick," *Billboard*, June 9, 1951; "Kiss of Fire" in "Most Played Juke Box R&B Records," *Billboard*, June 14, 1952.

136 *Of the top ten singles*: "Rock Around the Clock" was written by Max Freedman and Jimmy DeKnight; "The Yellow Rose of Texas" was an 1853 marching song adapted by Don George into a pop hit. See Fred Bronson, *The "Billboard" Book of Number One Hits*, 5th ed. (New York: Billboard Books, 2003), 1–2.

136 *"King of Mambo"*: See "Perez Prado Deal for Films Reported," *Los Angeles Times*, July 15, 1957.

136 *Elton John's anthem*: "Philadelphia Freedom" was co-written by Elton John and Bernie Taupin; "Fame" was co-written by David Bowie, John Lennon, and Carlos Alomar; "One of These Nights" was co-written by Don Henley and Glenn Frey. See Bronson, *"Billboard" Book of Number One Hits*, 401, 411, 416.

137 *before Michel Foucault noticed*: The French philosopher Michel Foucault's famous essay "What Is an Author?" proposed that creative works are the product of the many influences on an author. See Michel Foucault, "What Is an Author?," in *The Foucault Reader*, ed. Paul Rabinow (New York: Pantheon Books, 1984), 101–20.

137 *Eva Tanguay*: For more on Tanguay, see Andrew Erdman, *Queen of Vaudeville: The Story of Eva Tanguay* (Ithaca, N.Y.: Cornell University Press, 2012).

138 *"I started writing songs"*: John Sebastian, interview with author.

139 *Mick Jagger and Keith Richards*: See Gordon Thompson, *Please Please Me: Sixties British Pop, Inside Out* (New York: Oxford University Press, 2008), 207.

139 *Muddy Waters's "I Want to Be Loved" and Bo Diddley's "Road Runner"*: See Sean Egan, *The Rough Guide to the Rolling Stones* (New York: Rough Guides, 2006), 15.

140 *while Jagger and Richards watched*: See Keith Richards, *Life* (New York: Little, Brown, 2010), 141.

140 *locked Jagger and Richards in a kitchen*: Ibid., 142.

140 *"Keith likes to tell"*: Quoted in Mick Jagger et al., *According to the Rolling Stones* (New York: Chronicle Books, 2003), 84.

140 *"Will You Love Me Tomorrow"*: See Philip Norman, *John Lennon: The Life* (Toronto: Anchor Canada, 2009), 229.

140 *"Chains"*: The song appears as track four on the Beatles' debut studio album, *Please Please Me*, EMI Records, 1963.

140 *"When Paul and I first got"*: John Lennon, interview with Raoul Pantin, *Trinidad Express*, May 4, 1971. Quoted in Mark Lewisohn, *Tune In: The Beatles All These Years* (New York: Crown Archetype, 2013), 1:706.

141 *understood to have written "Please Please Me"*: See Robert Christgau, *Grown Up All Wrong: 75 Great Rock and Pop Artists from Vaudeville to Techno* (Cambridge, Mass.: Harvard University Press, 1998), 109.

141 *three fifteen-minute shows*: Walter Everett, *The Beatles as Musicians: The Quarry Men Through "Rubber Soul"* (New York: Oxford University Press, 2001), 213.

141 *Sylvie Vartan*: See Kenneth Womack, ed., *The Cambridge Companion to the Beatles* (New York: Cambridge University Press, 2009), 72.

141 *"In Paris in 1964"*: Quoted in *The Beatles Anthology* (New York: Chronicle Books, 2000), 114. George Harrison would later claim to have been the Beatle who introduced *The Freewheelin' Bob Dylan* to the Beatles in Paris in January 1964. Harrison referred to the album by its French title, but the French edition was not released until later in 1964. Regardless of who brought the album to the hotel, the Beatles agree to have listened obsessively to it while in Paris. See Simon Philo, *British*

Invasion: *The Crosscurrents of Musical Influence* (Lanham, Md.: Rowman & Littlefield, 2015), 74.

141 *from Minnesota in 1961*: See Stephen Petrus and Ronald D. Cohen, *Folk City: New York and the American Folk Music Revival* (New York: Oxford University Press, 2015), 255.

141 The Freewheelin' Bob Dylan: For more on the album, see Anthony Varesi, *The Bob Dylan Albums: A Critical Study* (Toronto: Guernica, 2002), 24.

142 *"Nottamun Town"*: See Dennis McNally, *On Highway 61: Music, Race, and the Evolution of Freedom* (New York: Counterpoint, 2014), 369.

142 *"Lord Randall"*: See Kevin J. H. Dettmar, ed., *The Cambridge Companion to Bob Dylan* (New York: Cambridge University Press, 2009), 19.

142 *"Scarborough Fair"*: See David Hajdu, *Positively 4th Street: The Lives and Times of Joan Baez, Bob Dylan, Mimi Baez Fariña, and Richard Fariña* (New York: Farrar, Straus and Giroux, 2001), 126.

142 *"Who's Gonna Buy You Ribbons When I'm Gone?"*: See Dave Van Ronk, *The Mayor of MacDougal Street*, with Elijah Wald (New York: Da Capo, 2005), 85.

142 *her death in 2011*: See William Grimes, "Suze Rotolo, a Face, with Bob Dylan, of '60s Music, Is Dead at 67," *New York Times*, March 1, 2011.

143 *Little Richard numbers*: See Clinton Heylin, *Bob Dylan: The Recording Sessions, 1960–1994* (New York: St. Martin's Press, 1995), 113.

143 *Elston Gunn*: See Seth Rogovoy, *Bob Dylan: Prophet, Mystic, Poet* (New York: Scribner, 2009), 25.

143 Peter Gunn: See Hajdu, *Positively 4th Street*, 67.

143 *"Did you hear that?"*: Quoted in ibid., 197.

143 *album of pre-rock pop standards*: Dylan's album was titled *Shadows in the Night*, Columbia Records, 2015.

143 *"That's me in my Dylan period"*: Quoted in David Sheff and G. Barry Golsen, *The "Playboy" Interviews with John Lennon and Yoko Ono* (New York: Playboy Press, 1981), 165.

144 *"I started thinking about my own emotions"*: Quoted in Jann Wenner, *Lennon Remembers* (New York: Verso, 2000), 83–84.

145 Hullabaloo *or* Shindig!: *Shindig!* ran from 1964 to 1966 on ABC, and *Hullabaloo* ran from 1965 to 1966 on NBC. For more on these programs, see Jake Austen, *TV-a-Go-Go* (Chicago: Chicago Review Press, 2005), 37–40.

145 *"Bob used to ask me"*: Joan Baez, interview with author.

145 *"Sweet Sir Galahad"*: Baez performed the song at the 1969 Woodstock Festival and recorded it on her 1970 album *One Day at a Time*.

145 *"I had something"*: Baez, interview with author.

146 *"Oh my God"*: Quoted in Michelle Mercer, *Will You Take Me as I Am: Joni Mitchell's Blue Period* (Milwaukee: Backbeat Books, 2012), 32.

146 *"It was James"*: See David Hajdu, "Billboard Goddesses," *New Republic*, April 20, 2012.

147 *Taylor's third album*: Warner Bros. released *Mud Slide Slim and the Blue Horizon* in 1971. See Nathan Brackett and Christian Hoard, eds., *The New "Rolling Stone" Album Guide* (New York: Simon & Schuster, 2004), 804.

147 *"Bobby has a lot to answer for"*: Dave Van Ronk, conversation with author.

148 *joint credit*: See Jon Wiener, *Come Together: John Lennon in His Time* (Urbana: University of Illinois Press, 1991), 99.

148 *Berry's publishing company sued*: See Wenner, *Lennon Remembers*, 90.

148 *"The thing was created"*: Quoted in Sheff, *All We Are Saying*, 201.

149 *"Hey, hey, hey"*: Lyrics from "Blurred Lines," credited to Robin Thicke, Pharrell Williams, and Clifford Harris Jr., Star Trak/Interscope, 2013.

149 *plagiarism suit*: For more on the trial, see Ben Sisario and Noah Smith, "'Blurred Lines' Infringed on Marvin Gaye Copyright, Jury Rules," *New York Times*, March 10, 2015.

149 *"wanted some credit"*: Quoted in Eriq Gardner, "Robin Thicke Admits Drug Abuse, Lying to Media in Wild 'Blurred Lines' Deposition," *Hollywood Reporter*, Sept. 15, 2014.

149 *"This is what happens"*: Quoted in Ben Sisario, "Industry Issues Intrude in 'Blurred Lines' Case," *New York Times*, March 1, 2015.

149 *"people are made to look"*: Quoted in August Brown, "Thicke Deposed to Clear Up Those 'Blurred Lines'; The Singer Details His Role in Writing the Controversial Song," *Los Angeles Times*, Sept. 16, 2014.

9. THE ALBUM: A PAIR OF TWENTY-MINUTE THINGS

151–52 *Dino in a cowboy hat*: The album was *Dean "Tex" Martin Rides Again*, Reprise Records, 1963.

152 *Goddard Lieberson*: Eventually, CBS would buy out Lerner and Loewe's royalty share of 30 percent, raising the company's share to 70 percent.

See Russell Sanjek, *American Popular Music and Its Business: The First Four Hundred Years*, vol. 3, *From 1900 to 1984* (New York: Oxford University Press, 1988), 352.

152 *bestselling album in America*: Craig Rosen, *The "Billboard" Book of Number One Albums: The Inside Story Behind Pop Music's Blockbuster Records* (New York: Billboard Books, 1996), 2. The soundtrack would sell more than one million copies by 1957. See "New Musicals on Disks," *Billboard Audition*, Oct. 28, 1957.

152 *seven more times*: Fred Bronson, "The Years in Music: How the Charts Beat 10, 20, 30, and 40 Years Ago," *Billboard*, Jan. 4, 1997.

152 *nineteen weeks*: See *British Hit Singles and Albums* (London: Guinness World Records Limited, 2004), 45.

152 *some thirteen million copies*: Andre Millard, *America on Record: A History of Recorded Sound* (New York: Cambridge University Press, 2005), 234.

153 *drug song*: Some accused "The Candy Man" of referring to Nembutal and amphetamines. See Mike Haskins, *Drugs: A User's Guide* (London: Ebury, 2003), 234.

153 Chariots of the Gods: Written by Erich von Daniken, the 1968 book argued that the religions and technologies of ancient civilizations were provided by aliens who were once welcomed on earth as gods. See Erich von Daniken, *Chariots of the Gods? Unsolved Mysteries of the Past* (New York: Putnam, 1968).

154 *"Cole Porter is definitive of an era"*: Quoted in Max Wilk, *They're Playing Our Song: Conversations with America's Classic Songwriters*, rev. ed. (Westport, Conn.: Easton Studio Press, 2008), 158.

156 *"Songs from successful plays"*: "Herbert Puts the Blame on Music Publishers," *New York Clipper*, Feb. 18, 1920.

156 *"I was Gilbert and Sullivan crazy"*: Quoted in Cole Porter, *The Cole Porter Story, as Told to Richard G. Hubler* (New York: World, 1965), 70.

156 *"first great literary idol"*: Harold Meyerson and Ernie Warburg, *Who Put the Rainbow in "The Wizard of Oz"? Yip Harburg, Lyricist* (Ann Arbor: University of Michigan Press, 1993), 15.

157 *Al Jolson was starring in* Sinbad: The show opened in February 1918 and played 388 performances. See Kay Green, ed., *Broadway Musicals, Show by Show* (Milwaukee: Hal Leonard, 1996), 29.

157 *imitation Stephen Foster tune "Swanee"*: See Arnold Shaw, *The Jazz Age: Popular Music in the 1920s* (New York: Oxford University Press, 1987), 266.

157	*Irving Berlin's "Blue Skies"*: See Allen Forte, *The American Popular Ballad of the Golden Era, 1924–1950* (Princeton, N.J.: Princeton University Press, 1995), 87.

158	*"At [one] time"*: Quoted in Stephen Citron, *Stephen Sondheim and Andrew Lloyd Webber: The New Musical* (New York: Oxford University Press, 2001), 271.

158	*demonstration record*: See Jerry Butler and Earl Smith, *Only the Strong Survive: Memoirs of a Soul Survivor* (Bloomington: Indiana University Press, 2000), 143.

159	*creaky* Mr. President: The musical comedy, starring Robert Ryan and Nanette Fabray, opened on Broadway on October 20, 1962. See Jeffrey Magee, *Irving Berlin's American Musical Theater* (New York: Oxford University Press, 2012), 290–300.

159	*the first long-playing albums*: Parts of the following text first appeared in slightly different form in David Hajdu, "Songbook Jam," *New Republic*, March 19, 2007.

159	*a mass-market product in 1948*: David Morton, *Sound Recording: The Life Story of a Technology* (Baltimore: Johns Hopkins University Press, 2006), xii.

160	*"Frank had his fill of singing crap"*: Billy May, interview with author.

161	*Ella Fitzgerald, working closely with Norman Granz*: For more on Granz and Ella Fitzgerald, see Barry Singer, "How Long Has This Been Going On?," *New York*, Nov. 1, 1993.

161	*"A great singer should sing"*: Norman Granz, interview with author.

162	*"Heartbreak Hotel"*: See Bronson, *"Billboard" Book of Number One Hits*, 10.

162	*"anti–rock and roll"*: Granz, interview with author.

162	*"He gave me the only advice"*: Quoted in Hemming and Hajdu, *Discovering Great Singers of Classic Pop*, 97–98.

162	*"you had to cater"*: Granz, interview with author.

163	*FCC opened up the FM radio band*: Sterling, *Concise Encyclopedia of American Radio*, 306–307.

163	*LPs were outselling single records*: See Geoffrey Cannon, "Bring Back the Single," *Guardian*, Oct. 22, 1968; Mike Gross, "LP Perils Single in Bowing Acts," *Billboard*, Aug. 19, 1967.

163	*full movement of a Berlioz symphony*: Peter C. Goldmark, the head of research at Columbia Records who helped develop the LP, recalled in his autobiography that his team was initially able to have one side of a disc play fifteen minutes of music, the average length of a musical movement. According to Goldmark, the Columbia Records president, Edward Wallerstein, then challenged him to record a full Berlioz movement, which runs about twenty minutes, on one side of the LP. See Peter C. Goldmark, *Maverick Inventor: My Turbulent Years at CBS*, with Lee Edson (New York: Saturday Review Press, 1973), 135.

163 *twenty to twenty-five minutes*: Frank Hoffmann, ed., *Encyclopedia of Recorded Sound* (New York: Routledge, 2004), 1246.

165–66 *overdubbing and double tracking*: Songs that featured these techniques included 1951's "How High the Moon" and 1953's "Vaya con Dios." See ibid., 660; Walter Everett, *The Foundations of Rock: From "Blue Suede Shoes" to "Suite: Judy Blue Eyes"* (New York: Oxford University Press, 2009), 346.

166 *Shadow Morton*: See Paul Gripp, "Party Lights: Utopic Desire and the Girl Group Sound," in *Sexual Politics and Popular Culture*, ed. Diane Christine Raymond (Madison, Wis.: Popular Press, 1990), 65.

166 *Kinks' Face to Face*: For more on the Kinks, see Rob Jovanovic, *God Save the Kinks: A Biography* (London: Aurum, 2013).

166 Pet Sounds: For more about the record, see Jim Fusilli, *The Beach Boys' "Pet Sounds"* (New York: Bloomsbury, 2005).

166 *stunned by the album's invention*: See Barry Miles, *Paul McCartney: Many Years from Now* (New York: Owl Books/Henry Holt, 1997), 281.

167 *"the album of all time"*: Quoted in Vic Garbarini, "Paul McCartney: Lifting the Veil on the Beatles," in *The Rock Musician: 15 Years of Interviews—the Best of "Musician" Magazine*, ed. Tony Scherman (New York: St. Martin's Press, 1994), 27.

167 *number one greatest album*: In 2003, the magazine pronounced the album to be the greatest in history. See June Skinner Sawyers, *Read the Beatles: Classic and New Writings on the Beatles, Their Legacy, and Why They Still Matter* (New York: Penguin, 2006), 97.

167 *the original idea*: Paul McCartney, interview with author.

168 *"I'm not interested in singles"*: Quoted in Morgan Ames, "Simon and Garfunkel in Action," *High Fidelity*, Nov. 1967.

168 *"I'm going to start writing"*: Simon's quotation as recalled by Art Garfunkel in Pete Fornatale, *Simon and Garfunkel's "Bookends"* (New York: Rodale, 2007), 86.

169 *the Mark Hellinger Theater*: See Citron, *Stephen Sondheim and Andrew Lloyd Webber*, 187.

10. PUNK VERSUS DISCO: WHO NEEDS LOVE?

171 *April 19, 1978*: See George Gimarc, *Punk Diary: The Ultimate Trainspotter's Guide to Underground Rock, 1970–1982* (San Francisco: Backbeat Books, 2005), 132–33.

171 *four people left CBGB*: Details of these events come from Legs McNeil and Gillian McCain, *Please Kill Me: The Uncensored Oral History of Punk* (New York: Grove Press, 2006).

171 *Sticca would later recall*: Ibid., 314.

172 *"I'll kill 'em!"*: Quoted in ibid., 316.

172 *black T-shirts*: To see Arturo Vega's shirt design, visit http://blogs .villagevoice.com/music/2009/07/johnny_blitz_of.php.

172 *Robert Fripp*: For more on Fripp's career, see Eric Tamm, *Robert Fripp: From King Crimson to Guitar Craft* (London: Faber and Faber, 1991).

173 *breakthrough on the pop charts*: Blondie's 1979 single "Heart of Glass," album *Eat to the Beat*, and 1980 single "Call Me" would become major hits. See William Ruhlmann, *Breaking Records: 100 Years of Hits* (New York: Routledge, 2004), 176.

173–74 *"Sister Midnight"* . . . *"I Feel Love"*: Visit the official Blondie website for archived performance lists: http://archive.blondie.net/gig_list.php.

175 *Love Unlimited Orchestra*: See John A. Jackson, *A House on Fire: The Rise and Fall of Philadelphia Soul* (New York: Oxford University Press, 2004), 268, 302.

175 *Paul Ramon*: Thompson, *Please Please Me*, 250.

175 *"I hate hippies"*: Quoted in Jonh Ingham, "The Sex Pistols Are Four Months Old," *Sounds*, April 24, 1976.

175 *"That long-hair shit"*: Frankie Valli, interview with author.

177 *Vernon and Irene Castle*: See William A. Shack, *Harlem in Montmartre: A Paris Jazz Story Between the Great Wars* (Berkeley: University of California Press, 2001), 3.

177 *Harry Fox*: For more on Fox's career, see Frank Cullen, *Vaudeville Old and New: An Encyclopedia of Variety Performers in America*, with Florence Hackman and Donald McNeilly (New York: Routledge, 2006), 1:403–404.

178 *At least forty tunes*: For a list of some of the titles, visit www.streetswing .com/music_archive/m1foxtrot.htm.

178 *"Do the Funny Fox Trot"*: See *Victor Records 1917 Catalogue, Second (November) Edition*.

178 *"Fox Trot Classique"*: See Chip Deffaa, *Voices of the Jazz Age: Profiles of Eight Vintage Jazzmen* (Urbana: University of Illinois Press, 1990), 66.

178 *"Black Satin Fox Trot," "The Raggy Fox Trot"*: See David A. Jasen and Trebor Jay Tichenor, *Rags and Ragtime: A Musical History* (New York: Dover, 1989), 157, 209.

178 *civic and church leaders*: See "The Dances and What Has Been Done and Said to Have Them Suppressed," *Washington Post*, Dec. 14, 1913.

178 *"If I was presiding"*: See "Urges Prison for 'Trot': Priest Declares Dance Both Immoral and Criminal," *New-York Tribune*, July 8, 1912.

178 *juba dances*: See Marshall Winslow Stearns and Jean Stearns, *Jazz Dance: The Story of American Vernacular Dance*, rev. ed. (New York: Da Capo, 1994), 29.

179 *"Unless it is suppressed"*: See "Down the Line: Dangers of the Dance," *New York Herald Tribune*, Nov. 9, 1925.

179 *variable constant*: A "variable constant" is referred to by the University of Amsterdam mathematician and philosopher L.E.J. Brouwer in the context of measuring bodies on an expanding sphere. See L.E.J. Brouwer, *Collected Works: Philosophy and Foundations of Mathematics*, ed. A. Heyting (Amsterdam: North-Holland, 1975), 1:62.

180 *the pogo*: In punk mythology, Sid Vicious is said to have created the dance. See Paul Marko, *The Roxy London WC2: A Punk History* (London: Punk 77, 2007), 132.

180 *The very notion of "musicality"*: For an overview on the connections between musicality and gay identity, see Philip Brett, "Musicality, Essentialism, and the Closet," in *Queering the Pitch: The New Gay and Lesbian Musicology*, ed. Philip Brett, Elizabeth Wood, and Gary C. Thomas, 2nd ed. (New York: Routledge, 2006), 9–26.

181 *"Disco was the soundtrack"*: Edmund White, interview with author.

181 *"a symbolic call for gays"*: See "Disco Takes Over," *Newsweek*, April 2, 1979.

181 *Sylvester*: For more on Sylvester and the liberation movement in the 1970s, see Joshua Gamson, *The Fabulous Sylvester: The Legend, the Music, the Seventies in San Francisco* (New York: Picador, 2006).

182 *"A gay man in the '70s"*: White, interview with author.

183 *"I didn't make a punk album"*: See Lester Bangs, *Blondie* (New York: Fireside/Simon & Schuster, 1980), 62.

184 *"some rock critics"*: Lester Bangs, "Review: Blondie, *Eat to the Beat*," *Stereo Review*, vol. 43, December 1979.

II. VIDEO: MOONWALKERS

185 *Ringo shouts*: At this moment in the film, Ringo's mouth doesn't move. His voice was clearly added in postproduction.

185 *listening obsessively*: See Miles, *Paul McCartney*, 161.

186 *"I remember meeting"*: Quoted in ibid., 162.

186 *video for MTV*: See Jeffrey Paul Smith, *The Sounds of Commerce: Marketing Popular Film Music* (New York: Columbia University Press, 1998), 160.

186 *demanding a paternity test*: See Sam Kashner, "Making Beatlemania: *A Hard Day's Night* at 50," *Vanity Fair*, July 2, 2014.

186 *Eva Tanguay*: Tanguay starred in two silent film comedies: 1916's now lost *Energetic Eva*, which might have been a filmed version of her vaudeville routines, and 1917's *Wild Girl*, a romance in which she played a woman who, after being abandoned as a baby, was reared as a boy by a Gypsy tribe. See Erdman, *Queen of Vaudeville*, 198–202.

186 Le mélomane: Méliès's film, also known as *The Melomaniac*, was released in 1903. See Elizabeth Ezra, *Georges Méliès* (Manchester, U.K.: Manchester University Press, 2000), 30.

186 The Play House: Keaton's film was released in October 1921. See James L. Neibaur and Terri Niemi, eds., *Buster Keaton's Silent Shorts, 1920–1923* (Lanham, Md.: Scarecrow Press, 2013), 107–17.

186 *no laboratory effects*: See Marion Meade, *Buster Keaton: Cut to the Chase* (New York: HarperCollins, 1995), 112.

187 *"Coming Up"*: See Paul Du Noyer, *Conversations with McCartney* (London: Hodder & Stoughton, 2015), 146.

187 The Jazz Singer: The film opened on October 6, 1927. See Arnold Shaw, *The Jazz Age: Popular Music in the 1920s* (New York: Oxford University Press, 1987), 184.

187 *thousand-seat theaters*: When it opened in 1911, the Winter Garden had 1,590 seats. See Charles Samuels and Louise Samuels, *Once upon a Stage: The Merry World of Vaudeville* (New York: Dodd, Mead, 1974), 199.

188 *Frank Tashlin*: Before making *The Girl Can't Help It*, Tashlin was an animator, directing such Looney Tunes cartoons as 1943's *Puss n' Booty* and *Porky Pig's Feat*. See Ethan de Seife, *Tashlinesque: The Hollywood Comedies of Frank Tashlin* (Middletown, Conn.: Wesleyan University Press, 2012), 17.

188 *novelty shorts*: In 1959, Lester directed *The Running, Jumping, and Standing Still Film*. The short film, featuring the BBC Radio *Goon Show* stars Peter Sellers and Spike Milligan, caught the Beatles' attention. The Beatles producer George Martin had previously produced Spike Milligan, and band members, particularly John Lennon, were big fans of *The Goon Show*. See Steven Soderbergh, *Getting Away with It; or, The Further Adventures of the Luckiest Bastard You Ever Saw, Also Starring Richard Lester as the Man Who Knew More Than He Was Asked* (London: Faber and Faber, 1999), 20; Iain Ellis, *Brit Wits: A History of British Rock Humor* (Bristol, U.K.: Intellect Books, 2012), 24; Peter Brown and Steven Gaines, *The Love You Make: An Insider's Story of the Beatles* (New York: New American Library, 2002), 70–71.

189 *cut down their need*: See *Beatles Anthology*, 214.

189 *short music films called Soundies*: See Maurice Terenzio, Scott MacGillivray, and Ted Okuda, *The Soundies Distribution Corporation of America: A History and Filmography of Their "Jukebox" Musical Films of the 1940s* (Jefferson, N.C.: McFarland, 1991).

190 *Lack initiated MTV*: See Robert Sam Anson, "When Music Was Still on MTV: The Birth of an Iconic Channel," *Vanity Fair*, Nov. 21, 2000; Bill Roedy, *What Makes Business Rock: Building the World's Largest Global Networks* (Hoboken, N.J.: Wiley, 2011), 28–29.

190 *MTV's first office*: Information in this paragraph is derived from the chapter "We Were Just Idiots in Hotel Rooms: John Lack, Bob Pittman, and the Creation of MTV," in Ron Tannenbaum and Craig Marks, *I Want My MTV: The Uncensored Story of the Music Video Revolution* (New York: Plume, 2011), 14–30.

191 *August 1, 1981*: See Richard Defendorf, "New Channel Hopes to Be Music to Adults' Ears," *Orlando Sentinel*, April 12, 1985.

191 *early broadcasts did not go well*: Details in this paragraph are derived from Anson, "When Music Was Still on MTV."

191 *still a novelty*: About 18 million out of 79 million U.S. households had some form of cable television service in 1981. By 1986, about 37.5 million

households would be cable subscribers. See Ronald Garay, "Politics and Cable Television: The Case of Houston, Texas," in *Communication Yearbook 7*, ed. Robert N. Bostrom (New York: Routledge, 2012), 443; *Statistical Abstract of the United States 1987*, 107th ed. (Washington, D.C.: U.S. Bureau of the Census, 1986), 531.

192 *"If it weren't for MTV"*: Gerald Casale, conversation with author.

192 *there was a delay*: See Nancy Griffin, "Michael Jackson's 'Thriller': How an Iconic Music Video Was Made," *Vanity Fair*, July 2, 2010.

192 *Cholly Atkins*: See Megan Pugh, *America Dancing: From the Cakewalk to the Moonwalk* (New Haven, Conn.: Yale University Press, 2015), 254–55.

193 *backsliding*: Ibid., 262.

193 *Fred Astaire called Jackson*: Ibid., 275.

193 *sales of the album doubled*: See Nancy Griffin, "The 'Thriller' Diaries," *Vanity Fair*, Jan. 2010.

193 *fifteen hundred Filipino prisoners*: See Francis Pakes, *Comparative Criminal Justice*, 3rd ed. (New York: Routledge, 2015), 156.

193 *thirteen thousand people danced*: See Shreeya Sinha, "Mexico Chases World Record: Biggest Selfie," *New York Times*, June 13, 2015.

194 *Madonna had emerged*: For more on Madonna's early music videos, see Carol Vernallis, *Experiencing Music Video: Aesthetics and Cultural Context* (New York: Columbia University Press, 2004).

194 *twenty-seven-city tour*: Madonna's first major tour was dubbed "The Virgin Tour." See "Talent in Action," *Billboard*, May 18, 1985; Dafydd Rees and Luke Crampton, eds., *Rock Movers and Shakers* (Santa Barbara, Calif.: ABC-CLIO, 1991), 321.

12. HIP-HOP: BEATS WANT TO BE FREE

198 *Clive Campbell*: For more on Campbell, see Jeff Chang, *Can't Stop, Won't Stop: A History of the Hip-Hop Generation* (New York: St. Martin's Press, 2005).

198 *The DJs in Kingston, Jamaica*: For more on the Kingston music scene, see Lloyd Bradley, *This Is Reggae Music: The Story of Jamaica's Music* (New York: Grove Press, 2000); David John Howard, *Kingston: A Cultural and Literary History* (Northampton, Mass.: Interlink Books, 2005), 166–93.

198 *moved to the South Bronx*: Chang, *Can't Stop, Won't Stop*, 68–72.

198 *hosting sound system parties*: Jennifer 8. Lee, "An Effort to Honor the Birthplace of Hip-Hop," *New York Times*, July 23, 2007.

198 *merry-go-round*: Kool Herc uses this term in Will Hermes, "All Rise for the National Anthem of Hip-Hop," *New York Times*, Oct. 29, 2006.

198 *break-beat style*: See Kembrew McLeod and Peter DiCola, *Creative License: The Law and Culture of Digital Sampling* (Durham, N.C.: Duke University Press, 2011), 53–57.

199 *"Don't turn it loose"*: From the single "Funky Drummer," written by James Brown, King Records, 1970.

199 *"I wanna give"*: Ibid.

200 *Universal Zulu Nation*: See Dan Charnas, *The Big Payback: The History of the Business of Hip-Hop* (New York: New American Library, 2010), 18–20.

200 *roughly the same period*: See Murray Forman, *The 'Hood Comes First: Race, Space, and Place in Rap and Hip-Hop* (Middletown, Conn.: Wesleyan University Press, 2002), 71–77; Radcliffe Joe and Nelson George, "Rapping DJs Set a Trend," *Billboard*, Nov. 3, 1979.

201 *Kraftwerk*: See Cheryl Lynette Keyes, *Rap Music and Street Consciousness* (Urbana: University of Illinois Press, 2004), 75.

201 *"Bridge Is Over"*: See Imani Perry, *Prophets of the Hood: Politics and Poetics in Hip Hop* (Durham, N.C.: Duke University Press, 2004), 84.

201 *"Rapper's Delight"*: For more on the song, see Loren Kajikawa, *Sounding Race in Rap Songs* (Berkeley: University of California Press, 2015), 19–48.

201 *made the* Billboard *chart*: The single reached number thirty-six on *Billboard*'s Hot 100. See Paul Grein, "Chart Beat," *Billboard*, Aug. 23, 1986.

202 *Sylvia Robinson*: For more on Robinson, see Marcia Gillespie, "Sylvia Robinson: Rap Music Queen," *Ms.*, Oct. 1983.

202 *on the single "The Magnificent Seven"*: See Chang, *Can't Stop, Won't Stop*, 154–55.

202 *Sugarhill released "The Message"*: See Charnas, *Big Payback*, 32–38.

203 *among the first rap records*: "The Message" was named 1982's top album by *The New York Times* and top single by the *Los Angeles Times*. See Robert Palmer, "'The Message' Is That 'Rap' Is Now King in Rock Clubs," *New York Times*, Sept. 3, 1982; Robert Palmer, "The Pop Life," *New York Times*, Dec. 22, 1982; Robert Hilburn, "Top 10 Singles Dance to Another Tune," *Los Angeles Times*, Dec. 28, 1982; Geoffrey Himes,

"Urban Anthems of Rap Music," *Washington Post*, Dec. 30, 1982; "Grandmaster Flash and the Furious Five, 'The Message'—the 50 Greatest Hip-Hop Songs of All Time," *Rolling Stone*, Dec. 5, 2012.

204 *Violent imagery*: Much of the text from this point until the words "Rhythm Racketeers" was published in a different form in David Hajdu, "Guns and Poses," *New York Times*, March 11, 2005.

204 *"32-20 Blues"*: See Paul Oliver, *Screening the Blues: Aspects of the Blues Tradition* (New York: Da Capo, 1968), 112.

204 *"Black Mountain Blues"*: See Eric Sackheim, ed., *The Blues Line: Blues Lyrics from Leadbelly to Muddy Waters* (New York: Thunder's Mouth Press, 1969), 51.

205 *"Got the Blues for Murder Only"*: See Peter Stanfield, *Horse Opera: The Strange History of the 1930s Singing Cowboy* (Urbana: University of Illinois Press, 2002), 112.

205 *"Duncan and Brady"*: See Moses Asch and Alan Lomax, eds., *The Leadbelly Songbook: The Ballads, Blues, and Folksongs of Huddie Ledbetter* (London: Oak, 1962), 74.

205 *"free from the chain gang now"*: See Barry Mazor, *Meeting Jimmie Rodgers: How America's Original Roots Music Hero Changed the Pop Sounds of a Century* (New York: Oxford University Press, 2009), 38.

206 *Woody Guthrie used*: See Sullivan, *Encyclopedia of Great Popular Song Recordings*, 1:62.

206 *Mozart quoted*: See David Gordon and Peter Gordon, *Musical Visitors to Britain* (New York: Routledge, 2005), 74.

206 *Ravel quoted*: See Michael Thomas Roeder, *A History of the Concerto* (Portland, Ore.: Amadeus Press, 1994), 358.

206 *Stravinsky quoted*: See Eric Walter White, *Stravinsky: The Composer and His Works* (Berkeley: University of California Press, 1979), 413.

206 *"I could go through Stravinsky's"*: Quoted in Jonathan Cott, *Dinner with Lenny: The Last Long Interview with Leonard Bernstein* (New York: Oxford University Press, 2013), 33.

206 *Ives quotes*: See J. Peter Burkholder, "'Quotation' and Paraphrase in Ives's Second Symphony," in *Music at the Turn of the Century: A 19th-Century Music Reader*, ed. Joseph Kerman (Berkeley: University of California Press, 1990), 52.

206 *Charlie Parker*: See Alex Ross, *The Rest Is Noise: Listening to the Twentieth Century* (New York: Farrar, Straus and Giroux, 2007), 476.

206　*Sonny Rollins*: See Tom Piazza, *The Guide to Classic Recorded Jazz* (Iowa City: University of Iowa Press, 1995), 169.

207　*portable equipment*: See Scot Solida, "The 10 Most Important Hardware Samplers in History," MusicRadar.com, Jan. 24, 2011.

207　*Hank Shocklee*: For more on Shocklee, see Tom Moon, "Public Enemy's Bomb Squad," in *The Rock History Reader*, ed. Theo Cateforis, 2nd ed. (New York: Routledge, 2013), 265–68.

207　*seventy-one samples*: See Jennifer C. Lena and Mark C. Pachucki, "The Sincerest Form of Flattery: Innovation, Repetition, and Status in an Art Movement," *Poetics* 41 (2013): 248.

208　*in O'Sullivan's favor*: See Ronald Sullivan, "Judge Rules Against Rapper in 'Sampling' Case," *New York Times*, Dec. 16, 1991.

208　*"They Reminisce over You (T.R.O.Y.)"*: See Joseph Schloss, *Making Beats: The Art of Sample-Based Hip-Hop* (Middletown, Conn.: Wesleyan University Press, 2004), 36.

208　*"Information wants to be free"*: Stewart Brand, creator of the *Whole Earth Catalog*, used this phrase in 1984. See Michael Schrage, "Hacking Away at the Future: Market's Realities Undermine Thrills," *Washington Post*, Nov. 18, 1984.

13. DIGITIZATION: THE IMMATERIAL WORLD

211　*"New Victor Artists in Popular Field"*: To see the ad, visit the Library of Congress National Jukebox website at www.loc.gov/jukebox/features /victor-advertising.

212　*Marian Anderson*: See Allan Keiler, *Marian Anderson: A Singer's Journey* (New York: Scribner, 2000).

212　*Noble Sissle and Eubie Blake*: See Robert Kimball and William Bolcom, *Reminiscing with Noble Sissle and Eubie Blake* (New York: Cooper Square Press, 1973).

212　*the Yale Collegians*: See Judith Ann Schiff, "Rudy Vallee, the First Crooner," *Yale Alumni Magazine*, Nov. 2002.

212　*"There is nothing stranger"*: See www.loc.gov/jukebox/features/victor -advertising.

212　*installed in cars*: The Galvin Manufacturing Company built the first commercially successful car radio, the Motorola 5T71, in the early 1930s. See Justin A. Williams, "Cars with the Boom," in *The Oxford Handbook of Mobile Music Studies*, ed. Sumanth Gopinath and Jason Stanyek (New York: Oxford University Press, 2014), 2:110.

212 *the invention of the Walkman*: Sony introduced the Walkman in Japan on July 17, 1979, and began selling it in the United States at Christmastime 1979. See Ron Alexander, "Stereo-to-Go—and Only You Can Hear It: For the Thinking Man," *New York Times*, July 7, 1980; John Nathan, *Sony: The Private Life* (New York: Houghton Mifflin Harcourt, 1999), 154.

212 *the trademark Soundabout*: See V. Elaine Smay, "Big Sound from a Tiny Stereo Cassette Player," *Popular Science*, July 1980; Hans Fantel, "Sound," *New York Times*, July 10, 1980.

212 *Stowaway*: See "The Incredible, Shrinking Tape Player," *New Scientist*, May 7, 1981.

213 *"My Sweet Lord"* . . . *"He's So Fine"*: In 1971, Bright Tunes, the publishing company that held the rights to the Chiffons' 1962 song "He's So Fine," written by Raymond Mack, sued George Harrison for plagiarizing the song in his 1970 track "My Sweet Lord." In *Bright Tunes Music v. Harrisongs Music*, the U.S. District Court of the Southern District of New York ruled in 1976 that Harrison, even if he didn't consciously plagiarize "He's So Fine," was guilty of copyright infringement. See Siva Vaidhyanathan, *Copyrights and Copywrongs: The Rise of Intellectual Property and How It Threatens Creativity* (New York: New York University Press, 2001), 126–30; Donald E. Biederman et al., *Law and Business of the Entertainment Industries*, 5th ed. (Westport, Conn.: Praeger, 2007), 62; Columbia Law School–USC Gould School of Law Music Copyright Infringement Resource: http://mcir.usc.edu/cases/1970-1979/Pages/brightharrisongs.html.

213 *"Surfin' U.S.A."* . . . *"Sweet Little Sixteen"*: The Beach Boys' 1963 "Surfin' U.S.A." used the melody of Chuck Berry's 1958 "Sweet Little Sixteen." After Berry's organization threatened legal action, Brian Wilson gave Berry songwriting credit. See Randy Lewis, "After 'Blurred Lines' Verdict, Brian Wilson Talks Chuck Berry and 'Surfin' U.S.A.,'" *Los Angeles Times*, March 12, 2015; Philip Lambert, *Inside the Music of Brian Wilson: The Songs, Sounds, and Influences of the Beach Boys' Founding*

Genius (New York: Continuum, 2007), 64; Paul McGrath, "It's the Same Old Song, Nearly: 'Adapting' Other People's Work Is Part of the Rock Tradition," *Globe and Mail*, March 7, 1981.

213 *"Happy Xmas (War Is Over)"... "Stewball"*: John Lennon and Yoko Ono's "Happy Xmas (War Is Over)" used the melodic structure of the 1963 Peter, Paul, and Mary version of the folk song "Stewball." See Joe Hickerson, "The Songfinder," *Sing Out! The Folk Song Magazine*, Summer 2009.

214 *copyrightable as creative works*: In Section 101 of the U.S. Copyright Act 17 U.S.C. §§ 101–810, it is noted that a collective work or compilation is copyrightable if there is authorship in the selection and arrangement of materials. See Deborah Bouchoux, *Intellectual Property: The Law of Trademarks, Copyrights, Patents, and Trade Secrets*, 3rd ed. (Clifton Park, N.Y.: Delmar Cengage Learning, 2009), 191; the Cornell University Law School Legal Information Institute website at www.law.cornell.edu /uscode/text/17/101.

214 *IBM Personal Computer*: IBM introduced its personal computer to consumers in August 1981. See James L. Rowe Jr., "IBM to Sell Personal Computer in Fall," *Washington Post*, Aug. 13, 1981.

214 *Apple Macintosh*: In 1984, Apple unveiled the Macintosh personal computer at its January 24 annual meeting. See Andrew Pollack, "Apple Expands Product Line: Macintosh Entry Near," *New York Times*, Jan. 16, 1984.

214 *Kane Kramer*: See Barry Fox, "The Mother of Idiocy," *New Scientist*, Dec. 24–31, 1987; Richard James Burgess, *The History of Music Production* (New York: Oxford University Press, 2014), 151.

215 *take more than an hour*: In the 1990s, it could take up to two hours to transfer an audio file. See Bill Kovarik, *Revolutions in Communication: Media History from Gutenberg to the Digital Age* (New York: Continuum, 2011), 234.

215 *Karlheinz Brandenburg*: See Jonathan Sterne, "How the MP3 Became Ubiquitous," in Gopinath and Stanyek, *Oxford Handbook of Mobile Music Studies*, 1:39; Greg Milner, *Perfecting Sound Forever: An Aural History of Recorded Music* (New York: Faber and Faber, 2009), 359; Doug Nairne, "MP3 Creator Says He Knows Pain of Ripped-Off Musicians," *South China Morning Post*, Dec. 12, 2000.

215 *Fraunhofer Society*: See Jack Ewing, "An Idea Incubator Tries to Grow Cash," *Business Week*, March 12, 2007; John Schmid, "German Cre-

ators of MP3 March to Different Tune," *New York Times*, Nov. 5, 2001; Douglas Heingartner, "Patent Fights Are a Legacy of MP3's Tangled Origins," *New York Times*, March 5, 2007.

216 *Motion Picture Experts Group*: See Rachel Powell, "Digitizing TV into Obsolescence," *New York Times*, Oct. 20, 1991.

216 *MPEG Audio Layer III*: See "MPEG Mania," *Maximum PC*, March 2001.

216 *Shawn Fanning*: See Greg Miller and P. J. Huffstutter, "File-Sharing PC Software Shakes Up Music World; Technology: 'Napster,' Created by a 19-Year-Old, Has the Recording Industry and Some College Campuses Up in Arms," *Los Angeles Times*, Feb. 24, 2000; G. Beato, "Trading Spaces," *Spin*, May 2000.

216 *nickname*: See Warren Cohen, "Napster Is Rocking the Music Industry," *U.S. News & World Report*, March 6, 2000; Nick Paton Walsh, "Mom, I Blew Up the Music Industry," *Guardian*, May 20, 2000.

217 *twenty-six million users*: See Bruce Kogut, ed., *The Global Internet Economy* (Cambridge, Mass: MIT Press, 2003), 462.

217 *Ninth Circuit Court of Appeals*: The three-judge panel on the court found that Napster contributed to the wholesale infringement of copyright-protected music and recordings. See Matt Richtel, "The Napster Decision: Appellate Judges Back Limitations on Copying Music," *New York Times*, Feb. 13, 2001.

217 *name would later resurface*: See William Glanz, "Napster Resurfaces, but Once-Free File-Sharing Service Now Charges Fee," *Knight Ridder Tribune Business News*, Oct. 29, 2003.

217 *"the wireless"*: See Robert H. Marriott, "'What's in a Name?' Radio or Wireless—Denote Same Thing," *New York Herald Tribune*, Dec. 11, 1927.

218 *exchange value*: See Karl Marx, *Grundisse: Foundations of the Critique of Political Economy* (New York: Penguin Classics, 1973), 140–49.

218 *$.99*: See Michael Prager, "Online Music Store Has a Core Following; Apple Users Find New iTunes Site Hard to Resist," *Boston Globe*, May 21, 2003.

218 *one million songs*: See Mike Himowitz, "A Platinum Debut Shows iTunes Has Hit Potential," *Baltimore Sun*, May 8, 2003.

218 *"Nobody was going to pay"*: Roger Ames, interview with author.

219 *homemade video clips*: The first video on YouTube was "Me at the Zoo," shot by Yakov Lapitsky and uploaded on April 23, 2005. See Randall Stross, *Planet Google: One Company's Audacious Plan to Organize Everything*

We Know (New York: Free Press, 2008), 236; Joel Landau, "Tube Perfect 10: 'You' Grew from a Single Elephant Video to a Stampede," *New York Daily News*, Feb. 15, 2015.

219 *YouTube was using*: See Andrew Murray, *Information Technology Law: The Law and Society* (Oxford: Oxford University Press, 2010), 27.

219 *such as Spotify*: Some of the material on Spotify in this section appeared in different form in David Hajdu, "Next to Nothing: The Economics and Aesthetics of Streaming," *Nation*, Aug. 24, 2015.

220 *the week it was introduced*: See Katherine Boehret, "The Digital Solution: New Way to Stream Music Crosses the Pond," *Wall Street Journal*, July 21, 2011.

220 *Apple Music*: See Brian X. Chen, "Apple Music Is Unveiled, Along with Operating System Upgrades," *New York Times*, June 8, 2015.

220 *most often as a lyricist*: See Clark Collis, "Music Critic David Hajdu Releases Album—with Help from Jill Sobule," *Entertainment Weekly*, Aug. 27, 2015.

220 *symposium on copyright*: For the transcript of the symposium, titled "Creation Is Not Its Own Reward: Making Copyright Work for Authors and Performers," see *Columbia Journal of Law and the Arts* 38 (Spring 2015).

220 *"middle-class economic status"*: Quoted in ibid., 425.

220 *"a pretty good pizza"*: Quoted in ibid.

221 *"the aural equivalent"*: See Elvis Costello, "Joni's Last Waltz?," *Vanity Fair*, Nov. 2004.

221 *Swift declined*: See Tim Bajarin, "How Taylor Swift Saved Apple Music," *Time*, June 30, 2015.

223 *The ur-text of Auto-Tune*: Much of the following text on Auto-Tune was first published in different form in David Hajdu, "Imperfect Pitch," *New Republic*, June 22, 2012.

223 *Arthur Freed*: For more on Freed's career, see Hugh Fordin, *M-G-M's Greatest Musicals: The Arthur Freed Unit* (New York: Da Capo, 1975).

224 *Invented as an afterthought*: See Melissa Ragona, "Doping the Voice," in *The Oxford Handbook of Sound and Image in Digital Media*, ed. Carol Vernallis, Amy Herzog, and John Richardson (New York: Oxford University Press, 2013), 165.

224 *transistor*: The transistor was discovered at Bell Labs when Walter Brattain and John Bardeen realized that amplification was occurring when a

contact was placed on a semiconductor. See Charles Townes, "The Creative and Unpredictable Interaction of Science and Technology," in *A Century of Ideas: Perspectives from Leading Scientists of the 20th Century*, ed. Burra Sidharth (New York: Springer, 2008), 128.

224 *Teflon*: First sold commercially in 1948, Teflon was invented inadvertently in 1938 when the DuPont scientist Roy J. Plunkett discovered that the residue of refrigeration gases could serve as a nonstick coating. See Andrew F. Smith, ed., *The Oxford Encyclopedia of Food and Drink in America*, 2nd ed. (New York: Oxford University Press, 2013), 342.

224 *microwave oven*: In 1946, the Raytheon Manufacturing Company engineer Percy Spencer invented the microwave. Spencer was testing magnetron tubes when he noticed that the tubes had melted his candy bar. Finding that the magnetrons could cook food, Spencer would patent his discovery in 1950. See Ben Ikenson, *Patents: Ingenious Inventions—How They Work and How They Came to Be* (New York: Black Dog and Leventhal, 2004), 214.

224 *Frisbee*: The Frisbee originated when students began flinging around empty pie tins that were made by the Connecticut baker William Russell Frisbie. In 1948, Walter Frederick Morrison and Warren Franscioni created a plastic version of the pie tin. After their partnership ended, Morrison patented the flying disc in 1958 and sold the rights to Wham-O, which eventually named it the Frisbee. See Johnny Acton, Tania Adams, and Matt Packer, *Origin of Everyday Things* (New York: Sterling, 2006), 97–98.

224 *"Well, I don't know"*: Quoted in Andrew Matson, "Inventor of Auto-Tune: 'I'm Innocent,'" *Seattle Times*, June 26, 2009.

225 *"the Cher Effect"*: See Ragona, "Doping the Voice," 164.

226 *"Auto-Tune can be used"*: See the NOVA website article "Auto-Tune: Expert Q&A," July 7, 2009.

227 *inheritability of artistic talent*: Researchers have suggested that the gene AVPR1A may be connected to music perception, music memory, and music listening and that the gene SLC6A4 may be connected with music memory and choir participation. See Yi Ting Yan et al., "The Genetic Basis of Music Ability," *Frontiers in Psychology*, June 27, 2014.

229 *The spark for the idea*: Much of the following text was first published in different form in David Hajdu, "Principia Electronica," *New Republic*, Dec. 7, 2012.

229 *West Berlin*: See Marc Spitz, *Bowie: A Biography* (New York: Three Rivers Press, 2009), 443.

229 *funk music hater*: See Eric Tamm, *Brian Eno: His Music and the Vertical Color of Sound* (New York: Da Capo, 1995), 35.

229 *"Eno came running in"*: From the liner notes in David Bowie's CD compilation *Sound+Vision*, Rykodisc, 1989.

230 *"If you're 15 to 25 years old now"*: Quoted in Ben Sisario, "Electronic Dance Concerts Turn Up Volume, Tempting Investors," *New York Times*, April 5, 2012.

231 *"Music was born free"*: See Ferruccio Busoni, *Sketch of a New Esthetic of Music* (New York: G. Schirmer, 1911), 5.

231 *"We have formulated"*: Ibid., 4.

232 *at odds with Adorno*: Theodor Adorno and Max Horkheimer saw new technologies as perpetuating a "culture industry" that oppressively created a uniformity of desire. See Theodor W. Adorno and Max Horkheimer, "The Culture Industry: Enlightenment as Mass Deception," in Theodor W. Adorno and Max Horkheimer, *The Dialectic of Enlightenment* (New York: Verso, 2008), 120. In contrast, Walter Benjamin, Adorno's Frankfurt school contemporary, believed that some machines—especially those involved with the cinema—could possibly fulfill the human yearning for union with nature. See Benjamin, "Work of Art in the Age of Its Technological Reproducibility," 35; John Tresh, *The Romantic Machine: Utopian Science and Technology After Napoleon* (Chicago: University of Chicago Press, 2012), 14–15.

232 *"The history of electronic music"*: George Lewis, conversation with author.

232 *the Warehouse*: See Michaelangelo Matos, *The Underground Is Massive: How Electronic Dance Music Conquered America* (New York: Dey Street, 2015), 4.

233 *"The Detroit underground"*: Quoted in Tim Barr, *The Rough Guide to Techno* (New York: Rough Guides, 2000), vii.

233 *Dubstep*: See Paul C. Jasen, *Low End Theory: Bass, Bodies, and the Materiality of Sonic Experience* (New York: Bloomsbury, 2016), 179.

233 *138 to 142 bpm*: See Peter Dowsett, *Audio Production Tips: Getting the Sound Right at the Source* (New York: Focal Press, 2016), 199.

234 *Andy Stott*: See Will Hermes, "Faith in Strangers," *Rolling Stone*, Nov. 20, 2014.

234 *"There was a lot of criticism"*: Quoted in David Hajdu, "Birthday of the Cool," *New Yorker*, March 11, 1996.

CODA

239 *more than a dozen songs*: These include Katy Perry's "Last Friday Night (T.G.I.F.)," written by Katy Perry, Lukasz Gottwald, Max Martin, and Bonnie McKee, *Teenage Dream*, Capitol Records, 2010; Adam Lambert's "Fever," written by Lady Gaga, Rob Fusari, and Jeff Bhasker, *For Your Entertainment*, RCA Records, 2009; Nicki Minaj and Lil Wayne's "Roman Reloaded," written by Onika Maraj, Dwayne Carter, and Ricardo Lamarre, *Pink Friday: Roman Reloaded*, Young Money/Cash Money/Universal Republic, 2012; Pusha T's "What Dreams Are Made Of," written by Terrence Thornton, *Fear of God II: Let Us Pray*, GOOD/Deacon/Re-up, 2011; Tal and Flo Rida's single "Danse," written by Tal Benyerzi, Bruno Damas, Silvio Tristan Lisbonne, Manon Lisa Romiti, and Julio Masidi Biau, Warner Music France, 2013; Jay Rock, Rick Ross, and BJ the Chicago Kid's "Finest Hour," written by Johnny McKinzie, Erik Ortiz, Kevin Crowe, William Roberts, and Bryan Sledge, *Follow Me Home*, Top Dawg/Strange, 2011; Yelawolf's "Everything I Love the Most," written by Michael Atha, William Washington, Jason "Pooh Bear" Boyd, and William Martin Joel, *Radioactive*, Ghet-O Vision/DGC/Interscope/Shady, 2011; Obie Trice's "Bruh Bruh," written by Obie Trice, *The Hangover*, Black Market Entertainment, 2015; Big Sean's "Mona Lisa," written by Sean Anderson, Marcos Palacios, Ernest Clark, and Alexander Izquierdo, *Hall of Fame*, GOOD/Def Jam, 2013; Britney Spears's "3," written by Max Martin, Shellback, and Tiffany Amber, *The Singles Collection*, Jive Records, 2009; Rich Boy's "Drop," written by Jamal F. Jones and Marece Benjamin Richards, Interscope, 2009; Cam'ron's "Triple Up," written by Cam'ron, *Killa Season*, Diplomat/Asylum, 2006; Trick Daddy's "Menage a Trois," written by Brandon Holleman, Tony Castillo, Darion Crawford, Mark Bryan Seymour, and Maurice Young, *Thug Matrimony: Married to the Streets*, Atlantic Records, 2004; and Ludacris's "Teamwork," written by Christopher Bridges and Mickey Davis, *Chicken-n-Beer*, Disturbing tha Peace/Def Jam, 2003.

239 *"Lesley Gore was there"*: Gloria Steinem, conversation with author.

239 *"Elvis was so cool"*: Edmund White, interview with author.

240 *fluidity of sexual partnership*: For studies that examine how popular music has destabilized sexual and gender binaries, see Shana Goldin-

Perschbacher, "The World Has Made Me the Man of My Dreams: Meshell Ndegeocello and the 'Problem' of Black Female Masculinity," *Popular Music*, Oct. 2013; J. Jack Halberstam, *Gaga Feminism: Sex, Gender, and the End of Normal* (Boston: Beacon Press, 2012); Judith Peraino, *Listening to the Sirens: Musical Technologies of Queer Identity from Homer to Hedwig* (Berkeley: University of California Press, 2006); Francesca T. Royster, *Sounding Like a No-No: Queer Sounds and Eccentric Acts in the Post-soul Era* (Ann Arbor: University of Michigan Press, 2013).

240 *growing acceptance of polyamory*: See William Baude, "Is Polygamy Next?," *New York Times*, July 21, 2015; Michael Carey, "Is Polyamory a Choice?," *Slate*, Oct. 16, 2013; Elizabeth Emens, "Monogamy's Law: Compulsory Monogamy and Polyamorous Existence," University of Chicago Public Law and Legal Theory Working Paper, 2004; Ronald C. Den Otter, *In Defense of Plural Marriage* (New York: Cambridge University Press, 2015).

240 *The music that's most popular today*: Portions of this text were published in different form in David Hajdu, "It's an Old Trope, but How Well Does the Factory Model Explain Pop Music?," *Nation*, Nov. 16, 2015.

243 *number one on the pop charts*: "Billboard Hot 100," *Billboard*, March 4, 1967.

ACKNOWLEDGMENTS

My thanks go, first, to my former editor at FSG, Paul Elie, who initially encouraged me to write this, as well as to my current editor, Sean Mc-Donald, who made invaluable suggestions and saw the book through to its completion. I'd also like to thank:

Leon Wieseltier, my longtime editor and mentor at *The New Republic*, and John Palattella, my first editor at *The Nation*. During the many years I was working on this book, I drew on several occasions from the text in progress for pieces in both magazines.

Alisa Solomon, my dear friend and colleague at Columbia, for her support and inspiration.

James Marcus, Bud Kliment, John Carey, and David Yaffe, all of whom read the text as I was writing and offered advice along the way.

Jon Moskowitz, who also read most of the text in progress and contributed significantly to the chapters on MTV and hip-hop.

Ross Yelsey, who worked diligently on the research and organized the endnotes.

The former dean Nick Lemann, the current dean, Steve Coll, and their fellow deans at the Columbia Graduate School of Journalism, for their support.

Franklin Bruno, Matthew Salganik, Andrew Gelman, Dan Goldstein, and Eric Bradlow, for their expertise.

Michael Kubin and Ingrid Sterner, who copyedited the manuscript.

The staffs at the Lincoln Center Library for the Performing Arts, Butler Library at Columbia University, Bobst Library at New York University, the Institute of Jazz Studies at Rutgers University, the Experience Music Project, the Rock and Roll Hall of Fame, and the Belfer Audio Archive at Syracuse University.

My agent and pal Chris Calhoun.

And, above all, as always, my wife, Karen, and the rest of my family, for their help, tolerance, and love.

INDEX

"Red Wagon," 110
Regency, 127
Reilly, Harry, 151, 152
Reinhardt, Django, 80
religious music, 17
R.E.M., 146
Republic Pictures, 98, 99
Reynolds, Debbie, 223, 229
Rhapsody in Blue, 41
rhythm and blues, 108, 112–14, 116, 118, 119, 121, 232–33
Rhythm and Blues Revue, 118
Rice, Tim, 168
Richards, Keith, 139–40
Rifkin, Joshua, 165
Rihanna, 226, 243
Rite of Spring, 176, 206
Ritter, Tex, 85, 93
Ritz, Tootie, 26
Robbins, Everett, 102
Robbins, Jerome, 187
Robertson, Eck, 212
Robinson, Bill "Bojangles," 48, 49
Robinson, Smokey, 133
Robinson, Sylvia, 202
Rock, Pete, 208
rock and roll, 25–26, 30, 54, 59, 60, 101–21, 162, 179, 182–83, 187–88, 201, 230–31, 238
"Rock Around the Clock," 59, 114–16, 136, 178, 201
rock criticism, 58, 60
Rock 'n' Roll Revue, 118
Rodgers, Jimmie, 80, 91–94, 96, 104, 205
Rodgers, Richard, 154, 156, 157, 159–61

Rogers, Arline, 98
Rogers, Ginger, 187
Rogers, Roy (Len Slye), 80, 95, 98–100, 111
Rolling Stone, 167, 233
Rolling Stones, 9, 10, 139–40, 164, 189, 243
Rollins, Sonny, 4, 206–207
"Roll Over, Beethoven," 109
Romberg, Sigmund, 157
Roosevelt, Theodore, 82
Rose, Vincent, 40
Ross, Jerry, 158
Ross, Lanny, 71
Rossini, Gioachino, 17–18
Rotolo, Suze, 142
Rotten, Johnny, 175
Rubin, Rick, 197, 201, 203
"Ruby Tuesday," 10, 243
Rush, Art, 99
Ryders, 26–27

Sacre du printemps, Le, 54
Salome, 22
"Salt Peanuts," 206
sampling, 205–209, 241
Sampson, Edgar, 105
Sancious, David, 58
San Francisco Chronicle, 54
Sanjek, David, 153–54
Santana, 17
Sartre, Jean-Paul, 74
Schaeffer, Pierre, 165
Schneider, Doc, 93, 94
Schneider, Jack, 190
Schoenberger, John, 40

A NOTE ABOUT THE AUTHOR

David Hajdu is the music critic for *The Nation* and a professor at the Columbia University Graduate School of Journalism. He is the author of three books of narrative nonfiction and one collection of essays: *Lush Life: A Biography of Billy Strayhorn* (1996), *Positively 4th Street: The Lives and Times of Joan Baez, Bob Dylan, Mimi Baez Fariña, and Richard Fariña* (2001), *The Ten-Cent Plague: The Great Comic-Book Scare and How It Changed America* (2008), and *Heroes and Villains: Essays on Music, Movies, Comics, and Culture* (2009). He lives in Manhattan.